THE WHITE RAJAH

THE
WHITE RAJAHS
OF SARAWAK

by

ROBERT PAYNE

Fear nothing for me; the decision is in higher Hands; and I am willing to die as live in the present undertaking, if my death can benefit the poor people.

James Brooke

SINGAPORE OXFORD NEW YORK
OXFORD UNIVERSITY PRESS
1986

Oxford University Press

Oxford New York Toronto
Petaling Jaya Singapore Hong Kong Tokyo
Delhi Bombay Calcutta Madras Karachi
Nairobi Dar es Salaam Cape Town
Melbourne Auckland
and associates in
Beirut Berlin Ibadan Nicosia
OXFORD is a trademark of Oxford University Press

Originally published by Robert Hale Limited 1960
First issued as an Oxford University Press paperback 1986
ISBN 0 19 582687 6

Printed in Malaysia by Peter Chong Printers Sdn. Bhd.
Published by Oxford University Press Pte. Ltd.,
Unit 221, Ubi Avenue 4, Singapore 1440

CONTENTS

To the happy memory of
my friend
HASSOLDT DAVIS

LIST OF ILLUSTRATIONS

ACKNOWLEDGEMENT

The National Portrait Gallery holds the copyright of illustrations nos. 1 and 8.

ACKNOWLEDGEMENTS

Above all, I am deeply indebted to His Highness the Rajah of Sarawak, Sir Charles Vyner Brooke, who kindly placed his own and his father's letters at my disposal, and to Lady Jean Halsey, who gave me free access to the correspondence of her grandmother, the Ranee Margaret, and many other documents. Mrs. Evelyn Hussey overwhelmed me with kindness, and Mr. Charles Martine of the Borneo Company magically opened many doors. Mr. Anthony Brooke led me gently through the problems of the cession, and to Mr. T. S. Page I owe my knowledge of the multitudinous documents in his possession. To Mr. J. C. Swayne, Mr. T. Stirling Boyd, and Mr. J. A. Smith I am indebted for many illuminating insights.

SARAWAK

N

0 10 10 10 10 50 100
Scale of English Miles

BRITISH
NORTH
BOREO

DUTCH
BORNEO

Long Nawang

Mallulu Bay

Lake Kini Balu

LAWAS (1904)
TRUSAN (1884)
LIMBANG

Kimanis Bay

Labuan

BRUNEI (1890)

Tutong

Baram R.

Miri

BARAM (1882)

CHINA SEA

Cape Kidurong

REJANG (1861)

Sakarran R.

Batang Lupar R.

Simanggang

Muka

Oya

Matu

Bruick

Balor

Serikei

Rejang R.

KUCHING

Sadong R.

Mt.

Santubong

Batthat

Cape Datu

Talang-Talang Island

Sibuloot R.

(1846)

SARAWAK

Sirhassen Island

SAMBAS

CHINA SEA

Tumyassuk

Philippines

New Guinea

SULU SEA

SARAWAK

KUCHING

Borneo

Celebes

Penang

Malacca

Singapore

Pontianak

JAVA SEA

Sumatra

Java

I

THE ENCHANTED ISLANDS

THOSE WHO have never been in the East have missed the better part of the earth. The sun is never so splendid as when it rises over the Eastern seas; the moon and stars are closer to us in the Eastern skies; the Eastern earth is warmer, richer, nobler—or so it seems to be. From Jerusalem eastward we enter a brighter and more intense world, where the people seem to belong to another universe—small dark people with burning eyes and delicate skins. They are earthier than we are, and more spiritual; the fiery element has touched them; they move with a grace we can never equal. To live among them is to know a contentment unknown to the West; and sometimes a wanderer in the East comes closer to Paradise than anywhere on earth.

Today, the maharajahs have departed, but we still dream of them; and soon the sheiks will depart, but we shall dream of them for generations. There are no more diamonds in the mines of Anaconda; all the emeralds in the foreheads of Buddha have been plucked; the painted elephants no longer go in procession. The barbaric splendour of the East has been tamed. The Forbidden City in Peking has become a public garden, and the Living Buddha has crossed the mountain passes to the suburban comfort of an Indian hill-station. So it goes on, the legends rotting away and the mysteries explained. It is perhaps a pity.

The mind needs legends to feast on. Without legends, without the sense of a vast mysterious magnificence, unreachable and yet close by, we cannot balance ourselves as we walk on a tightrope over those abysses and chasms which lie within us. We need emperors, because we are all emperors in ourselves, and for the same reason we need sorcerers and magicians and holy texts to be recited in the darkest hours of the night. We need the palpable and sumptuous magnificence of Oriental temples to remind us of the sumptuous miracle which is a human being. Today, we are in danger of receiving from the East only statistics and travel folders.

In the early years of the nineteenth century Asia was still a land of legends. Men fought with swords and spears, wore chain armour, rode to battle with their women beside them, and slipped poison into the cups of their enemies. In those days Japan was a mysterious land where only a few foreigners had penetrated, and China was an imperial power ruled by an Emperor who believed that the whole world was tributary to him. India had been conquered, but was it really a conquest? The conquerors remained in the fortified towns, while the peasants lived exactly as they had lived for three thousand years.

No wonder adventurous Europeans flocked to the East to make their fortunes, and many of them stayed, spell-bound by what they saw. The luckiest were those who went to the islands of the East Indies, where most of the accepted conventions of Western civilization are thrown to the winds. In those islands a man does not have to work to live: he has merely to sit under a palm tree or throw a fishing line through a hole in the bamboo floor. Even those who live in the equatorial forests need only work for a few months of the year, clearing the land and watching the rice grow. The people are small and beautifully built, with the darkest eyes in the world. The rice fields are terraces on the hills, and when under water gleam like a thousand mirrors. The air is scented with the perfume of casuarina trees. Immense butterflies float across the forests, and rainbow-coloured pheasants sail into the air. The problems of such an existence were solved in Bali by making all the inhabitants artists—painters, sculptors, dancers, performers in ancient plays. We envy them, but we know we are incapable of following their example.

In all history only one man succeeded in coming from the West and making himself king over an Eastern race and founding a dynasty which lasted for a hundred years. This man, a debonair young Englishman called James Brooke, became a legend in his lifetime. He lived a life such as schoolboys dream of—he attacked pirates, marched unarmed into the palaces of sultans who were his declared enemies, and went into battle at the head of armies of head-hunting savages, whose women were sometimes as beautiful as princesses. These savages were the Dyaks of the forests and the river banks, who went about naked except for brightly coloured loincloths and helmets of plumes. They wore tigers' teeth in their ears, and decorated their long-houses with human heads which they hung up like garlands of flowers, filling the sockets of the eyes with sea shells.

These Dyaks were ruled by Malay Sultans and Rajahs, descendants of the freebooting Arab pirates who in the fifteenth century swept over the East Indies. They, too, were handsome and unscrupulous. James Brooke, who loved and hated them, once described them in his journal:

These Rajahs, born in the purple, bred amid slaves and fighting-cocks, inheriting an undisputed power over their subjects, and under all circumstances, whether of riches or poverty, receiving the abject submission of

those around their persons, are naturally the slaves of their passions—
haughty, rapacious, vindictive, weak, and tenacious unto death of the
paltry punctilio of their court.

James Brooke ruled over the Malays and Dyaks with a firm hand.
He looked like a romantic hero, and behaved like one. His successor
was his nephew Charles Brooke, who for fifty years ruled Sarawak
and extended his empire until it stretched nearly across the whole of
North Borneo. The last Rajah of Sarawak was Charles's son Vyner,
who stepped down from the throne only at the end of the Second
World War. He, too, looked like a romantic hero. In old age, sitting alone in his London apartment near Hyde Park, with a healthy
glow on his cheeks, surrounded by mementoes of long-forgotten escapades in the East Indies, he still carries himself with a heroic air,
debonair as all heroes should be, Ulysses home at last after throwing
a kingdom away.

So this is the story of the three white Rajahs who came to a savage
land and ruled it wisely, fought wars, dispensed justice, worked hard,
and kept faith with their Malay and Dyak subjects.

In 1841 James Brooke wrote: 'Fear nothing for me; the decision
is in higher Hands, and I am willing to die as live in the present
undertaking, if my death can benefit the poor people.' So it was
with all the Brookes—those tempestuous and dedicated men, who
sometimes quarrelled violently among themselves, but closed ranks
whenever the fortunes of their people were at stake. They were
proud and possessive, but also humble. They showed the way to win
men's hearts in the East. It is a lesson we have still to learn.

II

THE YOUNG SAILOR

No one would ever have guessed that James Brooke of Widcombe Crescent, Bath, would become a white Rajah, the sovereign ruler of a small Eastern empire. He had all the ordinary virtues. He was charming, handsome, well-mannered, gentle to women. He believed wholeheartedly in the Christian virtues of justice, charity, and common sense. He rode well, and drank well. He liked playing practical jokes, and he was never a particularly brilliant student, and he was often silly. There were perhaps ten thousand young Englishmen like him, and if you passed him in the street you would not have turned your head. Yet a fire burned in him, blazing with such heat that it drove him nearly out of his mind and sent him to one of the loneliest and most dangerous places on earth, to become the sole possessor of a land of raging rivers and haunted forests.

His father, Thomas Brooke, was a judge of the High Court of Benares, a dull, precise man who served the East India Company well and retired early on a pension. They said of him that he talked well, read interminably, and with his stateliness and habitual solemnity resembled a judge to perfection. He married a Scots girl, Anna Maria Stuart, who came out to India to visit her brother, a member of the Bengal Council. She was lively and vivacious, but no beauty. Though she had soft blue eyes, delicate bones, and a rich colouring, she had a heavy, lumpy nose and a curiously unattractive mouth. Her children loved her, and paid only perfunctory attention to their father. She was warm and trusting, liked dressing up, wore jewels well, and adored her six children.

There was nothing in the least remarkable in her ancestry, but Thomas Brooke could claim among his ancestors a man who had been the richest money-lender in England. Sir Thomas Viner (or Vyner) had been the power behind Cromwell, supplying him with large quantities of bullion, at the same time advancing money to the East India Company. He became Lord Mayor of London, one of Cromwell's closest advisers and a pillar of society under the republic of England.

His son, Sir Robert Viner, chose to fight on the opposite side in the Civil War and was one of the first to welcome Charles II when he returned to the throne. He too became Lord Mayor of London, lending large sums of money to the King to pay for the extravagances of the Court. Pepys, the diarist, knew him well. 'No man in England lives in greater plenty,' he wrote. 'He commands both King and Council with the credit he gives them.' He did not, however, command the King for long. In 1672 the King owed him the enormous sum of £400,000, and suspended payment: the richest man in England was reduced to bankruptcy.

Pepys tells an odd story of a visit to Sir Robert Viner's country estate in Middlesex. There in the great house, luxuriously furnished, where the window frames, door cases, and chimneys were made of marble, he was shown a black boy who had died of consumption: the body was dried in an oven and placed in a box for the amusement and delectation of visitors. Two hundred years later James Brooke was to live in a land where the drying and public exhibition of human heads was one of the commonplaces of life.

The Viners were a short-lived dynasty, wielding great power during the rule of Cromwell and the reign of Charles II. With the death of Sir Robert's son George the baronetcy became extinct. Their inheritance—for there was still great wealth in the family—was handed down through daughters.

Judge Thomas Brooke was a wealthy man: he had independent means and received a considerable salary from the East India Company. He could afford to bring up his children in comfort. James was his fifth child—there was an older brother Henry who died young, and four daughters. He was born on April 29, 1803, and spent the first twelve years of his life in India. This in itself was unusual: officials of the East India Company usually arranged to send their children home to England to escape the pestilences which periodically swept over the country. James, growing up in a suburb of Benares, soaked up the colours and sounds of the Holy City, and to the end of his life felt a strong attraction for India.

In the year of his birth Major-General Arthur Wellesley was preparing to crush the power of the Mahrattas, so bringing all India under the control of the East India Company. In the year James came home the same general, then known as Duke of Wellington, destroyed the power of Napoleon on the battlefield of Waterloo. They were stirring times, but James seems to have known very little about the great historical events which happened in his childhood. In England he was put under the care of his grandmother, who lived in Reigate, and a friend of his father who lived in Bath: which meant that he was under no one's care. He hated Norwich Grammar School, where he was sent as a boarder; but he hated it no more than schoolboys hate their schools.

He made little impression at school. Later, when legends surrounded his name, it was remembered that he never told a lie and demonstrated at an early age a character of the utmost nobility. James remembered chiefly his great friendship for his schoolmate George Western, who suddenly at the end of the holidays decided to go to sea instead of returning to his lessons. James was heart-broken. He could not stand being at the school without George Western. He decided to run away, borrowed money from another boy, announced that he was going to sea, and was accompanied to the coach by a group of cheering schoolfellows.

He did not go to sea. Instead to went to the house of his grandmother in Reigate, who took pity on him and applied to the school to have him readmitted. The school authorities were adamant. Many years later they would proclaim James Brooke to be one of their most gifted pupils, but now they were glad to wash their hands of him. They had no liking for rebels, and were happy to be rid of him.

Messages were sent off to India to ask what should be done with the young rebel. James spent some happy months waiting for replies to these messages. His father was shortly returning to England for retirement, and it was decided to do nothing until the family returned. He went briefly to another school, with no more success than before; and when Thomas Brooke finally arrived with his wife and five children, setting up an establishment in Bath, James was perfectly amenable to the idea of abandoning school for ever: he was given a private tutor.

He had wanted to be a sailor, but he became a soldier. Shortly after his sixteenth birthday he received an ensign's commission in the 6th Madras Native Infantry, and sailed for India. Two years later he was promoted to a lieutenancy. A restless schoolboy, he became a restless lieutenant. A progress report on James and a young fellow officer reads: 'Lieutenants Brooke and Fendall during the attendance at Cawnpore were attentive, and willing. They possess excellent abilities, and will, we hope, receive an early impression of the necessity of steadiness and decision.' It is an illuminating report, and suggests the absence of many of the qualities which make a good soldier.

James was, in fact, a bad soldier, with a happy-go-lucky attitude towards the Army. His main task was drilling the native troops, and he liked to tell the story of how he was once drilling them and marching them across the parade ground, when it occurred to him to tell them to march over a neighbouring hill. He never saw them again. He collected scandalous stories about the officers and their wives, and liked retailing them. The Army amused him, but made few demands on him. There were occasional big-game hunts; there was always some pig-sticking somewhere; but it was altogether more pleasant to bait the senior officers.

He knew obscurely that something was wrong—he was bored by the society of white men, thirsting for action and devilment. He was in a strange mood, caring and not caring, decided and undecided. No women seem to have interested him in India, and he spent a good deal of time composing poems, no better and no worse than hundreds of poems written by his contemporaries. Only one of these poems has been preserved. Here is the first verse:

> *The future hath no dream of joy to give,*
> *   Sad Memory vainly clings unto the past:*
> *Ah! wherefore should the wretched wish to live?*
> *   Sweet hope is gone, and life is ebbing fast—*
> *A shatter'd wreck, that yields to every blast*
> *   Of stormy passion, or of wild despair,*
> *Full soon to be what all must be at last,*
> *   A clod of earth, an unknown thing, or air,*
> *Wildly roaming in space, and fix its wandering—where?*

There are five more verses on the theme of 'Wherefore should the wretched wish to live?'

It is clear that he was in a Byronic mood, full of inner restlessness and frustration. His 'wild despair' was real enough; so, too, was his desire to put an end to his wandering, to serve a cause greater than himself.

The opportunity came when the Burmese invaded Assam in 1824, and Lord Amherst, Governor-General of Bengal, declared war on Burma. James offered to raise a troop of native cavalry irregulars. He was in his element at last. The irregulars rode with the advance guards, and acted as scouts. They did their work so well that his volunteer troops were commended by the general in command, and James himself was mentioned in dispatches for 'most conspicuous gallantry'. On January 27, 1825, he saw his first battle, and two days later, he saw his last.

At a place called Rungpore the Burmese were occupying a heavily fortified position. Native troops were ordered to attack, but when the Burmese opened a withering fire, the English captain panicked and bolted into the jungle. James was riding nearby on a reconnoitering expedition. He had made careful observations of the stockade, thought to be undefended, and he was on his way back to warn headquarters when he heard the firing. He wheeled round, threw himself from his horse, assumed the command, and led the charge. A moment later he felt a stunning blow in his chest, and fell unconscious. His colonel hurried up with reinforcements, and after some bloody fighting the fort was taken. Some time later the colonel asked what had happened to Lieutenant Brooke, and was told he was dead. The colonel insisted on seeing the body. James was still breathing, but he was close to death with a bullet in the lungs.

He was carried to a hospital, where for some months he hovered between life and death, frail and painfully thin. Too ill to be moved by carriage, he was put in a canoe and paddled down a branch of the Brahmaputra and so by slow stages to Calcutta. The Medical Board reported on him; he was ordered back to England, where his chances of recovery were thought to be better. He was granted a four-and-a-half-year furlough.

He left for England in August, 1825. He was a hero, a very sick man, and a very thoughtful one. For many years to come he would remember vividly the sensation of gliding down the Brahmaputra with the jungles crowding the river's edge and the kingfishers flying overhead, while he lay at the bottom of the canoe, too weak to move. It was like an opium dream, all time flowing out before him, time and the earth coloured by the light of the Orient. Twenty years later he told his friend Spenser St. John that this journey through the obscure tributaries of the Brahmaputra had changed him. Henceforth he belonged to the East.

He spent the next years with his family in Bath, gradually recovering his health. His father had a large library, and he read contentedly. His brother was in the Army, and he was surrounded by his adoring sisters, who acted very much like characters out of the novels of Jane Austen. Yet he was very remote from their world. Because he was strangely pale and took very little interest in their social activities, they called him 'Moonbeam'. Wealthy, unattached, handsome, he was sometimes inveigled into attending one of the local balls, and there is a story of him at a ball, sitting on a blue satin settee and scornfully smiling at the dancers. A girl asked who he was, and was told he was the son of those very eminent and respectable pillars of society who were always driving about Bath in a big green coach; and having observed his arrogant smiles, the girl asked no more questions.

On the whole, however, he was content. He derived a wicked amusement from the frivolities of Bath, comparing them with the realities of Assam. Bath was a precise town, neat as a new pin. He did not like it, but he had a small pension from the East India Company and he was in no hurry to return into their service. He spoke of journeys into the interior of unknown lands, but without conviction. He was still living the opium dream of the Brahmaputra.

At last, in July, 1829, he set sail for India on the Company's ship *Carn Brae*, which was almost immediately wrecked off the Isle of Wight. James was saved, but his health was affected by long immersion in the water, and he asked for six months' further leave. This was granted, but he was warned not to overstay his leave under penalty of being written off the Company's books. He must report for work in Calcutta by July 30, 1830, at the very latest.

At the time the East India Company's demand seemed reasonable: he had a whole year to reach India. At the beginning of 1830 he made inquiries about a passage, but few Indiamen were sailing and it was not until March that he obtained a berth on the *Castle Huntley*, bound for China and ports of call. It proved to be an unusually slow voyage; he did not reach Madras until July 18, and this left him only twelve days to reach his regiment in Calcutta. He made application of the Company officers in Madras for a short extension of his leave. It was refused. Harsh words were spoken. James had no very deep feelings for the Company and suddenly he decided to quit. He decided to go to China with the *Castle Huntley*. 'I bade farewell to John Company and all his evil ways,' he wrote triumphantly to his sister.

He kept a journal during his voyage. It is a strange journal, at times oddly immature, often remarkably perceptive. He made sweeping judgments; his enthusiasms were quickly kindled; he spoke sometimes with an air of authority about things he knew nothing about. Maturity and immaturity crowd those hurried pages.

The days he spent cooling his heels in Madras had given him a new insight into John Company's method of government. He wrote about Madras:

> The natives are despicable, and here, as at every other place I have seen, have been corrupted by their intercourse with Europeans. They lose their particular virtues arising from their habits and their religion. and become tainted with the vices of those around them. The subject would be worth a more minute inquiry: Africans and North and South Americans corrupted, enslaved—or extirpated? How is it in the Pacific? I don't know. But no rational Englishman can observe the deterioration of the native character arising from their intercourse with the whites, without a blush.

These jejune notes are important: for the first time we see him wrestling with the problems of corruption, which he was to write about later with far greater authority. But if Madras displeased him, Penang, which he reached towards the end of August, delighted him beyond measure. He found all the virtues in that romantic island, perhaps the most beautiful of all the islands of the East. It was a place, he thought, eminently suited for colonization:

> If European colonization is to be tried in the East, Penang is the spot on which the experiment should be made. The ground is fertile, the climate cooler and better than the greater part of the continent of India, inhabitants scarce, and religious prejudices almost unknown. Here a settler might hack and hew away to his heart's content if they would give him the land he cleared of jungle. Here, likewise, with the industry and activity of the European and the care of a fostering government, various articles of commercial produce might be grown. But the Company have the monopoly. *Basta cosi!*

Already in embryo he was stating the ideas which were to ride him when he came to settle in the East. He wanted to see colonies growing freely, no longer at the mercy of the Company's Board of Directors in Leadenhall Street, with its niggling regulations. He wanted 'the care of a fostering government', meaning perhaps financial advances and the protection of His Majesty's ships. His colonizers were to be free citizens in communities where those who opened up the land would become possessors of it.

He was considerably disturbed when he reached Singapore to see the colonizers in the flesh. Singapore then as now was largely controlled by Chinese merchants and coolies who grew rich by trading and by exploiting the Malays. James regarded them as interlopers. He hated them at first sight with a venomous hatred. He could find nothing to say in their favour:

Their habits are the most filthy, their dress the most unbecoming, their faces the most ugly, and their figures the most ungraceful of any people under the sun. They appear cut out of a log of wood by the hand of some unskillful savage. Their mouths are wide, their noses snub, their eyes small and set crooked in their heads. When they move, they swing arms, legs and body, like a paper clown pulled by a string, and to sum up, all their colour is a dirty yellow, nearly the hue of a Hindustani corpse.

It was unfair, and it was untrue; and the deliberate catalogue of horrors may owe something to De Quincey, who also painted a terrifying picture of those graceful people as they appeared to him, wearing the colours of an opium dream. James never changed his mind about the Chinese. He could tolerate them on occasion, but he never liked them.

He found further reason to detest the Chinese when the *Castle Huntley* put in at Canton. Once again they reminded him of wooden figures jerked by strings. He fell ill in Canton, and his hatred of them seems to have been exasperated by a long bout of influenza, from which he was nursed by the ship's doctor, who engaged him in long adolescent conversations on theology. James had no high opinion of theologians: after reading the Gospels, he had the curious feeling that all had been said, and there was nothing left for the theologians to say.

Already he was the prisoner of the Eastern islands. When the *Castle Huntley* returned to England by way of the Cape and the island of St. Helena—he visited Napoleon's tomb, finding it 'shaded by willows and peach-trees, with a fount of crystal water and refreshing greenness'—he could talk of nothing but buying a schooner and filling it with merchandise to trade among the islands. For him the East was paradise, England a purgatory.

In Bath he tried to convince his father that a ship loaded with merchandise would be a good investment, but the old judge spoke only of the advantages of a career in the government. There was some talk of allowing him to stand for Parliament and he wrote a pamphlet on the Reform Bill. He was restless. He smoked too much. He wrote disconsolate little notes to the officers of the *Castle Huntley*, reminding them of his plan to buy a schooner and begging them to join him. But his mind veered like a weathercock: where to go? what to do? 'I am cut up root and branch,' he wrote in the spring of 1832, 'dying of wretchedness and the slow stupor of inactivity.'

He had lost interest in balls and flirtations. There was a brief and unhappy affair with the daughter of a Bath clergyman. To escape from his father's house he spent whole days in the fields collecting flowers, and amusing himself by learning their proper botanical names. At such times he would remember with peculiar poignancy the days he had spent on the green island of Penang or that other day when for a few hours the *Castle Huntley* anchored off the shores of Sumatra and he saw 'clear water, gemmed with three or four islands called The Sisters, through which peep the white cliffs'. Beyond the cliffs lay the wild jungle, creepers hanging from the giant trees, game birds flying through the branches and the tracks of elephants. 'Here,' he wrote, 'we were lords of all we surveyed.'

But in Bath there were no virgin forests, and no elephants. Instead there were tea parties, interminable discussions on the subject of the Reform Bill, walks in a bland countryside. He told himself he was nearing thirty, and he had accomplished nothing at all. He had made a journey to the Far East and he had been wounded in a forgotten skirmish in Assam—he was not permitted to forget that he had been wounded, for his mother kept the bullet which had been extracted from his lungs in the drawing-room under a glass case.

The letters he wrote during this time are painfully similar. He writes always about going to sea—to hunt whales off Greenland, to visit the Azores, to sail up the Amazon. He wanted to be a sailor, but knew nothing about sailing. He hoped some ship's captain would have mercy on him and train him. He spoke of taking lessons in navigation, and never took them. He read everything he could lay his hands on concerning colonial policy in the Far East; and having written a pamphlet about Reform, he wrote and published another called *The Justification of our Foreign Policy towards Holland*.

For a while he even thought of outfitting a ship against the Dutch in the Far East, for the Dutch annoyed him almost as much as the Chinese. Towards the end of the year he wrote:

Our present plan is to go and take a tract of land in New Holland, and turn farmers in the back settlements, which will give us the opportunity of exploring an unknown country, and making discoveries in certainly

one of the wildest and least-known frontiers of the globe. I feel myself,
however, disposed to buckle to anything that offers, and I only wish I
had money enough to carry a letter of marque against the Dutch vaga-
bonds in the Eastern Seas.

The months passed, and there was still no ship. He was almost
out of his wits with misery. Restless, he began to travel a little, visiting friends all over England and Ireland, and when he returned
from these forays he would settle down to a contest of wits with his
father, hoping to wear down the old man's objection to a sailor's
life. He kept asking for a ship—any ship. At last, in February, 1834,
his father relented and promised to buy a ship for him and to furnish
it with merchandise. James heard of a promising brig in Liverpool,
and hurried off to examine it. It was everything he wanted. It resembled a privateer—'low and wicked and black, with a black hull
and black mast'. He wrote to his friend Cruikshank, the ship's
doctor on the *Castle Huntley*:

> *Me voilà donc!* I have a vessel afloat, and nearly ready for sea—a rakish
> slaver brig, 290 tons burden—one that would fight or fly as occasion
> demanded, and made to pay her expenses. The Indian Archipelago, the
> north-east coast of China, Japan, New Guinea and the Pacific is the
> unlimited sphere of our adventure.

On May 6, 1834, the *Findlay* sailed from England, laden with
merchandise. Her captain was his friend Kennedy from the *Castle
Huntley*, with another friend, Harry Wright, as first mate. James
accompanied them merely as owner, in charge of trading. He
had not chosen his officers well. Kennedy and Wright fell out;
there were constant quarrels; and with near mutiny on his hands,
James decided abruptly to sell the vessel and cargo, and cut his
losses. His first adventure in trading with the East was a complete
fiasco.

He returned to Bath, and once again he was the aimless man-
about-town, more famous for his defeats than for his victories. He
went foxhunting; he spent the summer evenings yachting along the
south coast of England and among the Channel Islands. He seemed
to have no purpose in life.

When his father died in December, 1835, his mind was made up.
With his inheritance, which amounted to £30,000—a huge sum in
those days—he was free to do as he pleased, and immediately set
about buying a ship for a voyage of discovery in the Eastern islands.
He bought a yacht, the *Royalist*, armed with six six-pounders, a
number of swivel guns, and every kind of small arms. She was 142
tons burden, and carried four boats. She was fast and graceful, and
he was particularly delighted because, having belonged to the Royal

Yacht Club, she possessed the same privileges as a man-of-war, and was permitted to fly the white ensign. She could carry provisions for four months.

This time he had learned to proceed cautiously: he would choose his officers with special care. First, he would invite some relatives and chosen companions to take part in a shake-down cruise in the Mediterranean. It was a quiet journey. There were no tantrums. The *Royalist* put in at Malaga in southern Spain, and he rode on donkey-back to Granada, coming to the conclusion that the Court of the Lions in the Alhambra was the most majestic thing he had ever seen. They went on to Malta and the Bosphorus, and visited Cnidus, Halicarnassus, and Rhodes. At Ephesus, with his young nephew John Johnson, the son of his sister Emma who had married a clergyman, he shot woodcock. As they sailed among the islands of the Aegean they occasionally landed and carried off whatever statues and inscriptions they could easily transport to the ship. Most English travellers in the Mediterranean were doing the same thing; and when he returned at last to Bath it was accounted a feather in his hat that he had plunder to show for the voyage.

James was still convinced that his destiny was bound up with the islands of the Far East. He kept the *Royalist* at Greenwich, and there set about reading as many books as he could find on navigation and the islands of the East Indies. The cruise had ended in June, 1837. For eighteen months he studied, and the *Royalist* did not set out to sea again until December, 1838.

He published the fruit of his studies in Greenwich in a long paper printed in the *Athenæum* magazine in October, 1838. It is a good article. It showed that at last his mind was made up, and he knew exactly where he was going. He explained that he had given himself the task of entering Malludu Bay on the north-eastern tip of Borneo, and he would then attempt a journey into the interior to the mysterious Lake Kini Ballu, where the great rivers of Borneo were thought to have their source. Somewhere in this region he hoped to discover the descendants of the ancient Hindu rajahs who ruled over Borneo before they were conquered by the Mohammedan invasion, and he hoped to study the natives of the interior and do a small amount of prospecting, sending his finds periodically back to England through Singapore. After eighteen months among the islands he proposed to visit Australia, returning to England by way of the Pacific islands and Cape Horn.

The article however was more than the statement of a purpose. It was a careful examination based on available sources of the political position in the Eastern Archipelago: of the prospects of the Dutch and Spanish, of the errors committed by the British; of the empty spaces on the maps, which in those days showed little more

than the outlines of Africa, Australia, Japan, and New Guinea. He
wrote ironically about fashions in discovery:

> Whilst the folly of fashion requires an acquaintance with the deserts of
> Africa, and a most ardent thirst for a knowledge of the usages of Tim-
> buctoo, it at the same time justifies the most profound ignorance of all
> matters connected with the government and geography of our vast acquisi-
> tions in Hindoostan. The Indian Archipelago has fully shared this
> neglect; and even the tender philanthropy of the present day, which
> originates such multifarious schemes for the amelioration of doubtful
> evils, which shudders at the prolongation of apprenticeship for a single
> year in the west, is blind to the existence of slavery in its worst and most
> aggravated form in the east. Not a single voice is upraised to relieve the
> darkness of Paganism, and the horrors of the eastern slave-trade.

But only a few passages in the prospectus are written in that
ironical tone. On the whole it describes humbly and modestly what
he hoped to discover in Borneo and the neighbouring islands. There
were rumours of a race living in the interior 'little better than
monkeys, who live in trees, eat without cooking, are hunted by the
other tribes, and would seem to exist in the lowest conceivable grade
of humanity'. These, too, he hoped to see and report on. He also
hoped to make comparisons between the Dyaks in Borneo and the
inhabitants of the islands of Bali and Lombok, known to be 'fair,
good-looking and gentle'. Already he seems to have been fascinated
by the Dyaks, who were as gentle as he hoped, though they indulged
in the murderous game of head-hunting.

The prospectus published in the *Athenæum* was based upon a much
longer report intended for private distribution, which included
some hard-hitting attacks on Dutch policy. He accused the Dutch
point-blank of occupying the islands of the Indies 'more to injure
others than for any advantage to themselves'. During the Napo-
leonic Wars the British governor, Sir Stamford Raffles, had occupied Java; at the end of the war Java was restored to Dutch sovereignty. 'The consequences', wrote James, 'are well-known: all the
evils of Dutch rule have been re-established, and the British watch-
fully excluded, directly or indirectly, from the commerce of the
islands.' He did not believe the Dutch were in a strong position.
'Their position, though apparently so imposing, is in reality far
from strong, and their power would easily sink before the vigorous
opposition of any European country.' He hoped for another general
war, which would allow the British to take over the possessions they
had so cavalierly abandoned.

Again and again in the prospectus James returned to the subject
of Malludu Bay. He hoped to establish a settlement there, 'having
sufficient authority to cultivate a good understanding with the
native governments, and spread inferior posts over the Archi-

pelago'. He hoped, in fact, to make a landing and then rule over an ever-increasing territory. But nothing of this was stated in the shorter version published in the *Athenæum*. He hinted; he suggested; he even mentioned, in a roundabout way, the possibility of a settlement. In fact, his voyage of discovery was to be a voyage of conquest.

He did not know he was to become a conqueror. He saw himself as a discoverer, one of those who go out and explore unknown lands. On November 14, 1838, he described his feelings just before he sailed to the East:

> Could I carry my vessel to places where the keel of a European ship never before plowed the waters, could I plant my foot where white man's foot has never been before—could I gaze upon scenes which educated eyes have never looked on—see man in the rudest state of nature—I should be content without looking to further rewards. I can indeed say truly that I have no object of personal ambition, no craving for personal reward; these things sometimes flow attendant on worthy deeds or bold enterprises, but they are at best consequences, not principal objectives.

So he wrote in a letter to his friend Cruikshank, and there is no reason to disbelieve him. In his own eyes he was intent upon a virtuous adventure. The officials of the Dutch Foreign Office, who had read the prospectus, submitted a report to the Foreign Minister and trembled at the thought of what he might do when he reached the Far East.

The *Royalist* sailed from Devonport on December 16, 1838, with a crew of nineteen. Twelve days later she was coasting past the island of Madeira. Prevailing winds bore her to Rio de Janeiro, which she reached a month later. Progress was slow, and she seems to have had difficulty tacking across the South Atlantic, for she did not reach Cape Town until the middle of March. He had hoped to be in Singapore in March. At last on the first of June he arrived in Singapore, already after only twenty years of existence a large port.

In his prospectus James had spoken of a stopover at Singapore for reconnaissance lasting perhaps two months. In his view a man could discover the present history of all the islands if he went about Singapore with his ears open. He had been there three days when his plans were drastically changed. The journey to Malludu Bay was temporarily abandoned for a journey to Brunei, the seat of the Sultan of Brunei, then known as Borneo Proper. He wrote home on June 3:

> The accounts from Borneo are favourable; the Sultan of Borneo Proper is favourably inclined to the English, and hates the Dutch. The government of Singapore has offered me letters to him; and from Borneo Proper

I hope to penetrate the interior, or else fall back on my old plan of Malludu Bay. Of course I visit the latter at any rate; but from the capital, and with the kingly protection much may be done.

With the kingly protection. . . . . It was not quite in that way he had thought of entering Borneo when he was writing his prospectus.

For a few more weeks he remained in Singapore, listening to travellers' tales and fitting out his ship. He had a keen ear for the latest story. He learned that the Sultan of Brunei was the notorious Omar Ali Saifuddin, who if he hated the Dutch despised the English. He learned that the Sultan's uncle, the Rajah of Sarawak, had recently shown unusual consideration to some shipwrecked sailors, giving them clothes and gifts and then sending them back to Singapore in safety. The Rajah of Sarawak went by the name of Rajah Muda Hassim. In Singapore people spoke of him with affection and gratitude, and looked forward to the time when, as heir presumptive to the throne, he would come to power in Brunei.

James made inquiries about Sarawak. He learned that the antimony ore, which gleamed with a dull silvery gleam and which he could see being unloaded in Singapore harbour, came from Sarawak. He learned, too, that the Rajah was fighting some obscure rebels in the interior. There had been no mention of Sarawak in his prospectus. Now he was on fire to enter Sarawak and meet the young prince who showed such a genuine delight in being merciful. Once again his plans were altered. Only July 16 he wrote home:

My intention is first to visit Sarawak—a river whence they get antimony ore, as yet unknown and unmarked on the charts. At Sarawak I hope to get hold of the Rajah of Borneo Proper, and go up to the capital with him, and, if possible, make an excursion up the river. I feel *confident* something is to be done.

When he announced that he proposed to sail up the Sarawak River, the Singapore merchants were delighted, and gave him presents to be offered to Rajah Muda Hassim in recognition of his services to the shipwrecked sailors. James himself proposed to offer valuable gifts to the Rajah and the nobles—'Gaudy silks of Surat, stamped velvet, scarlet cloth, gunpowder, etc., besides a large quantity of confectionary and sweets, such as preserved ginger, jams, dates, syrops, and, to wind up all, a huge box of China toys for his children.' For purposes of barter he brought £100 worth of coarse nankeen cloth.

Three accidents had come together and changed his plans. If there had been no shipwreck, if there had been no fighting in the interior, if he had not seen a Chinese ship loaded with antimony ore and discovered that it came from Sarawak, he might have gone on to Malludu Bay. That would have been the end of the story, for the bay was then in the possession of Ilanun pirates, and if he had landed he would have been killed.

On July 27 he sailed from Singapore towards Borneo. He was in no hurry. He corrected charts, surveyed the coast and took soundings. After a night of heavy squalls the *Royalist* rounded Cape Datu, the western tip of Borneo, and sent a boat ashore to an island called Talang-Talang. There were some Sarawak Malays on the island, members of a party sent by the Rajah to collect turtle eggs (immense numbers of these eggs are still found there).

The leader of the party was a young Malay chieftain called Bandari Daud, who was polite without being obsequious. He wore a sarong and a dark green velvet jacket, and he carried two krisses in his sarong. James gave him some syrup, a glass of sherry, three yards of red cloth, and a little tea and gunpowder. In the evening he landed again at the foot of a white granite hill, and found a fort, defended by Malays armed against the Ilanun pirates. Cream-coloured pigeons were everywhere. Eagles circled overhead. The scent of casuarina trees filled the summer air.

There were monsoon rains that evening, and again the next night, but the rain cleared during the day. At last, on August 11, they came in sight of Santubong Mountain at the mouth of the Sarawak River, a wonderfully shaped mountain, very majestic, over 2,000 feet high, covered with a thick cloak of trees nearly to the top, with a soft sandy beach and casuarina trees below. And facing it lay the low banks of the river covered with pale green mangroves.

The next day the *Royalist* lay at anchor, and a landing party was sent ashore. They found only wild hogs, and these so shy, said James, 'that they might have been fired at all their lives'. He sent a boat up-river to Kuching to inform the Rajah of his arrival, and the next day the boat returned accompanied by a Malay prahu loaded with important dignitaries of state—a prince of the royal house, the Rajah's secretary, an officer of his guard, and a well-mannered Parsee, who seems to have been a merchant. James came to the conclusion that the Parsee's manners were the product of training, while the Malay's exquisite deportment came from good breeding.

Prince Aladin was one of the brothers of the reigning Rajah. He was the only one who was armed with a kriss. He wore a black velvet jacket trimmed with gold lace, green cloth trousers, and a red sarong. All the visitors were in good humour. They talked incessantly, and some, abandoning their Mohammedan prejudices, drank wine. The Prince complained of a European captain who had spoken insolently to his Malay crew, and was then properly murdered.

James was a little disturbed by the complaint, wondering whether he was expected to approve. 'No Malay in Borneo,' the Prince went on, 'will ever injure a European if he is well-treated and in a manner suitable to his rank.' It was a good omen for the future: James could play the game of rank and honours as well as anyone, and he had long ago determined to treat all Malays with deference.

The visitors remained on board all day. At sunset they boarded their prahu, but were turned back by the ebb tide; they remained on the *Royalist* until midnight when the tide turned. The Prince slept in James's cabin, while the others slept on couches and carpets all over the ship.

The Sarawak River winds for thirty-five miles between thick forests and mudbanks before it reaches Kuching. Mangroves and nippah palms line the shore. Crocodiles bask; monkeys gibber; water snakes fling themselves across the river with their heads raised in the air. The heat steams up from the forests. On August 14 the *Royalist*, favoured by a light breeze, sailed slowly up-river. Once she grounded against a hidden rock, and for an hour James wondered whether he had not come to an end of his adventures. Prahus, sent by the Rajah, hurried from Kuching, but they arrived too late, for she had already been heaved off the rock. James was touched by the kindness of the Malays. At night, less than two miles from Kuching, he dropped anchor.

At first dawn the *Royalist* rounded a bend in the river, and at seven o'clock came in sight of Kuching.

III

THE BATTLE WITH THE PRINCES

On that bright morning, when the *Royalist* was anchored in mid-stream and the mist hung over the jungles, James Brooke saw for the first time the town which was to become his home and his capital. It was a very small town of brown huts and long-houses made of wood or the hard stems of the nippah palm, sitting in brown squalor on the edge of mudflats. There was one long-house larger than the others and this was pointed out to him as the residence of Rajah Muda Hassim, the heir to the throne of Brunei.

At seven o'clock James ordered the firing of a royal salute of twenty-one guns. When the smoke cleared, there came an answering salute of seventeen guns. He was pardonably pleased with his reception, and still more pleased when a few minutes later there came a second salute in his honour, this time of eight guns. These were being fired by the brother of the Rajah, Prince Mohammed.

It was one of those soft August mornings when everything shimmers, when the blue sky is filled with blue pigeons, and when the great blue mountain of Matang in the distance seems to have been carved out of ice. Even the pathetic little town looked delightful in the early morning sun.

Prince Aladin was already making arrangements for the official reception. Small boats plied back and forth between the royal long-house and the *Royalist*, while the English took breakfast. At about nine o'clock a small party from the *Royalist* was rowed ashore and taken to the Rajah's reception hall, a large shed erected on piles, one side open to the river.

James delighted in the barbaric splendour of his reception—the spears, the silks, the great walls decorated with banners, and the Malay princes sitting impassive beside the Rajah Muda Hassim, the senior princes in front and their younger brothers behind. The Rajah was in full ceremonial uniform: a silk jacket with a high stiff collar, silk trousers, and a sarong of gold brocade, the ivory handle of a kriss, protruding above the sarong. He was about forty, a little fat, pleasant, with a delightful smile and winning manners; there was something curiously feminine about him. Beside him stood his atrociously ugly brother Prince Mohammed, 'a sulky looking, ill-favoured savage, with a debauched appearance', so James described him. There was the handsome Prince Budrudeen with his quick intelligence and intense sensitivity; he was a man of resolution, and James loved and admired him in time above all the Malay princes he encountered.

There was also Prince Makota, a man of exquisite charm, great resolution, and diabolical cunning. He did not look like a Malay. He may have had some Chinese blood in him. He possessed all the talents. He wrote poetry, he talked well and quickly—a little too quickly for people's comfort. Above all he was committed to a career of ruthlessness and terror practised with the utmost effrontery and good manners. He was capable of astonishing acts of evil, but all this was unknown to James, who was impressed by his tact and intelligence. In later years he came to regard Prince Makota as a man of satanic gifts, who practised crimes for pleasure. Altogether fourteen of the Rajah's brothers were present.

The reception was formal, and very little was accomplished. James sat stiffly in a chair beside the Rajah, while attendants supplied rolled tobacco leaves about a foot long and small cups of tea. Musicians played, and the slow music played by the Malay orchestra proved to be strangely soothing. There were the inevitable polite inquiries about the health of the Rajah and his visitor, and many professions of friendship.

Very tentatively James raised the subject of the war in the interior which had brought the Rajah to Sarawak, for normally he would be living in Brunei. When James went on to ask whether the war was proceeding favourably, the Rajah answered tartly that there was no war, only some 'child's play among my subjects'. Someone, perhaps Prince Makota, hinted that the war would go even better if James remained in Sarawak, for evidently the presence of the *Royalist* was regarded as a stroke of good fortune. After half an hour all the English left the reception hall and returned to their ship.

Outwardly nothing had been accomplished; actually a good deal had been accomplished. James had taken the measure of the Rajah. He knew he was valuable. He did not know yet what was expected of him or how he would use his newfound influence, but he knew already that his destiny was bound to Sarawak.

The next day the Rajah announced by messenger that he intended to visit the *Royalist*. He asked James to come ashore and escort him to the ship, and he particularly wanted to know whether he would receive a full royal salute. James, who had some doubts about whether he should leave the ship simply to escort the Rajah, satisfied him on both counts; and shortly after breakfast the Rajah, accompanied by all his brothers, and a crowd of attendants, came on board. James loved the barbaric trappings of Oriental royalty,

Rajah Sir James Brooke: the portrait painted in 1847 by Sir Francis Grant

The town of Kuching as Brooke first saw it in August 1839, "a very small town of brown huts and long-houses made of wood . . . sitting in brown squalor on the edge of mudflats"

The Sarawak River at Kuching, 1846; from a sketch by Captain Bethune, R.N., made from Rajah Brooke's "palace"—the bungalow named "The Grove"

and he was delighted by the procession. In front of the Rajah servants carried his sword of state with its gold scabbard, a shield, a jewel-hilted kriss and flowing horse tails. In just such a manner, to the accompaniment of plaintive music, might Tamerlane or Genghis Khan have walked from their palaces.

This time formality was thrown to the winds. The Malays were all over the ship, examining everything with childlike curiosity and exclaiming over the wonders they saw. They crowded into James's cabin, where it was oppressively hot. They ate up his food and drank his wine. The Rajah showed signs of almost embarrassing familiarity, and James was sufficiently disturbed 'to wish them in another place'. They left two and a half hours later to a salute of twenty-one guns, and James was so glad to be free of them that he sent them presents. To the Rajah went some Chinese toys for his children, biscuits, sweetmeats, tea, knives, scissors, a pistol, a silk sarong, some yards of velvet and red cloth. To the princes went bricks of soap, writing paper, cigars, lucifers, knives, scissors, and small pierglasses. All these presents were well-received, but James was bedeviled by their request for scent bottles—there were not enough scent bottles to satisfy them.

Slowly, a little awkwardly, he was feeling his way. He knew his Malays by now, but he was still puzzled by the intricacies of protocol.

He decided to pay a diplomatic visit on Prince Mohammed. He was kept waiting in an anteroom for an unusual length of time, and suddenly he jumped to his feet, announcing that he intended to leave forthwith. At once all the nobles and princes who were closely watching him in the anteroom assured him that there had been a misunderstanding, and begged him to remain. James could see no reason to remain. When he visited the Rajah, he had been admitted at once into the reception hall. It was explained to him that Prince Mohammed was perhaps changing his clothes, and that he would be overwhelmed with grief if he heard that his distinguished visitor had left. A few moments later the Prince entered, saying that he had been unaware of James's arrival, the servants had not informed him, they had indeed said that the distinguished Englishman would not be arriving for an hour. James accepted the excuse with good grace, though privately incensed. He was beginning to learn how to deal with these Malay noblemen. Once again there were cups of tea, foot-long cigars, empty conversations, sudden departure. Protocol was further observed when the Prince sent him a present of fowl and some goats. James was glad of them. He was beginning to weary of the fare provided on the *Royalist*.

He was weary, too, of the incessant rain. Every day there were thunderstorms, and every day he saw the sun. The storms ended as

C

quickly as they began, but he was not yet accustomed to those sudden thundering downpours which shake the earth to its foundations and blot everything from sight.

There were more violent thunderstorms later when he made a journey up-river in the *Royalist*'s longboat with an escort of war prahus provided by the Rajah. Prince Aladin and Prince Mohammed accompanied him. It pleased him to travel where no European had travelled before; and he was especially delighted by his night journeys under the brilliant stars, the trees festooned with fireflies, and the presence of the Dyaks, those small and beautifully formed people who cultivated their sparse patches of rice and collected human heads as other people collect butterflies.

As he looked out from the longboat and talked with those who lived on the banks of the river, he came to the conclusion that Sarawak was a trader's paradise. He made long lists of the produce of the land, and constantly revised them. There were antimony, timber, Malacca cane, rattan, beeswax, birds' nest for the Chinese epicures, pipe-clay, rice, sago, vegetable tallow, perhaps gold and diamonds. These could be bought in exchange for brilliantly coloured velvets and beads—velvets for the Malays, beads for the Dyaks. He did not, however, regard himself as a trader: he was an explorer, one who opens up the land. He did not yet know what he would do in Sarawak.

After three days Prince Mohammed suggested it was time to turn back to Kuching. 'There is nothing to see,' the Prince said, when they were approaching the rapids. 'The river here is narrow, rapid, and obstructed by trees; the Dyaks hostile; the Rajah's enemies in ambush.' James was in no position to disobey. He suspected that the real reason for the order came from the Prince's desire to return to the fleshpots of Kuching. Also, the Prince was running out of tobacco.

At the end of the month he was off again, with the Rajah's permission to explore the Lundu River to the west. In a long-house on the shores of the river he saw human heads for the first time: thirty were hanging in the apartment of a chieftain called Sejugah, who explained that all the heads belonged to his enemies, the Sarebas, and every young man had to obtain a head before he could get married. Except for this deplorable habit of head-hunting, these Dyaks were delightful people. They were gentle, chaste, honest, touchingly kind. They were very curious about the white men, and showed amazing tact. Their women were beautiful and completely fearless; in the presence of strangers they bathed naked, laughed, and played games. They worshipped no gods except a long-dead hero, and they had no priests, and therefore no religious ceremonies. A little sententiously, James wrote in his diary: 'The simplicity of their characters, the purity of their morals, and their present ignorance of all forms of worship and all idea of future responsibility, render them open to conviction of truth and religious impression.' James may have had his tongue in his cheek. He was in no hurry to see them converted.

The native dances delighted him. His rapid notes, written down while watching a sword dance in the long-house at night, were later copied out into his diary. He wrote:

> The room partially lighted by damar torches—the clang of noisy instruments—the crowd of wild spectators—their screams of encouragement to the performers—the flowing hair and rapid evolutions of the dancers, formed a scene I wish could have been reproduced by such a master as Rembrandt or Caravaggio.

One would like to know more about the days he spent in the long-house, while the rain thundered on the roof and the torches spluttered and the heads with beads inserted in the eye sockets looked impassively down. The long-house was a whole village; fifty families lived in it, and he was free to wander where he wished. He observed the Dyaks at work and at leisure; he admired their primitive iron-furnaces, their shipbuilding yards—they constructed canoes fifty feet long—and their paddy fields. They seemed to him the most enviable people, with a natural nobility of their own, quiet, industrious, with no hint of malice in them.

From the long-house he went a few miles up-river and encountered another race, still more industrious. Here there was a small Chinese settlement, of people newly arrived from Sambas over the border: thirty Chinese men and five Sambas women. They were mining antimony; they had found diamonds, and hoped to find tin; they had already planted many acres of rice, betelnut, Indian corn, and sweet potatoes. The settlement had been in existence for only four or five months, but already it was flourishing. James noted in his diary: 'The race are worthy of attention, as the future possessors of Borneo.' It was not one of his happier prophecies, but there was enough truth in it to make him think seriously about the Chinese as competitors of the English. When he returned to Kuching, he could think only of trade.

The Rajah and Prince Makota were also thinking about trade, and they plied James with questions about trading prospects with Singapore. For the first time James became aware of the complexity of the mind of *der Makota*, that corrupt and smiling prince, who never smoked tobacco nor chewed betelnut, who kept asking searching questions about how the trade would be managed, and who seemed to have a prodigious knowledge of the government, laws, and customs of Borneo. The Prince already saw himself as the accomplished entrepreneur, controlling all the trade that passed through Sarawak.

Wearying of the Prince, James turned his attention to the Rajah, who was one of those rare men who inspire immediate affection, 'a mild and gentle master', generous to a fault, always excusing the faults of others. James explained that he was leaving Kuching, to explore the coast. The Rajah was alarmed, and begged him to stay, and when James made it clear that he had no intention of staying at this point, the Rajah gave him as a parting gift a gold-handled kriss which had belonged to his father; in exchange James gave him a small pearl-handled dagger. Already they were brothers. And when at last James took his leave, the Rajah exclaimed: 'Tuan Brooke, do not forget me!'

The *Royalist* sailed down-river with the Rajah on board. Some six or seven miles from Kuching the Rajah left to return to his capital, and then James fired the proper salute of twenty-one guns. In return he received a salute of forty-two guns. 'At least we counted twenty-four,' he wrote, 'and they went on firing afterwards, as long as ever we were in sight.'

Henceforth there was to be an indissoluble bond between the Rajah and the young Englishman, which would be broken only by death.

James however was still uncertain about his plans. He had made no promises. He had not yet identified himself completely with Sarawak. He was still on a voyage of discovery. He had met the Malay rulers and their Dyak and Chinese subjects; he had yet to meet the pirates.

His first encounter with the pirates took place when he was sailing up the Sadong River to the north-east of Sarawak. Here he met two local chieftains, Serip Sahib and Datu Jembrong, the one an Arab, the other a native of Mindanao in the Philippines. Datu Jembrong was a pirate, an old man but well-built and still active in his trade, capable of much kindness. Serip Sahib was tall and heavy, with a fine nose and clean-cut features, very indolent; it was clear that he encouraged and perhaps financed the pirate raids. These two charming ruffians made no secret of their passion for piracy. James was wary. He gave them gifts, listened to their stories, and accepted their friendship with reservations.

One evening when the *Royalist* was moored in midstream and the Malay prahu which had accompanied him during his journeys was at anchor near the shore under the dark shadow of a hill, he heard the Malays shouting at the top of their voices: 'Dyaks! Dyaks!' Sarebas pirates were attacking the Malay prahu.

James ordered all hands on deck, fired a blank from the gun, sent up a blue flare, and lowered a boat to go to their rescue. Afraid that the Sarebas pirates would attack his ship, and not knowing how many they were, he loaded his guns, ran up the boarding netting, and saw that his men were at battle stations. The brilliant blue flare frightened the pirates, and they vanished in the darkness as silently as they came. Four men lay wounded in the prahu, and the pirates left a dozen spears behind.

For the first time James became aware of the power of the pirates. He had not in fact seen them; he had felt their invisible presence. The least he could do was to take the wounded back to Kuching. He was still debating with himself whether to return to Kuching when Prince Makota providentially arrived with an invitation from the Rajah: would James kindly come to stay with him in his palace? It was an invitation which could not be ignored.

James sailed for Kuching, and was at once escorted into the Rajah's apartments. That night he slept on a crimson silk mattress embroidered with gold. He was a little drunk, for he had attended a banquet *à l'anglaise* given in his honour—one of those immense royal banquets where the host himself plied the guests with wine and sweetmeats, and whispered into their ears: 'You are at home!'

James had no intention of making Kuching his home. He was overwhelmed by the Rajah's kindness, but he was in no mood to surrender his freedom. He could feel the attractions of Sarawak— the buried treasure, the high mountains, the mysterious valleys inhabited by a casual, handsome people who amused themselves by head-hunting—but he resisted these attractions steadily. He sailed for Singapore, and it was six months before he returned.

Why he left at this moment when his power over the Rajah was increasing daily is something of a puzzle. He may have wanted to wait until the civil war in Sarawak was over; he may have thought that a few months' absence would improve his prospects; he may have been hoping for happier adventures in other islands of the Indies. At any rate, he was in a mood for voyaging. He was perfectly free to travel wherever he liked, and he suffered all his life from a kind of spiritual restlessness.

Suddenly he decided to sail for the Celebes—someone in Singapore had told him about the great qualities of the Bugis warriors. He was particularly anxious to visit the court of the King of Boni, who owned allegiance to his Dutch conquerors. Unlike Rajah Muda Hassim, the King of Boni was anxious to avoid a meeting with an English adventurer, especially since the Dutch had quite formally forbidden such meetings. James was made to kick his heels, waiting for the invitation which was continually delayed.

At last he was granted an audience, and after riding for an hour across an empty plain, he was greeted with a show of force. Several thousand Bugis, naked to the waist, were waiting for him at the

palace gates. There were spearmen in bright chain armour in the
palace courtyard. The King sat on a throne, wearing a skullcap and
a long robe studded with gold buttons. The audience was brief, and
the King seems to have been especially interested only in the fact
that James had once visited Constantinople, a city which many
Moslems regarded with favour because it was the residence of the
Sultan of Turkey. James was not deeply impressed with Celebes.

When he returned to Singapore he was ill with a lingering disease
which seems to have been malaria, complicated by an infection in
the foot brought about when he stupidly walked barefoot through
the jungle. He was in a bad temper. He raged against inactivity,
made plans, changed them, wrote endless letters, and dreamed of
seeking adventure in China. He wrote to his friend John Templer:
'I sail for Borneo tomorrow morning; from Borneo I go to Manila;
and from Manila probably across to China; beyond that I know
nothing.' He did not reach China, and never saw Manila. Towards
the end of August, 1840, he sailed to Sarawak. He had come home
at last.

In the eight months which had elapsed since his last visit very little
had changed. The small rebellion, which Rajah Muda Hassim
once described as 'child's play', was still going on, with the Dutch-
protected Sultan of Sambas favouring the rebels and sending them
small supplies of guns and ammunition. The indolence of the Rajah
sustained the rebellion. The weeks passed, while the Rajah spoke
of bringing up an army of Malays and Dyaks to put an end to the
war once and for all, and then he would go on to speak of how much
he needed James and how happy he was to have James by his side.
He hinted at dark plots among the princes. James constantly visited
the palace, and the Rajah came nearly every day to the ship.

Meanwhile small bands of insurgents were continually deserting
to the Rajah; or perhaps they were not deserting. No one seemed to
know what was happening. The rain fell. On board the *Royalist*
two men died suddenly of fever and were solemnly buried on shore,
with James conducting the funeral service—'that impressive and
beautiful service of the Church of England'. James was beginning
to weary of the Rajah's pleas, and there were rumours that he would
be assassinated if he remained. He was not perturbed by the
rumours, but he was deeply perturbed by the senseless rebellion, the
indolence and insolence of the Malay princes, the growing feeling
that the rebellion might go on for ever, because the Rajah had
neither the strength of purpose nor the weapons to put an end to it.

James was so angry that he decided to resume his journey to
China. He wrote in his diary for September 9, 1840:

I sent Williamson to intimate my approaching departure; and when I
went in the evening the little man had such a sorrowful countenance that

my heart smote me. When I told him I would remain if there was the slightest chance of a close to war, his countenance cleared, and he gaily repeated that my fortune and his would bring this struggle to an end, though others forsook him. I then consented to await the issue a few days longer . . .

Having at last decided to ally himself with the Rajah, James was in a quandary. The key to the enemy position was the stockade Balidah, only a few miles up-river. There were a number of small forts nearby, defended by men armed with spears and swords and a few muskets: the approaches to these forts were guarded by pointed bamboo stakes and lightly covered pits which were also provided with these fearsome stakes. The enemy was dispersed over an area of several miles, and if one fort fell, they could simply take cover in another.

Against perhaps 400 rebels there was a grand army consisting of 250 Malays with a handful of brass guns, 200 Dyaks who had gathered from all over the country, and some 200 Chinese without guns and scarcely any muskets, but with primitive bazookas. It was 'an incongruous army', James reported. In fighting, the Malays and Dyaks wore quilted jackets which covered only their bodies, 'the bare legs and arms sticking out from under this puffed-up coat, like the sticks which support the garments of a scarecrow'. How on earth, he kept asking himself, could these people be made to fight?

In fact, no one really wanted to fight. There was a great deal of shouting and the beating of silver-tongued gongs, and much aimless shooting. When the rebels opened fire from Balidah they took care that all their shots went over the tree-tops. They taunted one another, and when they wearied of hearing their own voices, they fired a few shots and went to sleep. The Dyaks were on the verge of fighting among themselves. According to Prince Makota there had been continual fighting for two months. James asked how many people had been killed.

'We killed five of the enemy,' the Prince replied.

'How many did you lose?' James asked.

'None at all!' said the Prince, and he seemed to be surprised that the question had been asked.

James brought up his own guns and fired a few shots at Balidah, but no one appears to have been impressed by this display of force; and the fort, which was loosely constructed, was easily repaired. Prince Makota was in no hurry to attack. There were interminable discussions, innumerable subtle alterations of the battle plan. By November 4, James was at his wit's end. He had once been excited by the prospect of seeing a war fought between Chinese, Malays, and Dyaks; now he completely lost interest, and told the Rajah that he intended to sail out of Sarawak for ever.

The Rajah begged him to stay for friendship's sake, and when James still refused, he offered to give him Sarawak, its government and trade, if only he would help to put down the rebels. James offered to stay on condition that the war was taken seriously.

It is in the nature of the Malay mind to possess more love for gesture than for direct action. If the Rajah said: 'Henceforth the war will be prosecuted seriously', and if he truly meant it, this was regarded as an action almost as comprehensive as an order to attack. After such an order fighting became an anti-climax.

James bore it all patiently. He suspected that Prince Makota was deliberately prolonging the campaign for his own mysterious purposes, but he hoped to impress on Prince Budrudeen the necessity for a quick war. On December 10 he visited the battle-front and reported his findings in his journal:

> We found the grand army in a state of torpor, eating, drinking, and walking up to the forts and back again daily; but having built those imposing structures, and their appearance not driving the enemy away, they were at a loss what next to do, or how to proceed.
>
> On my arrival, I once more insisted on mounting the guns in our old forts, and assaulting Balidah under their fire. Makota's timidity and vacillation were too apparent; but in consequence of Budrudeen's overawing presence, he was obliged, from shame, to yield his assent. The order for the attack was fixed as follows:—our party of ten (leaving six to serve the guns) were to be headed by myself. Budrudeen, Makota, Subtu, and all the lesser chiefs, were to lead their followers, from 60 to 80 in number, by the same route, while 50 or more Chinese, under their captain, were to assault by another path to the left. Makota was to take the paths as near as possible to Balidah, with his Dyaks, who were to extract the *sudas* [sharpened bamboo spikes] and fill up the holes.
>
> The guns having been mounted and their range well ascertained the previous evening, we ascended to the fort at about eight A.M., and at ten opened our fire and kept it up for an hour. The effect was severe; every shot told upon their thin defences of wood, which fell in many places so as to leave storming breaches. Part of the roof was cut away and tumbled down, and the shower of grape and canister rattled so as to prevent their returning our fire, except from a stray rifle. At mid-day the forces reached the fort, and it was then discovered that Makota had neglected to make any road, because it rained the night before!

So it went on, with nothing gained: bursts of gunfire, occasional skirmishes, shouts, taunts, the building of new forts, solemn promises by the princes to send reinforcements, the endless repetition of a confused stalemate. The Malays, Chinese, and Dyaks were fighting one kind of war; and thirteen Englishmen from the *Royalist* were fighting another. Characteristically, James, in command of his shipmates, charged across a paddy field and scattered a large enemy force in a bloodless victory. If he was surprised by his victory,

Prince Makota was still more surprised, saving his face by ascribing the victory to his own prowess, though he had done nothing all day. Shame spurred him to attack the enemy a little more vigorously, and soon the rebels, wearied beyond endurance by continual pin-pricks, offered to surrender if their lives were spared.

James was pleased. The senseless war was ending cleanly. He accepted their surrender, ordering them to burn their stockades and deliver up their arms. He had not counted on the Rajah, who was in favour of a general massacre. James, aghast, threatened for the third or fourth time to sail away. The Rajah explained that a general massacre was the only proper punishment for rebels, but James played successfully on his vanity, reminding him that he would receive great merit by pardoning them. 'I told him their lives were forfeited, their crimes had been of a heinous and unpardonable nature, and it was only from so humane a man as himself, one with so kind a heart, that I could ask for pardon.' He was beginning to understand the complicated game of flattery.

He played the game well, but not always with effect. The weak Rajah and the wily Prince Makota were more than a match for him, as month followed month, and intrigue followed war. James had an old-fashioned way of regarding promises: he thought they should be kept. The Rajah, frightened of Prince Makota, thought promises to James were part of the inevitable conspiracy with which he countered all the conspiracies against him. Wherever he looked, James saw 'the cunning and diabolically intriguing' hand of Prince Makota.

The war was over, but the terms of the armistice were broken within twenty-four hours. Some of the minor princes, sent an expedition up-river to pillage the enemy camp. James protested, and fired some shots at their war-prahus to prevent them going further. The Rajah remonstrated, but James was determined to stop a massacre. A few days later, when he had returned to Kuching, he heard that an Ilanun pirate fleet, consisting of eighteen war vessels armed with cannon and muskets, had been invited to seek its fortune along the river.

James was alarmed by this astonishing invitation, and came to the conclusion that Prince Makota had made some arrangement with the pirates. There were rumours, too, that the pirates intended to capture the *Royalist*. James protested again. The Rajah said the pirate fleet had only come for a visit; they did not intend to sweep up the river and raid the Dyaks. There was a naval review, with all the pirate vessels anchored in midstream. James went on board. He noted that the ships sometimes carried fifty oars, were not easily manœuvrable, and rarely ventured far from land. He asked questions about the beneficiaries of the plunder and learned that all slaves, money, and costly silks went to the ship's commander and the small number of free men around him, while everything else went to the slaves who manned the oars. For slaves they especially prized the woolly-haired Papuans. All the pirates were inveterate opium smokers.

James seems to have been fascinated by the pirates and described them at length in his diary. He admired their war dances, their head-dresses ornamented with the feathers of birds of paradise, their shields covered with small rings which clashed during the dances; and he hated them for the harm they did. Neither the English, the Dutch, nor the Spanish were doing anything to put them down. These 'pirates by descent, robbers from pride as well as taste' were the scourge of the East Indies, and he swore to destroy them. The pirates took a good look at the *Royalist*'s guns and sailed out to sea.

But though the danger from the pirates had been removed and the rebellion had ended, James was still uncertain about his own status in Sarawak. The Rajah had promised him the kingdom for helping him to put down the rebellion, but there was no transfer of power. The Rajah hesitated; Prince Makota intrigued; James brooded. To his journal he confided his most secret thoughts, which were sometimes at cross-purposes. One moment he speaks of placing himself at the service of the country, occupying the humble rôle of adviser. The next moment he sees himself as a conqueror holding sway over all North Borneo, Sarawak no more than a stepping-stone to greater conquests. The Rajah drew up an agreement permitting James to live in Sarawak and 'seek for profit'. James pointed out that this was far from being their original agreement, and the Rajah smiled, saying that this was only the beginning, and in any event the document was designed for the eyes of the Sultan in Brunei. James was suspicious. He could see no advantage in temporizing, and threatened to sail away, and did in fact sail to Singapore to buy at an excessive price a small schooner, the *Swift*, which could be used for exporting antimony ore. While he was away, the Rajah promised to build him a house. On his return, he was told, vast quantities of antimony ore would be waiting for him.

Already the frail Rajah had broken his promises seven times, and James was not unduly perturbed because the Rajah had broken his eighth promise. When he returned from Singapore he found that no house had been built and there was no antimony ore waiting to be loaded on to his ship. It was, after all, very much what he expected.

When he was on the spot, James usually got what he wanted. The Rajah ordered a house to be built for him—it was a good house, fitted with furniture from the *Royalist*—and in return for the cargo on the *Swift* the Rajah offered six thousand piculs of antimony ore.

It was a fair arrangement or would have been if the Rajah had carried out his side of the bargain. The Rajah took possession of the cargo, and forgot to provide the antimony. James, in his diary, slapped the Rajah gently on the wrist for this breach of contract:

> I did not much trouble myself about the deposit; and my attention was first roused by the extreme apathy of the whole party once the cargo was in their possession, overhauled, reckoned and disposed of among them.
>
> Yet I had confidence, and was loath to allow any base suspicion to enter my mind against a man who had hitherto behaved well to me, and had not deceived me before. From the time the cargo had been disposed of I found myself positively laid on the shelf. No return arrived; no steps were taken to work the antimony ore; no account appeared of the positive amount to be received; and all my propositions—nay, my very desire to speak of the state of the country—were evaded.

James was playing the game well. He would never explode, never show malice; he would, if necessary, be as evasive as the Rajah. He demanded, and got, a supply of antimony, not as much as he had hoped, but enough for a respectable shipload; and he got a house. He had just taken possession of the house when he observed an unseasonable number of boats manned by Malays and Sea Dyaks gathered at Kuching. He asked whether they were preparing to raid the interior, and was told that nothing of the sort was intended; he watched them sail up-river, and learned for the first time that a massive raid had been prepared with the Rajah's approval. Then he lost his temper. He announced that he would sail away for ever unless the raid was called off, and this time he meant it.

There were long discussions with the Rajah. There were rumours that some Englishmen were the prisoners of the Sultan of Brunei, and the Rajah had promised to have them released. He had done nothing. He had promised to free the women and children captured at the battle of Balidah; they were still under arrest. He had promised to forbid pirate fleets the use of the river, but a fleet of Malay and Dyak pirates, with two thousand five hundred men on board, had to be called back at the last moment. The Rajah listened and nodded, confessed himself at fault, smiled, assured James of his good faith, explained that it was only a matter of time before the whole country would be placed in James's hands, and then dismissed him. James, suspecting the influence of Prince Makota, decided that the time had come for a trial of strength.

He knew exactly what to do. He had an instinctive understanding of the Malay mind. He did what no one else would have dared to do. Only July 25, 1841, he sent the *Royalist* to Brunei to rescue the captured Englishmen, and the *Swift* off to Singapore with the antimony, while he remained alone and defenceless in Kuching.

It was a brilliant *coup de théâtre*, but a dangerous one. He was at the mercy of Prince Makóta and of everyone else who had a grudge against him. The Malays asked themselves how he could dare to put himself in such grave danger, and they reasoned that he must possess spiritual and physical forces superior to theirs. In two months the lonely man who had watched the ships sailing away from the steps of his small house became Rajah of Sarawak.

Those two months were the most critical months of his life. He remained a week in Kuching, daring his enemies to attack him. On August 2 a strange letter was placed in his hand. It read:

> Island Sirhassen, off Tan Datu,
> July 10th, 1841
>
> A boat leaves this tomorrow for Sarawak; perhaps this may fall into the hands of Mr. Brooke, or some of my countrymen, which, should I not succeed in getting to Singapore, I trust will lose no time in letting the authorities know, so that steps may be taken for the release of the remaining thirty-six British subjects now in Borneo; which I fear nothing but one of H.M. ships will effect.
>
> The pirates are cruising in great force between Sambas and this, and have taken thirteen Borneo prahus, or more; they know that there are Europeans in the prahu, and have expressed a wish to take them. Our situation is not very enviable. The bearer of this has just escaped from them. I have been living ashore with Abduramon, a native of Pulo Pinang, who knows Mr. Brooke, and has been very kind to me. Trusting penmanship and paper will be excused,
>
> I am etc., etc.
> G. H. W. GILL

On the back of this letter Willoughby Gill, late chief officer of the *Sultana* of Bombay, described how his ship had been totally destroyed by lightning and how forty-one of the survivors had reached Brunei in a longboat. Taken before the Sultan, they were ordered to pay an enormous ransom before being released. Gill with two passengers and some servants was allowed to go to Singapore to raise the ransom, but encountering pirates on the way they had taken refuge on the island of Sirhassen.

James saw at once that the letter was of crucial importance. The Rajah had repeatedly denied that his nephew, the Sultan of Brunei, was holding any English prisoners, yet he must have known what had happened. James demanded that a boat be sent to Sirhassan to rescue Gill, and then quite deliberately, knowing that he had stretched his luck, he vanished from Kuching.

His strength lay with the Land Dyaks, whose lives he had so often saved, and so he went among them, sailing up-river to Tudong and the mountains beyond. Once, when he was out hunting, a Dyak said, 'You will be fortunate: I heard the bird behind you.' His fortune was in fact turning rapidly. He was happy among the

Dyaks, who were gentle and undemonstrative. They spoke in a strange, delightful poetry. One day a Dyak, once a slave in the house of Prince Makota, spoke of how he had escaped from slavery, travelling through the woods and swimming the rivers until he came to his own country. Of the Malay prince he said:

He thought the Dyak had no eyes except in the jungle; he thought he had no ears except to listen to the bird of omen; he thought he had no wit except to grow rice; but the Dyak saw, and heard, and understood, that whilst his words were sweet, his heart was crooked, and that, whether they were men of the sea or Dyaks, he deceived them with fair sayings; he said one thing to one man, and another to a second; he deceived with a honeyed mouth.

So Homer might have spoken, describing the treacherous warriors on the plain of Troy; and indeed there was something wonderfully Homeric in all the wars and intrigues in the islands.

James was back in Kuching a week later. There was no news of the *Swift* and the *Royalist*; he began to be uneasy. Then on August 18 the *Royalist* returned at last to Kuching, bearing a letter for James from the Sultan, saying that it was perfectly true that some Englishmen were staying at Brunei; they were being well cared for; they had entered into a treaty with him, and it was for the purpose of implementing the treaty that Willoughby Gill had sailed for Singapore. James was advised not to meddle in affairs that did not concern him. Once more, and for the last time, James employed patience as his weapon.

On the next day the *Swift* returned from Singapore. Now with two ships on the river he could afford to show his strength, and when a third ship the *Diana*, arrived from Singapore, he was in a still stronger position. He demanded that the Rajah keep his promises; no more raids into the interior, the return of the prisoners from Brunei, good treatment for the Dyaks. He also mentioned the small matter of the transfer of power. The Rajah, according to his custom, counselled patience. James was weary of being patient, but decided to hold his fire for the sake of the prisoners at Brunei. The *Diana*, a ship belonging to the East India Company, was dispatched to rescue them. She was an impressive vessel, the first steamship the Sultan had ever set eyes on. He realized that he was powerless against people who could move their ships without oars or sails, and he allowed the prisoners to go. The *Diana* brought them to Kuching.

Prince Makota was now desperate. He saw, as never before, that his days as a princely racketeer were numbered. Once he had said, 'I was brought up to plunder the Dyaks, and it makes me laugh to think that I have fleeced a tribe down to its cooking-pots.' He had long contemplated murdering James, and determined to act. Arsenic was put in James's food, but James was warned. He was blazing with anger. A landing party, fully armed, was rowed ashore; the ship's guns were manned and trained on the palace; and James marched to the palace to issue an ultimatum. He expected some trouble from Prince Makota, but none came: the prince was hiding in his own palace. The Dyaks sent messages to say they supported James.[1]

Gracefully the Rajah signed the letter of abdication:

By agreement made in the year of the Prophet one thousand two hundred and fifty-seven, at twelve o'clock on the thirtieth day of the month of Rejab, Prince Muda Hassim, son of the late Sultan Mohammed, with a pure heart and high purpose, doth hereby transfer to the well-born James Brooke power over the country of Sarawak, together with all its dependencies, and present and future revenues.

To James Brooke shall belong all the revenues arising from the country, and he alone shall be responsible for all expenditures to be paid for the good of Sarawak. With a pure heart and high purpose he agrees to pay to the Sultan of Brunei one thousand Spanish dollars, and to the Prince Muda Hassim the sum of a thousand Spanish dollars. He further undertakes to respect the laws and customs of the Malays of Sarawak, formally subject to the Sultan of Brunei, Prince Muda Hassim and the Malay governors.

Furthermore it is agreed between us that if incidents arise inimical to the interests of the state of Sarawak, whether caused by the people, or by princes, or by rulers, then the Sultan of Brunei and his brother the Prince Muda Hassim shall uphold the power of James Brooke and permit interference by none.

The Prince's letter of abdication, signed and sealed on September 24, 1841, included a treaty of friendship. It was not, however, final, for it was necessary that the agreement be ratified by the Sultan. For the moment James was only acting Rajah, with the fullest powers.

Almost his first act was to issue a series of laws, which showed him to be a curiously Utopian lawgiver. He had the laws printed in Singapore in Malay:

[1] I have based this account on James's letters and diaries written at the time. Many years later, in a letter written to Lord Malmesbury on November 23, 1852, he summarized the events of those days in a neat, if not completely convincing paragraph:

The conduct of Makota soon brought affairs to a crisis; poison was attempted; I loaded the guns of the yacht and obtained an audience with the Rajah Muda Hassim. In a few words I pointed out the villainy of Makota; his tyranny and oppression of all classes; and my determination to attack him. I explained to the Rajah that several chiefs, and a large body of Seriawan Dyaks, were ready to assist me; and that the only course left to prevent bloodshed was immediately to proclaim me Governor of the Country.

I, James Brooke Esquire, Rajah of Sarawak, make known to all men the following laws:

1st. Murder, robbery and other heinous crimes will be punished accord to the *ondongondong* [i.e. the written law of Sarawak]; and no person committing such offences will escape if, after fair enquiry, he be proved guilty.

2nd. In order to ensure the good of the country, all men, whether Malays, Chinese, or Dyaks, are permitted to trade or labour according to their pleasure, and to enjoy their gains.

3rd. All roads will be open, that the inhabitants at large may seek profit both by sea and by land; and all boats coming from others are free to enter the river and depart, without let or hindrance.

4th. Trade, in all its branches, will be free, with the exception of antimony-ore, which the Rajah holds in his own hands, but which no person is forced to work, and which will be paid for at proper prices. The people are encouraged to trade and labour, and to enjoy the profits which are made by fair and honest dealing.

5th. It is ordered that no person going amongst the Dyaks shall disturb them, or gain their goods under false pretences. It must be clearly explained to the different Dyak tribes, that the revenue will be collected by the three Datus, bearing the seal of the Rajah; and (except this yearly demand from the governmènt) they are to give nothing to any other person; nor are they obliged to sell their goods except as they please, and at their own prices.

6th. The Rajah shall shortly inquire into the revenue, and fix it at a proper rate; so that everyone may know certainly how much he has to contribute yearly to support the government.

7th. It will be necessary, likewise, to settle the weights, measures, and money current in the country, and to introduce doits, that the poor may purchase food cheaply.

8th. The Rajah issues these commands, and will enforce obedience to them; and whilst he gives all protection and assistance to the persons who act rightly, he will not fail to punish those who seek to disturb the public peace or commit crimes; and he warns all such persons to seek their safety, and find some other country where they may be permitted to break the laws of God and man.

The eight laws are worth examining carefully, for James composed them with great care and with the utmost seriousness. At thirty-eight he had become acting Rajah of Sarawak: a complex civilization made up of Chinese gold miners, Malay princes and fishermen, Dyak pirates and head-hunters had fallen into his hands. The eight laws clipped the wings of the Malay princes, penalized head-hunters and pirates, and left the incomprehensible Chinese severely alone. He was demanding free trade, free passage of all goods, the abolition of slavery, especially debt-slavery, the imposition of an equitable tax system, and a fair profit for the antimony miners. It was an astonishing programme. James considered it a *minimum* programme, and acted accordingly.

To see that the laws were carried out, he held court in his own house every day. He punished murderers and thieves, saw to it that debtors were fairly treated, and protected the Dyaks against the Malays, who sometimes behaved as though there had never been any transfer of power. He decided to abandon the English custom of oath-taking, for it meant nothing to the happy savages he ruled over. He kept his witnesses apart, and developed a system by which he could learn more from their lies and prevarications than from their truthful statements. 'In one case about a slave', he wrote, 'three witnesses had resolved on the sex; but, questioned separately as to size and age, all disagreed. They were not prepared. One represented her a woman grown and marriageable; another, as high as my walking-stick; the third, as a child.' For himself the chief advantage of these daily trials lay in his increasing knowledge of the Malay and Dyak minds. Soon he would come to know them as no one else had ever known them.

Dyaks came to him and asked permission for a little head-hunting, 'as a schoolboy will ask for apples'. James sternly refused. He prepared to fit out a fleet against the pirates. There were small uprisings in the interior, and there was little he could do except to order the local chiefs to put them down. He arbitrated a dispute between Chinese gold miners in Upper Sarawak, and discovered that the Chinese settlers had carefully construed their original grant from Rajah Muda Hassim as an outright gift of land; and he cancelled the grant. He was generous and fair, and very lonely. He wrote home for 'an electrifying machine', a magic lantern, and a peepshow, explaining that he wanted them to amuse the Dyaks, but it is just possible that he wanted to amuse himself. The Dyaks especially enjoyed the peepshow, which showed Napoleon riding on a white horse at Waterloo.

They were dangerous months, for Rajah Muda Hassim and all his brothers remained at Kuching. They formed a kind of shadow government, ready to take over as soon as James had received the inevitable dose of arsenic or someone cut off his head. Even Prince Makota, who had hurried off to seek help in Sambas, returned a little sheepishly, with plans to dethrone the new Rajah. The old Rajah complained that he dared not go to the court of the Sultan of Brunei: someone, perhaps Prince Makota, would kill him as soon as he arrived. On January 1, 1842, when he had been acting Rajah for more than three months, James wrote in his diary: 'Whatever they bring—whether it be life or death, fortune or poverty—I am prepared; and in the deep solitude of my present existence I can safely say that I believe I could bear misfortune better than prosperity.'

Prosperity, real prosperity, was something he never came to

Prince Makota of Sarawak—"he possessed all the talents"

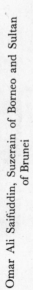

Omar Ali Saifuddin, Suzerain of Borneo and Sultan of Brunei

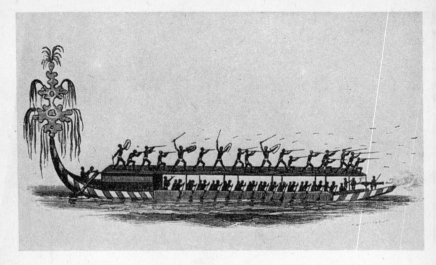

A war prahu—the standard warship of Dyak pirates

The recapture of Kuching, 1857, by the Borneo Company steamer, *Sir James Brooke*, from a painting by Helms in the possession of the Borneo Company

know; misfortunes lay around every corner. The Malays were continually plotting, and the Sarebas chieftains were looking forward to his downfall because he prohibited head-hunting. One of them even hung a basket on a high tree, a clear indication that there was a suitable resting-place for the new Rajah's head.

Occasionally he visited the interior, to put down wars or to install some local chieftain in office. He was on his way to install a friendly chieftain when he came upon the evidence of a skirmish—a heap of five heads was being guarded by warriors in full war-panoply.

> We found the five heads guarded by about thirty young men in their finest dresses, composed principally of scarlet jackets ornamented with shells, turbans of the native bark-cloth dyed bright yellow, and spread on the head and decked with an occasional feather, flower or twig of leaves. Nothing can exceed their partiality for these trophies; and in retiring from the 'war-path', the man who has been so fortunate as to obtain a head hangs it about his neck, and instantly commences his return to his tribe. If he sleep on the way, the precious burden, though decaying and offensive, is not loosened, but rests on his lap, whilst his head (and nose!) reclines on his knees. The retreat is always silently made until close to home, when they set up a wild yell, which announces their victory and the possession of its proofs.

James installed the chieftain, pronounced judgment on the heads, delivered lengthy lectures against head-hunting, took notes on the customs of the tribes. He was not very surprised when he returned to Kuching to find delegations of Dyaks proclaiming him as their Rajah and saying: 'The whole world has heard that a son of Europe was a friend to the Dyaks.'

He could count on the Dyaks; he could not yet count on the Malays. At all costs it was necessary to remove Muda Hassim from Kuching. Spring came, and then summer, but it was not until half way through July that arrangements were completed for sending a princely delegation to the Sultan of Brunei to obtain his consent to the transfer of power. A formal letter was written to the Sultan and put in the hands of Muda Hassim's brothers. Muda Hassim himself remained in Kuching to await the outcome of the embassy.

James was looking forward to his visit to Brunei, but the first sight of the place alarmed him. It was hardly larger than Kuching and consisted of the same brown huts on piles. He described it as 'a very Venice of hovels, fit only for frogs'. Prince Budrudeen was the first to go ashore with the letter, which lay in a brass tray covered with an embroidered yellow cloth. The Prince returned with the news that it had been received by the Sultan with exclamations of joy. With nothing to fear James stepped on shore and was received by the Sultan like a long-lost friend.

Like Prince Makota, the Sultan was one of those men who appear to belong to legend rather than to history. He was the incarnation of murderous imbecility. He was over fifty, a small, thin, bald man, who could neither read nor write; he had three thumbs, having an extra thumb, like a small claw, on his right hand. He suffered from cancer of the mouth, his arms and legs were painfully thin, and he wore an expression of permanent confusion. He was dressed in purple satin and cloth-of-gold, and wore a gold-headed kriss at his waist.

James was fascinated by the monster, who talked continually, often joked, and was unable to concentrate on a serious matter for more than a few seconds. Given handsome presents, he kept asking for more. When the *Royalist* was stripped clean to provide him with more gifts, he ingenuously demanded a list of the remaining objects on the ship. The month of Ramadan was coming up, and he begged James to return shortly so that he would not have to starve during that month when all good Mohammedans fast. 'What shall I do during the fast,' he complained, 'without sugar and dates?'

In the end, after sitting for six days in conference with the Sultan, James came to the conclusion that flattery and bad counsel had turned his head. In James's view he was a harmless madman, rapacious in the extreme but otherwise good-tempered. He was to learn later that Sultan Omar Ali, far from being mad, was cool, unscrupulous, and dangerous.

While the Sultan sat on his throne of state, occasionally popping betelnuts into his mouth with the help of his two right-hand thumbs, James listened to long disquisitions on the new friendship which had sprung up between the Sultan and the English Rajah. He approved of the transfer of power, though he pointed out that many things in Sarawak were his personal possession and would have to be paid for —he mentioned $10,000 as a sum which might be regarded as the basis of an amicable settlement. There had been another shipwreck, and the Sultan confessed to be only too glad to release the imprisoned Hindus who had taken refuge in Brunei.

As for Muda Hassim, the Sultan professed to love him to distraction and to be eagerly looking forward to his arrival in Brunei. He pretended to be overjoyed by James's new position in Sarawak. 'I wish you to be there,' he said. 'I do not wish anybody else. You are my amigo, and it is nobody's business but mine, and if I please to give you all, I can!' Holding James by the hand, the Sultan repeated endlessly the only foreign words he knew: '*Suya amigo.*'

To be the friend of the Sultan was one thing; to be Rajah was another. James waited impatiently for the letters which would put the seal on the transfer of power. They came at last, after interminable delays, wrapped in yellow silk, sealed with the royal seal, addressed to Muda Hassim. The *Royalist* pulled up anchor and sailed for Kuching.

On the evening of August 18 these letters were solemnly read by a man standing on a raised platform while the Malay princes stood below. They were all armed. Prince Makota was present. The last of the letters announced that James had been appointed Rajah of Sarawak, with the full permission of the Sultan of Brunei. At once Muda Hassim shouted: 'If anyone present disowns or contests the Sultan's appointment, let him now declare!' And when no one spoke, Muda Hassim turned again to the princes and said: 'Are there any of the princes who contest it? If anyone disobeys the Sultan's mandate, I will separate his skull! Prince Makota, what do you say?'

Prince Makota said he would obey. At that moment, as at a signal, ten of the Rajah's brothers leapt forward with drawn swords and danced around the Prince, striking the pillar above his head and pointing significantly in the direction of his heart. Any motion would have been fatal, but he kept his eyes on the ground. James, too, was quiet. He had reason to be quiet. At that moment, when the princes pointed their krisses at the enemy, threatening to run him through, the history of Sarawak had taken a new direction. He had become Rajah, entitled to dress in royal yellow, with a turban of lilac cloth-of-gold upon his head, with absolute rule over all the Malays and Dyaks in the country.

Afterwards, when he remembered the barbaric scene—the krisses flashing in the light of oil lamps, Prince Makota silent as in a dream, and Rajah Muda Hassim shouting grimly at the top of his voice—James pretended to an emotion he rarely possessed. 'I remained quiet', he wrote, 'and cared not, for one gets accustomed to these things.' But in fact he never grew accustomed to it. The beauty and the strangeness of that scene haunted him all his life; and long after he would tell the story, remembering new details, calling up the images of the Rajah and the princes as, waving swords, they surrendered their power into his hands.

IV

RAJAH BROOKE

James had reached full power, but in fact he was powerless. He had no army, no fleet, no court, no officials to administer the country, no police force except the small groups of Malays and Dyaks he could muster to put down uprisings in the interior, and he had no defence against pirates. There was almost no trade, and he had no treasury, and he was incapable of drawing up a balance sheet. He could command eight or nine Englishmen and perhaps two hundred Malays and as many Dyaks. He was Rajah of Sarawak, and power was a mirage.

Muda Hassim was in no hurry to return to Brunei, and all the Malay princes remained at Kuching. Even Prince Makota, who had been officially banished, remained for some months at the capital. Intrigue flourished, and rumours, invented perhaps by the very Malay princes who had surrendered to him their powers, spoke of how he would remain in authority for only a few days or weeks before being assassinated; and there were other rumours that 6,000 armed Chinese were about to invade the country.

He had been Rajah for only a few days when he heard that some of the Dyaks in the Singhé mountains refused to recognize his authority. An expedition was sent against them, and the ringleaders, Parimban and Pa Tummo, were captured, brought to Kuching and put on trial. They were sentenced to death. James entered the details of their execution in his journal:

> Sept. 7th at 6 o'clock in the evening, as the sun set, Parimban and Pa Tummo closed their earthly career. They were taken out to the rear of my house, and despatched by the knives of the Rajah's followers. I could not help being shocked, though the necessity was a stern one, and their death merited. Besides, their release would have entailed the destruction of numbers of my friends and supporters. Parimban died with courage. Pa Tummo shrank from the execution of the sentence. Both were laid in one grave.

It was a strangely heartless statement, and years later James came to regret the wording of it, even though he never regretted the necessity of stern measures when his power was in the balance. His enemies in England accused him of being a common murderer.

He was not a murderer: he was a man desperately anxious to maintain peace in a country on the verge of war. He was in peril from the Ilanun pirates along the coast, from the Sultan of Sambas on his western border, and from the armed bands of Serip Sahib who controlled the nearby Sadong River. At any moment there might be another Dyak uprising; at any moment the Malay princes might strike. In a mood of guarded enthusiasm, forgetting danger, he wrote to his mother in England:

> If it please God to permit me to give a stamp to this country which shall last after I am no more, I shall have lived a life which emperors might envy. If, by dedicating myself to the task, I am able to introduce better customs and settled laws, and to raise the feeling of the people, so that their rights can never in future be wantonly infringed, I shall indeed be content and happy.

Such statements are not written by murderers. They are written by men who carry a heavy load of responsibility on their backs.

James's power was the intangible power that comes from personal authority; almost it was invisible. He did not have to be physically present in Sarawak, for he could always leave someone behind to act in his name. He needed ships, money, guns, friends in high positions, the opening of large-scale trade between Sarawak and Singapore. For the moment the Dyaks were quiet, the Chinese were industriously working the gold mines, and the princes were more inclined to obey the faithful Budrudeen than the faithless Makota. 'My motives for going to Singapore are various,' he wrote. 'I hope to do good, to excite interest, and make friends; and I can find no season like the present for my absence.' On February 8, 1843, he sailed for Singapore.

He had hoped to make friends, and he found more than a friend. He found a man who shared his own enthusiasm for mysterious countries in the Far East and his own sense of mission. He was Captain the Honourable Henry Keppel, the thirty-four-year-old son of the Earl of Albemarle, in command of H.M.S. *Dido*, then being refitted in Singapore. Keppel was very short, standing little more than five feet, but he was tough and pugnacious, and he shared with James a high regard for good manners and a still higher regard for punishing offenders of the law. He had red hair and deep laughing blue eyes, and he walked with the rolling gait of a sailor.

To Keppel, James spoke of the need to put down pirates and to show the flag in Sarawak waters. Keppel at once offered to sail to Kuching in the *Dido*, with James as his most distinguished passenger. On the voyage Keppel complained about the charts supplied by the Admiralty, and said ruefully, 'I actually sailed by the best Admiralty charts eighty miles inland, and over the tops of mountains.'

The *Dido*, the first square-rigged vessel ever to enter the Sarawak River, fell in with pirates when she was only twelve miles from Kuching. There was a short running battle; most of the pirate ships escaped, but one, belonging to the Rajah of Rhio, an island near Singapore, was captured. If Keppel needed a lesson on the extraordinary power of the pirates, he already had it. The war prahu was well-armed, with three brass guns and a crew of thirty.

When the *Dido* anchored off Kuching the next day James was piped ashore with a salute of twenty-one guns. Keppel was delighted with his friend's reception, and wrote in his diary: 'The whole surface of the water was covered with canoes and boats dressed out with their various-coloured silken flags, filled with natives beating their tom-toms, and playing on their wild and not unpleasant-sounding wind-instruments, with the occasional discharge of firearms.'

The next business was a meeting with Muda Hassim, who received the *Dido*'s captain in state, sitting in his audience chamber hung with red and yellow silk curtains. Keppel was not over impressed by Muda Hassim, whom he described as 'a wretched-looking man; still there was a courteous and gentle manner about him which prepossessed us in his favour'. Keppel was uncomfortable during the long audience. It annoyed him that Muda Hassim sat with one leg crossed under him and continually picked at his toes, and he was still more annoyed by his habit of chewing betelnuts and spitting out the juice.

On the third day the former Rajah of Sarawak and his entire court visited the *Dido*. The royal brothers scrambled all over the ship. Muda Hassim was overawed by the size of the ship, and when Keppel explained that there were even bigger ships in Her Majesty's Navy, Muda Hassim politely assumed an air of incredulity. Someone told him not to spit betel juice in the captain's cabin. He waited until he was outside, and then spat a whole mouthful of the juice on the white deck. The first lieutenant shouted, 'Dirty beast!' Muda Hassim, who knew no English, simply smiled.

Keppel was fascinated by Kuching, and he was especially pleased with James's house, which was now comfortably furnished, the large dining-room, which was also used as an audience chamber, being neatly decorated with spears, daggers, and firearms of all kinds. James was in good form. So, too, was Dr. John Treacher, lately of Singapore, who told a strange story that Keppel wrote down in his journal. Shortly after the doctor's arrival in Kuching, he received a secret message from one of Prince Makota's wives, begging him to meet her in a secluded part of the jungle. The handsome doctor dressed in his finery and went to meet her, hoping for a conquest. She was young and pretty, but the doctor detected a look of determination which belied any hope of conquering her. She complained of the ill treatment she had received from the prince. She wanted to kill him, and she hoped the doctor would provide her with arsenic. The doctor refused. A few months later he may have thought it would have been wiser to accede to her wishes.

As part of his initiation into the affairs of Sarawak, Keppel was taken into the nearby Singhé mountains, where only a few months before James had led an expedition against the Dyaks. For the first time Keppel saw the long-houses with the dried human heads swinging from the rafters, sea shells in the eye sockets, tufts of dried grass protruding from the ears. He seems, like most visitors to Sarawak in those days, to have quickly accustomed himself to the sight.

He admired the young Dyaks with their ornaments of hornbill feathers and immense necklaces, and described a native dance:

In one house there was a grand *fête*, in which the women danced with the men. The dress of the women was simple and curious—a light jacket open in front, and a short petticoat not coming below the knees, fitting close, was hung round with jingling bits of brass, which kept 'making music' wherever they went. The movement was like all other native dances—graceful, but monotonous.

There were four men, two of them bearing human skulls, and two the fresh heads of pigs; the women bore wax-lights, or yellow rice on brass dishes. They danced in line, moving backwards and forwards, and carrying the heads and dishes in both hands; the graceful part was the manner in which they half turned the body to the right and left, looking over their shoulders and holding the heads in the opposite direction, as if they were in momentary expectation of someone coming up behind to snatch the nasty relic away from them. At times the women knelt down in a group, with the men leaning over them. After all, the music was not the only thing wanting to make one imagine oneself at the opera. The necklaces of the women were chiefly of teeth—bears' the most common—human the most prized.

But there were more important things than Dyak dances to attend to. It was learned that Prince Makota had suddenly left Kuching and had allied himself with the pirates of the Sarebas River. Keppel placed his entire resources at James's disposal. The armed cutters and pinnaces from the *Dido* with about eighty English seamen and marines, and a number of Dyak and Malay war prahus with about 500 men, sailed up the river. Keppel was in command. At the town of Paddi, seventy miles from the sea, there was a short sharp engagement, and the huge pirate fort, standing on stilts on high ground above the river, was taken and burned: the pirates surrendered. The expedition proceeded to Pakoo.

Pakoo fell, and then it was the turn of Rembas, which was

heavily defended, but this too was captured and burned. Keppel was hoping to repeat the expedition with a raid along the Sakarran River, when he was suddenly ordered to leave Sarawak and join the rest of the fleet in Chinese waters.

James returned to Kuching. He did not have long to wait before another warship, the *Samarang*, came to Kuching. The *Samarang* was under the command of Captain Sir Edward Belcher, a tight-lipped man who had been ordered to report on conditions in Borneo, especially with regard to the island of Labuan near Brunei, which was believed to have a good deal of coal. The British Admiralty was considering using Labuan as a coaling station.

Sir Edward Belcher took a dim view of James, and he seems to have been especially displeased by James's claim to be the Rajah of Sarawak. He suggested that if James considered himself Rajah, he should at least acquire from the Sultan of Brunei a grant of Sarawak in perpetuity. James agreed, and offered to accompany Sir Edward to Brunei. The *Samarang* had just started to descend the Sarawak River when it struck a rock and heeled over. There was nothing to be done except to abandon ship and wait until she could be got off the rock. Her seamen were delighted. They enjoyed being in Kuching. They liked James, and they intensely disliked their commander.

One of the midshipmen on board was Frank Marryat, the son of the novelist. He, too, went to see the native dances in the long-house. Unlike Keppel, who maintained a discreet reserve, young Marryat fell in love with the Dyak women. 'Their eyes', he said, 'are dark and piercing, and I may say there was something wicked in their furtive glances. Their hair was superlatively beautiful, jet black, and of the finest texture, hanging in graceful masses down the back and nearly reaching to the ground.' He had hoped the *Samarang* would remain where she was, but in eleven days she was floated off the rock. The journey to Brunei was continued.

Off Brunei, the Sultan himself came down to the *Samarang* for a audience with Sir Edward Belcher. James's rights over Sarawak were reaffirmed in a document which granted him full powers for-ever:

> In the era of the Prophet (God grant him peace!) the year one thousand two hundred and fifty-eight, the twenty-fourth day of Jamadalachir, the day being Monday and the time ten o'clock.
> His Highness Sultan Omar Ali Saifuddin, son of the late Sultan Mu-hammad Jamalu'l-Alam, appoints James Brooke Esquire to be his repre-sentative and in that capacity to govern the province of Sarawak, and James Brooke Esquire covenants and undertakes to observe the orders, customs, laws and regulations of His Highness the Sultan.
> James Brooke Esquire is responsible for all the affairs of the province

of Sarawak, and no one at all may interfere on any pretext except on the express command of His Highness the Sultan. Regarding the affairs of the other districts within our coasts James Brooke Esquire is not to exercise authority or concern himself in any way, but only within the province of Sarawak.

The Sultan seems to have composed this document because faced with a *fait accompli*. He was giving James what he demanded, but not an inch more. He expressed a desire to open all Borneo ports for trade and to co-operate in the suppression of piracy, and it is possible that he meant none of these things. James, watching him closely, was beginning to wonder whether he might not be able to dethrone the old Sultan and put Muda Hassim in his place. And he was not particularly impressed with the clauses in the deed which limited him to the small riverine area of Sarawak. He was still dreaming of becoming Rajah of the entire northern coast of Borneo.

He wrote a few weeks later: 'If we act, we ought to act without unnecessary delay. Let us push our interest along the coast to Sulu, and from Sulu towards New Guinea, gaining an influence with such states as are clear to the Dutch and the Spaniards.' In time Sarawak was to advance steadily to the borders of Brunei, until all that was left of the once great empire of Brunei was a small enclosed territory surrounded by Sarawak on three sides.

For the moment, however, James was content with his lot. Everything seemed to be conspiring towards furthering his plans. If Belcher had been boorish, inclined to regard the expedition to Brunei as a waste of time, Admiral Sir William Parker, famous for having led seventy-five sail of British ships up the Yangtse Kiang, regarded James as a man after his own heart. He especially approved of James's attacks on the pirates. They met in Penang, where the Admiral was about to start on an expedition against the pirates of Sumatra. Would James like to join? James assented with alacrity, and as a guest on board H.M.S. *Wanderer* he took part in the attack on Murdu—the Murdu Malays had recently attacked a merchant ship and killed many of the passengers.

There was a five-hour battle: two Englishmen were killed, and a dozen wounded; the pirates lost between fifty and seventy men. At one point in the battle, when James was being rowed ashore in the captain's gig, the boat was pushed under an enemy stockade by a strong current. James leaped ashore and led the attack. He was wounded inside the right arm and received a gash in the forehead from a spear. When the ship returned to Penang the sailors asked permission to man the yards and give three cheers to their distinguished visitor, who had shown himself to be insanely brave during the battle.

James had of course no right to wander abroad after Sumatran pirates: his job was to rule Sarawak. Keppel, just back from China, gave him a severe lecture. 'I took the liberty', he wrote, 'of giving him a lecture on his rashness, he having quite sufficient ground for fighting over in his newly-adopted country.' But James had enjoyed this short holiday and remained impenitent. Keppel was ordered to Calcutta, and it was some weeks before James was able to find a boat to take him to Sarawak.

In his absence his enemies had not been idle. Serip Sahib and Prince Makota were once more creating trouble, invading Sarawak territory and sedulously spreading the rumour that the new Rajah had no intention of returning. At the entrance to the Sadong delta Serip Sahib accumulated a fleet of 200 war-prahus which were seen from the bridge of the *Harlequin* by James while returning to Kuching. James wanted to fight, but the captain replied that he had no orders to attack pirates and it was better to let well alone. As soon as he reached Kuching, James wrote off a letter to Keppel, begging him to come quickly. If only he had been able to scatter the pirates! 'All the Queen's ships and all the Queen's men', he wrote, 'could not bring such a chance together again.'

Keppel arrived late in July, to be received in audience by Muda Hassim, who appeared to have not the slightest intention of leaving Kuching. To Prince Budrudeen Keppel suggested an attack against Serip Sahib. The Prince was overjoyed by the prospect.

On Tuesday, August 6, 1844, the *Dido* and the *Phlegethon*, belonging to the East India Company, having sailed down the Batang Lupar River, anchored off the small tributary called the Linga River. Messages were sent to the local chiefs warning them against giving any assistance to Serip Sahib, then known to be in his armed stronghold at Patusan, only a few miles farther down the river. Two days later, on the flood tide, the ships sailed against Patusan, which was taken by storm. Patusan was defended with sixty-four brass guns, and some iron guns. The guns were spiked and thrown into the river, and the fort was looted and set on fire. The Dyaks on board the ships secured several heads, and the expedition continued up-river, where more forts were taken and more heads were gathered by the Dyaks to decorate their long-houses.

One of those who fought at Patusan was a promising young midshipman from the *Dido*. He was James's nephew, Charles Anthoni Johnson, a slight youth with delicate, almost femine, features. He was standing in the bow of the *Jolly Bachelor* next to John Ellis, the captain of the maintop of the *Dido*, when a cannon ball cut John Ellis in two. Midshipman Charles Johnson, who was to become Rajah of Sarawak many years later, was unhurt.

Having destroyed the fortress of Serip Sahib, they went on to destroy the fortress of his brother, Serip Mullah. There was fierce fighting, with no quarter given: ambuscades, tropical storms; the river jammed with logs to prevent the English from moving upstream. The Sakarran pirates employed blowpipes and slingshots as well as muskets. The battle did not always go in favour of the English. Keppel describes the ugly encounter:

> Headless trunks, as well as heads without bodies, were lying about in all directions; parties were engaged hand to hand, spearing and krissing each other; others were striving to swim for their lives; entangled in the common *mêlée* were our advanced boats; while on both banks thousands of Dyaks were rushing down to join in the slaughter, hurling their spears and stones on the boats below.

So for four days, on both banks of the river, the fighting went on. When all the enemy settlements had been burned, and Prince Makota was a refugee in the forests, the ships returned to Kuching only to learn that a chieftain on the Linga River had allied himself with Serip Jaffar. The ships turned about to put down the new rebellion with the help of Belcher's ship, the *Samarang*, which had arrived on the Batang Lupar too late to fight effectively in the earlier war against the pirates.

The time had come for Muda Hassim and the Malay princes to return to Brunei. Accordingly, arrangements were made with Belcher to take them, together with their wives and concubines and an immense number of family retainers, by sea to Brunei. It was thought that the presence of the English ship would predispose Sultan Omar Ali to deal kindly with these princes who had surrendered their territory.

The Sultan greeted them cordially. 'If my father rises from the grave,' he said, 'I will not listen to him, but listen to Muda Hassim.' He was perhaps a little too explicit in his affirmations of continuing affection for the princes, but James seems not to have suspected treachery. After leaving Brunei he wrote that Muda Hassim was 'firmly established', and it needed only the occasional arrival of an English man-of-war to keep the Sultan in line.

Two months later, now Rajah of Sarawak *de facto*, with Prince Makota abandoned in the forests and all the other princes swept out of the way, James described his plans to a friend in London. They were the plans he had held ever since he set foot in Borneo, but they had acquired clarity and definition in the years of fighting and active participation in the affairs of Sarawak. He wrote:

> My intention, my plan, is to develop the island of Borneo. How to develop Borneo is not for me to say, but for them to judge. I have, both by precept and example, shown what can be done; but it is for the Government to judge what means, if any, they will place at my disposal. My intention, my wish, is to extirpate piracy by attacking and breaking

up the pirate towns; not only pirates direct, but pirates indirect. Here again the Government must judge. I wish to correct the native character, to gain and hold an influence in Borneo proper, to introduce gradually a better system of government, to open the interior, to encourage the poor natives, to remove the clogs on trade, to develop new sources. I wish to make Borneo a second Java. I intend to influence and amend the entire Archipelago, if the Government will afford me means and power. I wish to prevent any foreign nation coming on this field; but I might as well war against France individually, as to attempt all I wish without any means.

James's statement of intention concealed a multitude of intangible objectives. There is hidden rage in it, and some bafflement. One would like to know more about the 'pirates indirect', and what exactly did he mean when he said: 'I intend to influence and amend the entire Archipelago'? His secret intention may have been to destroy the last remnants of Malay power and to place himself in command of the Dyaks and all the tribes which had hitherto been under Malay domination. He wrote in his diary:

'If left to my own resources I must become the Chief of the Dyaks, and by my influence prevent mischief on a large scale. A gun boat, twelve good boats with 6-pounders and musketry, with two hundred Dyak prahus, will be a formidable force against Borneo itself, and this force may be needed if Muda Hassim is beaten there.'

The truth was that he was becoming increasingly worried about what would happen to Muda Hassim. He knew the cunning of Omar Ali, who was surrounded with some resourceful advisers. He knew, too, that without the help of Keppel and Parker, who whenever possible placed their ships at his disposal, he was defenceless. If the British acted quickly, the whole of Borneo and New Guinea would fall into their hands. But what if they did not act at all?

The British Government was in no hurry to acquire new colonies. Borneo was regarded as a strategic site for a possible coaling station, and there was a general belief that four or five small trading stations might be established along the coast without danger. James was continually speaking about the possibility of opening the *whole* of Borneo to colonial penetration, and his reports to London suggested that there might be advantages in sending a mission of inquiry. Accordingly in February, 1845, a certain Captain Bethune was sent out to inquire into the possibility of establishing a settlement on the north-west coast of Borneo.

About the same time James was appointed Confidential Agent in Borneo to Her Majesty. His powers were not strictly defined, but he was in effect a kind of consular agent, permitted to make representations to the British Government and to act independently on minor matters. As he interpreted his commission, his main task was to attack piracy wherever and whenever it occurred, and to see that Muda Hassim or another friendly prince was in effective power in Brunei.

With Captain Bethune, James sailed for Brunei to deliver a letter of friendship from the Queen. Omar Ali giggled during the audience, and behaved with his customary cunning. He stared miserably at the royal letter when it was presented to him on a yellow cushion. Muda Hassim, who appeared to be in charge of the Brunei government, was pleased with the expressions of friendship. It was a very hot day. There were twenty-one gun salutes. Banners waved. Prince Budrudeen, as usual, showed himself in command of the situation. Only Muda Hassim appeared to be a little frightened and lonely, saying that he wished the English were always nearby and complaining about the pirates of Malludu Bay. He had ordered the pirates to make no appearance in Brunei until they had given up piracy. 'This is good and candid,' James commented, perhaps guessing that more would be heard from Serip Usman, the pirate leader, who wrote to Brunei a little later daring the British to come to Malludu Bay and settle the matter by fighting.

Such threats, of course, were not to be taken seriously: the Malays were continually threatening one another, and these gestures were accounted part of the game of diplomacy. James however was in a mood for settling the issue of piracy once and for all. He returned to Singapore and discussed the matter with Admiral Sir Thomas Cochrane, who shared the views of Keppel and Parker. It was decided to pay a visit to Brunei and then to attack Malludu Bay.

An impressive fleet consisting of H.M.S. *Agincourt, Vestal, Daedalus, Vixen* and the sloops *Cruiser* and *Wolverine* sailed from Singapore, pausing long enough at Brunei to fire a shot at the palace of Prince Usop, who had threatened to engage the British and whose growing power in the affairs of Brunei was regarded with disfavour by the Confidential Agent in Borneo to Her Majesty. Prince Usop fled, and the twenty brass guns defending his palace were presented by Admiral Cochrane to the Sultan. The fleet sailed on to Malludu Bay.

Almost from the moment when he first dreamed of going to Borneo James had dreamed of acquiring possession of Malludu Bay. For him it was the key to Borneo, the jumping-off ground to New Guinea and the Philippines and all the unattainable islands of the Archipelago. He hoped to take part in the battle, but the Admiral wisely kept him on board his flagship; James, to his disgust, was compelled to watch from a distance. His nephew, Midshipman Charles Johnson, in command of the *Wolverine* pinnace, did fight and acquitted himself creditably.

The battle was hard-fought, in blazing heat, with no quarter shown on either side. The pirates' two forts stood at the mouth of a narrow river, guarded by a double boom formed of enormous tree trunks bolted together with iron plates. The British attacked in twenty-four boats, cut their way through the boom and advanced against the pirate outposts, which they took in fifty minutes' fighting. The pirates fought like tigers—their flag was a scarlet banner with a tiger painted on it. They were well-armed, and wore chain mail and a special armour made of sheet lead from the lining of tea chests. The British lost eight men and fifteen severely wounded; the pirates lost many hundreds, including the pirate chief Usman, wounded in the neck and carried away into the jungle to die. The battle started at nine in the morning. By two o'clock in the afternoon all the forts, towns, and vessels belonging to the enemy had been fired. James wrote in his diary: 'Thus Malludu ceased to exist.'

He was delighted with the victory for many reasons. It was not only that Malludu Bay had been cleared of the enemy and Muda Hassim was encouraged to exert authority where he had never possessed authority before, but James could foresee the time when he would himself exert a far greater authority in Borneo. He had impressed Cochrane with his wise conduct of affairs; he possessed an appointment from the British Government; and soon there would be an end to Sultan Omar Ali's government of Brunei, for it was inconceivable that the old man could rule much longer.

More good news came a few days later when he was sailing to Brunei to report on the expedition against the pirates. He learned that in his absence the wily Prince Usop, the illegitimate son of a former Sultan, had gathered a small force and attacked Brunei. Prince Budrudeen had been warned of the attack, gathered a thousand men armed with muskets, and defeated him. Usop fled, abandoning all his wealth, his gold, his wives and his children. He had been a great boaster in his time—they said of him that 'his mouth was brave, but his heart timid'—and now that he was removed from active participation in the affairs of Brunei, James was disposed to believe that Muda Hassim and Budrudeen would enjoy even greater power in the future. In this he was wrong, although Sultan Omar Ali issued a decree ordering the death sentence on Usop. As a member of the royal house he was put to death without indignity and without bloodshed—he was strangled.

James returned to Sarawak pleased with himself, pleased with the peace which had descended upon Borneo, pleased with Kuching, which was growing into a town of some importance—a hundred trading vessels had put in at Kuching during the past six months. Things were going well, almost too well. Prince Makota, repentant and penniless, came to borrow money—he asked for a loan of 2,000 reals, but received only three reals. 'A sheer waste of money,' James commented.

A more unusual visitor was a pirate chieftain called Lingire who one day walked into James's dining-room followed by a large party of his warriors, all fully armed. There were about eighty of these warriors, and James knew they had come to create trouble. He was helplessly at their mercy. Pretending to be delighted with the visit, he offered Lingire a chair, handed round cigars to his warriors, and asked what he could do for them. A Malay servant entered, and James said in English: 'Bring another bottle of sherry, and tell the Datus the pirates have come.'

The Datus were the Malay chieftains who ruled over their own communities under the Rajah of Sarawak, and it was some time before they could reach James's house, James whiled away the time by telling stories and asking Lingire about the greatest feats he had performed. The pirate fell into the trap. He described his feats of courage and strength at length, and about an hour later the powerful Datu Patingi entered with his bodyguard. For a moment the Dyak pirates and the Malays faced each other in silence, without moving; then the Datu Patingi demanded why the Dyaks had dared to enter the Rajah's house while armed. All the pirates might have been killed, but James decided it would be enough if he taught them a lesson. 'No one,' he said, 'shall come to me, and feel there is any danger in my presence. I forgive even those who come to me with evil intentions, and so I order you to go in peace.' Then like whipped dogs, between a hedge of Malays, the Dyaks went down to their ships.

At the close of 1845 there was peace within Sarawak. James wrote to London describing happily how the whole country was basking under the reign of justice. He did not know that Sultan Omar Ali had already ordered the complete destruction of the families of Muda Hassim and his brothers.

The massacre appears to have been organized by a certain Haji Seman, a man of low birth who had been raised to the position of chief adviser to the Sultan following the death of Prince Usop. Haji Seman seems to have hoped he would eventually become Sultan. He had four hundred men under him. One night at the end of December some fifty of them crept silently up to Muda Hassim's palace, which was supported on piles and hung above the river. Muda Hassim fought off the attackers until his house caught fire, then with his wife and children and three brothers who were staying with him, he escaped by boat to the other side of the river. He was badly wounded. His flight had been observed. He was outnumbered, and he saw that he had no alternative except to fight to the death. Suddenly a large number of the Sultan's boats came up to where he was hiding. His nerve failed him, and he decided on suicide.

Suddenly he shouted to his three brothers and his sons to join him in the cabin, where there was a quarter cask of gunpowder. The enemy was within earshot, calling on him to surrender, when he touched a match to the gunpowder. There was a tremendous blue flash, but the gunpowder was damp and though the boat rocked violently and everyone else in the cabin was killed, Muda Hassim was still alive and the boat still afloat. At the last moment, just before the attackers boarded the boat, he put a pistol to his head and blew out his brains.

His brother, Budrudeen, died more gloriously. When the attackers came to his house, he was ready for them. He had armed his servants, and had no intention of escaping. Some of the attackers succeeded in entering his house, but they were cut down. There was desperate fighting, with Budrudeen himself taking the lion's share in hand-to-hand encounters with the enemy. Towards the end, when he knew there was no more hope, he ordered most of his servants to escape by boat—most of them were killed a few minutes after leaving the house.

Only four people were left in the house: the Prince, Noor Salum, a woman who may have been his favourite wife, his sister, and a slave boy called Jaffar. All had been wounded in the fighting, but the Prince was the most seriously wounded. He had received a musket-ball in his left wrist, his chest and shoulder were slashed open by a sabre cut, and there were four or five separate wounds on his face and head. Worst of all his wounds was the sabre cut on his shoulder which had somehow cut the nerves controlling his right arm. When he saw that he could fight no longer, he ordered Jaffar to get down the cache of gunpowder hidden in the roof beams, to break in the head and scatter the powder in a small circle. Jaffar did all this, expecting to die with the others, but in his last moments Budrudeen remembered his affection for James and gave the boy the gold signet ring which James had given him shortly after their first meeting.

It was a heavy ring, bearing the arms of the Brooke family, and with the ring went a message. The message was a very simple one in the heroic style of a Malay prince about to meet his death: 'Tell the Rajah to remember me, and may the Queen know that I have kept my word.'

A few second later Jaffar lifted one of the mats covering the floor and slid down a post into the water, swimming to a small canoe hidden in the darkness about a hundred yards from the house. He had just reached the boat when he heard a tremendous explosion. Budrudeen's gunpowder was not damp; his house was blown sky-high; and the Prince and the two women were killed instantly.

Altogether, twelve of the fourteen brothers were killed that night The survivors may have wished they had been killed with the rest, for one of them, the ugly Prince Mohammed, was so dangerously wounded that he never regained his health, and the other went insane as a result of the horrors he had seen. The boy Jaffar did not escape. He was captured and brought before Sultan Omar Ali, who questioned him at length but decided that nothing was to be gained by killing a simple slave, whose only crime was to have escaped from a prince's palace. It was a mistake which very nearly cost him his throne, for the following March Jaffar found refuge on the British ship *Hazard* and told his story. At first no one believed him. Why should the Sultan massacre so many members of the royal family? In Kuching Jaffar told the story again, and gave Brooke the ring and the message. For a long time Brooke had feared for the princes. He believed every word of the story, and determined to avenge their deaths.

For him it was a nightmare. He could not escape the knowledge of his own complicity in the massacre, for in a sense he had sent them to their deaths. He had loved Budrudeen as he loved no one else in the world. That prince had been the gayest, the most charming, the most intelligent of them all; and to Budrudeen more than to anyone else he owed the fact that he was Rajah of Sarawak. In utter misery and despair he wrote in his diary, shortly after receiving the news:

> Violent passions and sleepless nights are hard to bear. I lay no blame on anyone. I look forward as much as I can, and backward as little, but I ought not and cannot forget my poor friends who lie in their bloody graves. Oh how great is my grief and rage! My friends—my most unhappy friends!—all perished for their faithful adherence to us. Every man of ability, even of thought, in Borneo, is dead, sacrificed. . . . But the British Government will surely act, and if not—then let me remember, I am still at war with this traitor and murderer—one more determined struggle—one last convulsive effort—and, if it fail, Borneo, and all for which I have so long, so earnestly laboured, must be abandoned——

He could not trust himself to write any more. In grief and horror, half-insane with rage, he drew a jagged line with a scratchy pen across the page.

E

V

TRIALS AND TRIBULATIONS

IN THE days when he was fighting pirates James wrote in his diary: 'Am I, then, really *fond* of war? And I answer—"Certainly", for what man is not?' These words, taken out of their context—James went on to say that he would not fight an unjust war—were later used against him by his enemies. But there was one war which he fought with extreme pleasure: the war against Sultan Omar Ali, the dangerous three-thumbed imbecile who had killed his friends.

News of the massacre did not reach him until March, 1846. Sometime in June Admiral Sir Thomas Cochrane, then sailing in Chinese waters, heard a curious story about a raid on Kuching by a large army of Brunei soldiers. He hurried to Kuching to investigate, learned that there was no truth in the story, but heard about the massacres. His fleet of six warships spent only one night anchored off Kuching. The next morning they sailed to exact vengeance from Sultan Omar Ali.

The Admiral decided to act cautiously. He had known for a long time that Brunei was well-fortified with brass guns made by the best brass-founders in the East. He sailed slowly along the coast while the Sultan, who knew of his coming, spoke to his soldiers, declaring that Brunei was impregnable. It was not impregnable. Bombarded by the British, it burst into flames. By evening the town was an empty shell, and the Sultan had fled with his court to the forest. An attempt to follow the fugitives in the forest was called off: the British sailors were not equipped for jungle fighting.

James had his revenge, but it tasted like ashes in the mouth—there was very little advantage to be gained from a burned city. The Sultan had vanished. No doubt, as soon as the fleet sailed away, he would return and rebuild it. Cochrane issued a proclamation, ordering the Sultan to mend his ways or face still further punishment. It was an astute move, for the fact that he had been publicly rebuked by the Admiral, acting in the name of Queen Victoria, would eventually reach him wherever he was hiding. Having lost 'face', he would almost certainly reappear and sue for peace.

The Admiral felt that enough punishment had been inflicted for the moment, and sailed northward along the coast. Soon he learned that a band of Ilanun pirates had sacked Ambong, a town friendly to the British. It was a simple matter to sail to the pirates' stronghold at Tampassuk and set fire to it. Cochrane was well-pleased with his excursion in Borneo waters: two towns put to the flames, a Sultan and a pirate chief humbled. Having accomplished so much, he was free to return to Chinese waters. For a while he toyed with the idea of proclaiming James Rajah of Brunei. The simplicity of the plan pleased him, but he knew that the idea was impractical. Parliament would have disapproved; and James's enemies in London would have had additional ammunition for their constant guerrilla war against him.

Meanwhile, Captain Rodney Mundy was ordered to Brunei to convey the survivors of the massacre back to Sarawak. When Mundy reached Brunei, there was still no sign of the Sultan. Once more a proclamation was issued, promising Omar Ali complete protection if he promised to mend his ways and demonstrate his friendship for Queen Victoria. Suddenly, for he had never been far away, the Sultan appeared, a small, contrite, bitterly disillusioned man, who preferred his ruined capital to the miseries of the jungle. He promised everything that was demanded of him. He swore undying loyalty to the Queen, and ceded to her the island of Labuan, which the Admiralty hoped to make into a coaling station. He was particularly gentle with Captain Mundy, who carried out the protracted negotiations. There was a singular tenderness in his demeanour when he realized that he was not going to be punished.

James assumed charge of Muda Hassim's relatives, 'a perfect menagerie of old women and children'. But while the old women were an encumbrance, the children delighted him. 'Several of the young sons are pleasant and intelligent boys,' he wrote. 'My dreams sometimes extend to the conversion of the Rajah's young family, for if a clever person managed them, amused them, and made them presents, they would likely enough become Christians.' There is however no record that any of them were converted to Christianity.

James himself was beginning to change. After the death of Hassim and Budrudeen, his face showed deep lines of worry, his finely curved lips were often compressed in a straight line, and the fire seemed to have gone from his eyes. He was a man oppressed by a sense of guilt. In his presence no one ever dared to talk of massacres.

There was a time when he had been happy leading expeditions, but now he spent more and more time in his palace. He held court, with the Malay Datus, or local governors, sitting at his side. He enjoyed the ritual of kingship, and he particularly enjoyed judging the cases which were brought to him, displaying an astonishing leniency in murder trials. When ships came in, there were usually some boxes of books for him, and then he would close himself up in his library and read far into the night. He had a large library, which was particularly rich in devotional literature. Sometimes he gave the impression of being a typical English squire administering an unusually large estate. Significantly he did not call his house a palace: he gave it the very English name of 'The Grove'.

Meanwhile Sarawak was prospering. There were now twelve thousand inhabitants in the booming town, including about a hundred and fifty Chinese. Ships plied up and down the river. The trade in antimony was flourishing. He had established peace throughout his kingdom, and the Sultan of Brunei was hardly more than a puppet in his hands. He had long ago anticipated that riches would begin to flow into the country once there was peace between the Dyaks and the Malays; and now at last the country was basking in the peace he had given to it.

He spent some months in the early part of 1847 in Penang, which he always regarded as the most beautiful of the islands of the Indies, and later in the year set sail for England. He had some misgivings about returning to his homeland. Nearly nine years had passed since he last visited England; his mother was dead; he had few friends there. He reached Southampton on October 1, 1847, still thinking that the journey might well be a mistake, and dangerous for the future of Sarawak. He changed his mind as soon as he landed. He was greeted everywhere as a conqueror. Had he not humbled the redoubtable Sultan of Brunei? Was he not the only existing White Rajah? He was a strange creature, endowed with royalty, yet still the subject of Queen Victoria.

The City of London hastened to give him the freedom of the city. Though he had never been to college, Oxford was delighted to honour him with the degree of Doctor of Laws. The Queen made him a Knight Commander of the Bath. He was now officially Sir James Brooke, K.C.B., Rajah of Sarawak, Governor of Labuan, Commissioner and Consul-General in Borneo. At the age of forty-four he had exhausted all his childhood ambitions.

Everywhere he went that winter he was showered with honours. He was entertained at Windsor Castle by the Queen and Prince Albert. He was a little oppressed by the formality of palace life in England. Invited to stay at the castle, he spent his first evening in complete seclusion. He wrote to his niece, Mary Anne Johnson, an account of that strange evening when the most honoured man in England was left alone to his own devices: 'I much regret to say that I have not met with one single adventure, nor have I seen one person's face since being in this celebrated Castle, excepting Prince

Albert's *valet de chambre*, who is a very well-spoken, well-dressed, civil gentleman—at which circumstance I am rather astonished, as I have always entertained an idea that all subordinate persons in all palaces were addicted to insolence and vainglory. Thus, my dear girl, you have the wonderful and entire history of all the events which have befallen me since I arrived.'

The next day, however, he had an entirely different story to tell. He kissed hands on his presentation and Queen Victoria astonished him with a little speech which showed that she had followed his career with profound interest. He bowed low to the ground. The Prince Consort, even more knowledgeable than the Queen, engaged him in conversation on Borneo. Brooke was sensibly casual about the honours which were being heaped upon him, but he seems to have been aware of their corrupting influence. He was succumbing to the demands of fame; succumbing with grace and tact. Nevertheless, he succumbed.

It pleased him to address large crowds of church-goers on the subject of raising mission funds for the encouragement of the Church in Borneo. He was delighted when all the principal clubs invited him to become a member. He was ingratiating in his interviews in Downing Street with the newly appointed Prime Minister, Lord John Russell. He was invited to the country houses of the great, and spent nearly every evening in London dining out and captivating the ladies with stories about head-hunters. He told stories well; he was genuinely liked; he behaved with exactly the proper decorum expected of a white Rajah; and he was growing increasingly bored. Suddenly, after spending only four months in England, he returned to Sarawak.

We know what he looked like at this time, for almost his first act after landing in England was to arrange for his portrait to be painted. The artist was Sir Francis Grant, and the portrait now hangs in the National Portrait Gallery. Those who knew him found it an excellent likeness. He looks straight out of the canvas with the air of a young Byronic hero, hair blowing in the wind, assurance written on every line of his features. He wears the uniform of the Royal Yacht Squadron: white shirt, a flowing tie, short midshipman's jacket, tight trousers, one knee bent in the conventional posture of the conqueror. The Sarawak River with its palms and mangroves flows at his feet, but he is not looking at the river, nor does he look out of the picture at the observer; he looks into the distance and the future, the faintest of smiles hovering on his lips. It is the portrait of a man gaily confronting a palpable destiny, and almost alone among the portraits in the National Portrait Gallery it suggests a deliberate and heroic romanticism.

Though James assumed the rôle of romantic hero to perfection,

he was full of gaiety when he left England, enchanted by the prospect of returning to the East and happy with his shipboard companions. His ship, the *Meander*, was commanded by his close friend,
Henry Keppel. His secretary, the faithful Spenser St. John, was on
board. So too was his young nephew, Charles Johnson, who had
fought in the pirate campaigns in Sarawak and at Malludu Bay.
Charles was losing his baby fat, and James kept a close watch on
him: it was just possible that Charles might be induced to abandon
his career in the Navy and assist him in Sarawak.

There were some young women on board, and James delighted
in their company. He was even more delighted by the behaviour of
the younger officers and midshipmen, who showed a welcome lack
of reverence by entering his large cabin whenever they felt like it
and helping themselves to his cherry brandy, singing and skylarking
to the confusion of Spenser St. John, who like an obedient secretary
was usually at his writing desk in a corner of a cabin. There were
twenty midshipmen on board, and all of them regarded the Rajah's
cabin as their clubroom. James was in high spirits, and took part in
all the dances. Once he whirled one of the ship's officers around the
cabin to the tune of a polka, and when the band broke into a waltz
he seized one of the young ladies round the waist and continued
dancing.

He was still in good humour when he reached Kuching, where the
whole population turned out to meet him. The river was filled with
war prahus, Chinese junks, canoes, and trading vessels all beflagged
in his honour. There followed the inevitable visit to Brunei and
Labuan, where James caught fever so badly that his life was des-
paired of, and there was a brief ceremonial interview with the
Sultan of Sulu, a young man with a dull and vacant expression, pale
and emaciated from smoking opium. This redoubtable Sultan,
whose pirate fleet once threatened the whole coast, was dressed in
red and green silks, with a large jewel in his turban. Behind him
stood a cupbearer in green silk who held up a purple finger-glass
into which at intervals the Sultan spat betel juice. The Sultan made
an odd remark about 'the recent revolution in France', but James
did not enlighten him. It was a purely formal interview, important
only in that the Sultan was privileged to see the *Meander*'s guns.
James was glad to return to Kuching.

Meanwhile the safety of Sarawak still depended upon freedom
of the seas, and in the early months of 1849 the seas off the northern
coast of Borneo were invaded by hordes of pirates in their war
prahus. Their ships were fast; they were completely merciless; and
they plundered and massacred at will. 'During the first six months
of 1849', wrote Spenser St. John, 'these pirates attacked Sadong
twice, as well as Sussang on the Kaluka, and Serikei, Palo, Mato,

Bruit, and Igan. Almost all intercourse by sea ceased, as few who attempted to pass the mouths of the pirate rivers escaped unhurt. I calculated at the time that above 500 of the Sultan's subjects had been killed or taken captive between January and July, 1849; and we know that one large fleet had passed the mouth of the Sarawak River to attack the subjects of the Sultan of Sambas.'

It was clear that something had to be done about the pirates, but it was no longer a question of sending a few small boats against them. A pirate fleet might consist of a hundred prahus, many of them equipped with swivel guns. They represented a vast, anarchic, and destructive force. Only a greater force could stop them.

Nearly every day people came to Kuching with tales about the pirates: how they had landed in a small creek, spread out, made their way to a village, looted everything in sight, murdered everyone they could lay their hands on, and then vanished as swiftly as they came. The Sultan of Brunei was begging for help against them. Even in the neighbourhood of Kuching the depredations of the pirates were felt. When the Rajah heard early in March that a pirate fleet numbering a hundred vessels had put to sea, he decided to act at once. By March 25, at great cost, he had equipped ninety-eight war prahus, manned by more than 3,000 men, and led them out to sea. The armada swept along the coast, sailed up the rivers and returned, hunted pirates wherever they were rumoured to be, and came back two months later empty-handed. The pirates had mysteriously vanished. It was a bitter blow, but the Rajah had learned his lesson. What was needed was a standing fleet which would periodically sweep the seas. In the end the pirates would be compelled to show themselves.

Two months later he set out again, this time with only about seventy war prahus and about 2,500 natives, but his fire-power immeasurably increased by the presence of the *Royalist* and the East India Company's steamer *Nemesis*. There were also two paddle-box boats, two cutters, a steam tender, and the gig, pinnace, and cutter of H.M.S. *Albatross*. This motley force sailed from Kuching on July 24 with the Rajah characteristically commanding the fleet from a war prahu called *Singh Rajah* (the Lion King). Nearly all the other war prahus bore the names of animals or insects—*Snake, Tiger, White Ant, Bee, Chicken*. There was also a war prahu bearing the happy name of *Brave Bachelor*.

On the evening of the next day the fleet anchored at the mouth of the Sibuyow River. There were no pirates in sight. It was a very calm evening, and nothing of any consequence occurred except that an enormous flock of bats issued out of the forests and for half an hour at sunset circled ominously above the fleet. The presence of the bats seemed to presage events of great importance. It was

Ramadan, the time when the Malays fast during the day and eat only at night; and they looked forward to a night encounter with the pirates.

They did not see the pirates that night, nor the next night. On July 28 when the fleet was anchored opposite the sand flats of the Sarebas River, they heard that only the day before the pirates had slipped out of the river and made their way northward, intending to strike at Serikei on the Renjang River before returning. By all accounts the pirates were well-armed with muskets and brass guns. They had been raiding continually. They had taken the town of Palo, which was rich and famous for its manufacture of salt and for its ricefields, and in the nearby town of Mato they had captured two vessels, one bound for Singapore with sago, the other lately arrived from Singapore with a cargo of cotton goods. Altogether about 150 boats were under the command of the pirates. Seventeen of these war prahus were under the command of the pirate chief Lingire.

The pirates built admirable ships, many of them over ninety feet long, and all of them supplied with a roof and strong bulwarks, with about seventy rowers at the oars. The roofs protected the ammunition from the rain, and the bulwarks were proof against grapeshot; cut into the bulwarks were the ports through which they worked their guns. The fighting men were provided with muskets, cutlasses, and *kampilans*, long straight-bladed Ilanun swords.

It was expected that the pirates, after their foray in the north, would return to their bases on the Kaluka or Sarebas Rivers. Accordingly it was decided to divide the fleet into two groups, the Rajah making for the mouth of the Kaluka River with twelve war prahus and two men-of-war cutters, while the remaining ships guarded the approaches of the Sarebas River. The ships were to keep close to the shore. Between the two fleets lay the sand bar of Tanjong Marau which stretched for two or three miles out to sea. They could not see each other, but they could easily communicate with one another by means of rockets. The Rajah had deliberately taken the more dangerous position, hoping to entice the pirates into offering battle.

As usual, nothing happened, and they began to fear that the pirates were aware of their preparations. Two days passed, days of strained silence and expectation. At last on the night of July 31, when it was very dark, for the moon was dimmed by misty clouds, the entire pirate fleet made for the Sarebas River and collided with the larger fleet waiting for it. The *Nemesis* sent up a rocket, to warn the Rajah that the battle had begun; and the rocket was followed by a blue flare, which illuminated the sea for miles around. In this eerie light the captain of the *Nemesis* saw that the pirates, by blundering into his fleet, were inextricably mingled with the war prahus of the Malays and Dyaks and it was almost impossible to tell one from the other. The blue flare went out; there was darkness again; and the only light came from the flashes of the guns and from the small fires which glowed on some of the boats, throwing reflections on the dark waters.

In the confused battle, which lasted for four hours, there were strange intervals of quietness, when it was possible to hear clearly above the lapping of the sea the sound of the bells which marked the watches of the night and the monotonous chanting of the Koran. There was the world of darkness, and there was the sudden bright blue world which opened up when the blue flares sailed across the sky; and there was nothing in between.

The pirates fought with the courage of despair. They were out-numbered, having only about a hundred boats, considerably less than the 150 originally reported. Lingire, at the head of his seven-teen boats, attacked the *Nemesis*. It was a foolhardy attack: the captain of the *Nemesis* simply ordered a concentrated fire from his thirty-two-pounders on their war prahus, sinking nearly all of them. The survivors, nothing daunted, swam towards the *Nemesis* with their swords in their mouths and attempted to climb up her bulwarks. Sailors on the *Nemesis* chopped off their hands and watched them sink back into the sea. In panic the surviving pir-ates, with a strong flood tide in their favour, ran their prahus ashore and escaped into the forests.

When morning came, the sea was seen to be littered with the dead floating amid baskets, mats, balks of timber, and strips of cloth. There were sixty abandoned war prahus beached on the sandy shore of Tanjong Marau. Here and there boats could be seen moving aimlessly backward and forward with the tide. Some 400 pirates had been killed, but an enormous number, perhaps 2,500, had suc-ceeded in taking refuge in the jungle. Though their fleet was largely destroyed, the pirates themselves were alive to fight again. Ac-cording to the captain of the *Nemesis*, the losses on his side amounted to no more than thirteen or fourteen natives killed and wounded.

The Rajah had no reason to be proud of his exploits that night. He had been suffering from a severe attack of fever, and he lay be-low in his cabin all night. The *Singh Rajah* had made no contact with the main fleet. He had heard the fighting which took place some seven or eight miles to the south, and rumours came to him that his own forces had been defeated. In the morning he sailed south, and discovered that almost the entire pirate fleet had been destroyed.

Two days later, on August 2, ships were sent up the Sarebas River, to find felled trees blocking their progress. The Malays and Dyaks were landed; there were brief engagements and about fifty pirates were killed in the jungles and some 450 more were said to have died as the result of fighting against native tribes. The pirates hid in the jungles and pounced on the landing parties, but were usually beaten off. Spenser St. John was one of those who penetrated a little way into the forests. He saw a coarse mat covering a body. The mat was lifted up, and there was a dead girl lying there naked, her head and breasts cut off, with obscene wounds on her stomach. This girl, and a few others who were discovered, had been captured by the pirates at Palo or Mato. In their flight through the forest the pirates in their rage had hacked them to death.

The Rajah hated the pirates for many reasons. They threatened Sarawak; they threatened law and order; they were violent beyond any reasonable degree of violence; and they were very numerous. It was calculated that there were altogether 25,000 men on the north coast of Borneo living off piracy and murder. It had to stop, and he was prepared to stop it whatever the cost.

In England the sea battle of Tanjong Marau came to be known as the *Albatross* affair. It was discussed endlessly. Richard Cobden thundered against the grave injustice of the mass slaughter of these innocent seafarers, whose only crime was that they were going about their normal business along the coast. The Rajah was painted as a reckless adventurer whose previous protestations of Christian philanthropy were now proved to be baseless. He was described as a bloodthirsty and despicable coward. It was conveniently forgotten that careful reports on the savagery of the pirates had been accumulating for years. A certain Joseph Hume, Member of Parliament for Montrose, asked in the House whether there was not some way of preventing this mad despot from committing further massacres; the editor of the Singapore *Strait Times* fulminated in editorials; Richard Cobden harangued large crowds on the virtues of pacific dealings with primitive tribes; and Lord John Russell trembled. Wilberforce's Emancipation Bill had been passed into law only sixteen years before. In England the Liberals were aroused against every kind of maltreatment of the dark-skinned races. Here, then, was the long-sought-for opportunity to chastise the impenitent sinner with a display of outraged public morality. The Rajah was cast in the rôle of King Herod, with the pirates as the slaughtered innocents.

At first the Rajah was stunned; then frightened; then resigned; then angered beyond endurance. He had allowed, and even encouraged, the publication of his journals; it was comparatively simple for his enemies to take isolated fragments from the journals to prove him guilty. Cobden spoke gravely of how the Rajah 'had gone out to the Eastern Archipelago as a private adventurer, had seized upon a territory as large as Yorkshire, and then drove out the natives; and then under pretence that they were pirates subsequently sent for our fleet and men to massacre them.' There were enough half-truths in the statement to make it disturbing. The curiously named Aborigines Protection Society was formed to combat him. Deputations visited the Prime Minister or sent memorials asking for the punishment of the Rajah; and when he answered the accusations his voice sounded strained, as though he could not shout loud enough to prove that black is black and white is white. He wrote in a memorandum:

All that is said amounts to this:

1st. That the Sarebas are *not* pirates.
Answer. A Court of Admiralty has said they are pirates.
2nd. That these excursions are in consequence of petty feuds between the tribes.
Answer. If this be so, these tribes are at war with the Netherlands Government, and with every other community, along a coastline of one thousand miles.
3rd. That there is no difference between the Malays and Dyaks of the Sarebas and the Malays and Dyaks of other communities, in the mode of conducting these warlike forays.
Answer. The difference is this—that the other thirty or forty communities do not go to sea on war-like or piratical expeditions, and all live at peace with one another; whilst the Sarebas constantly go to sea on piratical cruises, and devastate the other countries; and also, that the other tribes do not slaughter indiscriminately, which the Sarebas do.

When they talk of private motives of gain and wealth, etc., tell them that I am £10,000 out of pocket by Sarawak; and that the revenue of Sarawak is, like the revenue of any other place, applied for public purposes; and if it were twenty times as large as at present I could dispose of it for public purposes, strictly to advance the good of the country and people, and to cement the foundations of a government which will last when I have crumbled to dust.

The more the Rajah spoke of the pirates and their depredations, the more the word was flung back at him. Pirates, indeed! Does this puny adventurer think we shall be misled by a word? One of his most persistent enemies, James Foggo, took him to task for daring to use the word. He wrote:

James Brooke may exclaim *pirates, pirates, pirates,* against the Sarebas as the Spanish ambassador Gondomar thundered '*Pirato, pirato, pirato*' against Raleigh in the audience chamber of King James, but we have no doubt that the world will in time come to appreciate the outcry at its true value, and that the question will ultimately be decided on principles that can neither be derided as a weak and indiscriminate compassion, nor descried as an outrage against humanity.

Against these attacks the Rajah was often helpless, and he wearied of replying to them. There were limits to his patience. Once, when the mail brought him two furious onslaughts by Hume and Cobden, he sprang to his feet and cried: 'I wish I had the two before me, sword in hand, on the sands of Santubong!'

There was a curious unreality about the *Albatross* affair from the beginning. The fires were stoked by men who had not the remotest conception of life in the East Indies. They had chosen the wrong enemy. They sought a sacrificial victim, any victim, and they had chosen a man who was incapable of playing the rôle they had assigned to him. They were powerful; they attacked continually with their batteries of pin-pricks; and they were highly moral and indignant. James had his army of supporters, but sometimes his patience snapped. 'I believe there is not a cosy demagogue among the pack who would lead the life I lead for double the lucre I receive,' James wrote in a great rage. 'It would not suit any of those ranting lovers of peace and popularity, either in exposure to danger, or climate, or monotony.'

While Hume and Cobden thundered, James went about his own affairs. He paid official visits to Brunei and Labuan, where he caught fever again, this time so badly he was delirious for days, and would have died but for Keppel's careful nursing. Then he went on to Siam, where with the title of Her Majesty's Representative in the Further East, he hoped to conclude a treaty with the King of Siam. The Siamese were concerned to retain their independence and, suspecting James of attempting to bring them within the power of the British Crown, they did everything they could to make his mission a failure. They tried to prevent him from landing, and when he landed they made life so uncomfortable that he remained for a month in his quarters, 'as a defensive measure to avoid all chance of insult'.

It was a strategy calculated to please the Siamese, who might have permitted him to remain *incommunicado* for ever, and soon he had to admit that the mission was 'a dead failure'. James did succeed in interviewing the Phra-Klang, or Minister of Foreign Affairs, who deliberately insulted him by making him sit in a low chair below his own high-cushioned throne. James decided to teach him a lesson. He marched straight up to him and shook him firmly by the hand, and the mouth of the Minister of Foreign Affairs opened in surprise and terror. It was not a very successful interview. Some time later James was able to have a secret interview with Mongkut, the heir to the throne. He found Mongkut sensible and charming. Mongkut, who was then living in a monastery to avoid the persecution of the King, was the royal admirer of Anna Hariette Leonowens, more familiar to us as the Anna who severely tried the King of Siam.

James had discovered that he was not the most brilliant of diplo-mats and returned to Sarawak with the feeling that he was better occupied with his own business. His health was bad; the attacks on him were continuing, he decided to return to England. He dreamed of a holiday in Dorset. He wrote to a friend: 'We will dip in the sea, and go fishing until we are all sea-sick, and have picnics till we are all sick of roast goose and pigeon pies, and we will walk in the sun until we get fevers, and sit in the shade till we catch our death of cold.' He was in an unusually jaunty mood. His enemies were gloating over his imminent defeat, but his friends were jubilant. Gladstone said: 'I look on him with great respect as a man of an energy truly British; and I believe that in his heart and intentions, however liable he may be to errors of judgement, he is a man of philanthropy truly Christian.'

A public dinner was given for him. There were Members of Parliament, Governors of the Bank of England, directors of the East India Company, and a host of Army and Navy officers and merchants. Baron Alderson delivered an ornate speech of welcome, and James replied with deliberate modesty, disclaiming many of the virtues with which he was credited. In particular he disclaimed the accepted portrait of the high-minded philanthropist who had gone to the East with the intention of furthering justice, truth, and mercy. It had not been quite like that. He said:

> It has been stated, gentlemen, that when I set out for the shores of Borneo, now fourteen years ago, I carried a deep design in my bosom to suppress piracy, and to carry civilization to the Malayan race. This is most flattering to my wisdom and foresight, but unfortunately it is not true. I had but one definite object when I left England, and that was to see something of the world and come back again.

This was not, of course, the whole truth, but too much had been said of his manifest virtues. He complained bitterly of how the natives of the East Indies were 'betrayed by our carelessness, and British interests sacrificed to ignorance'. Those islands, 'the fairest and richest in the world', were, he said, at the mercy of 'an imbecility which hopes to attain everything by doing nothing, and which weakens every executive power in every distant part of the empire'. And he did not hide his hatred and contempt for his enemies who claimed he was a murderer because he stamped out piracy. He was in good heart, and those who saw him in London commented on the carefree appearance of the man who had looked so often sombre and close to despair.

When he returned to Sarawak, two blows fell one after another. He fell ill, and he was put on trial. His illness was so serious that he nearly died, and the trial seemed to be designed to destroy his spirit completely.

His illness was smallpox, which he probably caught on board the ship taking him to Kuching. A fleet of boats came to meet him; all the land around Government House was filled with welcoming throngs. It was observed that his face looked curiously puffed, covered with what appeared to be harvest bumps. The natives on board whispered that he had been struck by *purunasi*, but James could only guess at the meaning of the word. He realized he was desperately ill, probably of smallpox, and as soon as he came ashore gave orders that no one except those who had suffered from the disease should come near him. He had a high fever, and his mind began wandering. For some reason he thought he was fighting beside Simon de Montfort at the battle of Evesham, and when he tore at his cheeks he thought he was tearing at the battlefield.

He lay on a bed of plantain leaves, which were cool and therefore helped to assuage the fever. Native women sent perfumed water. An English missionary gave him brandy, which he at first refused, saying he had never heard of brandy as a cure for smallpox. There was a night when he was thought to be dying. Prayers were said in the mosques, votive offerings were made by the Malays and the Chinese, and the Dyaks were in despair. When the crisis passed, the native women sent delicate dishes to tempt his appetite, and more scented water for his bath. He was given opium, and slept round the clock. When he awoke, he realized for the first time that he had become permanently disfigured. There was no longer the handsome hero of the Grant portrait; there was an old man, lined and seamed by the pox, with his own claw marks on his face.

His hair was white; his face was pitted; only the eyes shone with a more intense fire. About this time an old Malay, who had known him well, reported on his appearance. James, he said, was nearly bald, with a fair or whitish moustache, and there were twelve wounds on his body. His eyes, said the Malay, were 'fierce like those of a crocodile'.

James never completely recovered his health. Some colour came back to his hair, and gradually some of the wounds on his face healed. He wrote to friends in Bombay: 'I am only simply ugly and pockmarked, instead of being hideous and disfigured.' He was, in fact, very cruelly disfigured. For many months he brooded on the reasons why God had chosen this time for chastening him.

Illness changed him, as it changes all people. He became gentler, fought his battles less violently, and sometimes fell into long periods of meditation, when he seemed to be withdrawn from the world. It was remembered that when he was ill, he could not sleep unless someone held his hand.

To hasten his recovery a hut was built for him high up in the mountain of Peninjau, a kind of hermitage, reached by a difficult path, very bare, looking down over the sheer forest-clad slopes. Here it was cooler than in the plains, and here, sometimes for weeks on end, he lived alone except for a servant.

His convalescence was brief. To his surprise and horror he learned that powerful forces within the British Government had decided to place him on trial, charged with the murder of natives peacefully practising their trade off the coast of Borneo. It was not called a trial. It was called a commission of inquiry. He was not in fact charged with murdering natives, but as the inquiry developed it became clear that this obscure naval battle against the pirates was the occasion for an attempt to deprive him of all his powers. Two Commissioners were sent to Singapore. They were Charles Prinsep, Advocate-General to the Government of India, and Humphrey Devereux, of the Bengal Civil Service. Prinsep was a sick man, on the verge of madness. Devereux was an austere and cautious man, in good health, who clearly found his task distasteful.

From the beginning James protested vigorously against the trial. Theoretically the inquiry was formed to pass judgment on 'certain anomalies in the position at present held by Sir James Brooke, Her Majesty's Consul-General and Commissioner in Borneo, and certain inconveniences therein arising'. It was suggested that there was a conflict of duties, and that James, as a sovereign ruler *de facto* and also a British subject, was in no position to carry out the duties he had accepted on behalf of the British Government. The accusations of murder were an afterthought, but the inquiry quickly degenerated into a battle royal between those who believed in the existence of pirates and those who did not.

James wrote a long and closely reasoned argument against the instructions received by the Commissioners—the instructions seemed to beg the question—and he demanded that the vague list of charges be defined. He also demanded that he should be allowed to confront his accusers and examine them. Witnesses, chiefly traders, spoke of their pacific dealing with the men James described as pirates. James called witnesses who spoke of the massacres which they had witnessed or which had come to their knowledge. Soon the the original charges were forgotten.

Often the exchanges were farcical. John Henry, a Singapore trader, was called to the stand. He was cross-examined as follows:

Have you any reason to believe, from what you heard or saw, that any Dyaks were pirates?

I found the Dyaks a more peaceable people than the Borneans and Malays of Sarawak, and more honest; they worked as coolies for me also in shipping antimony ore.

Have you ever visited the Dyak villages?

No, never.

In the voyages you made in Borneo, did you go armed?

Yes.

Why?

For fear of pirates.

James Guthrie, another merchant, was asked whether he had discussed the existence of pirates with Borneo traders. They told him there were many pirates around, but they were all Malays, Ilanuns, and Sulus. If there were any Dyak pirates, he could only conclude that they were pirates by compulsion, not by inclination. Of the battle fought against the Sea Dyaks, he said: 'I certainly think the attack was unjustifiable.'

He was however in a minority. As the Commissioners listened to the evidence and cross-examined the witnesses in the steamy court-room, it became abundantly clear that vast pirate fleets had sailed out of the rivers of Borneo and attacked defenceless coastal villages at their leisure. The Dutchman, C. F. Bondriot, formerly a Resident in the Dutch possession of Java, testified:

I know one instance where they killed about 400, and if I had my notes I could tell of other cases, where they carried away the heads; this happened in the Dutch possession. All the natives on the west coast are all aware of these tribes, and fear them; they are different from the other native pirates, who go all round the island. They do not kill you at once, should you wish to surrender, but in the end you are sure to be beheaded. Even children have heard about these pirates and express great fear for them when their name is heard. Had I had opportunity I should have killed even more than Sir James Brooke did. They sometimes use guns, but principally use bamboos, covered with iron at the point.

So the argument went on, with nothing accomplished, and most of the witnesses dazed and somnolent. A certain Madame Dutron-quoy, wife of Gaston Dutronquoy, landlord of the London Hotel, Singapore, was called to the stand and asked to recount her know-ledge of the pirates—she knew them well at Pontianak, and could not be convinced that they had no existence. A certain Thomas Tirendale, Singapore shipbuilder, testified that he had signed a memorial against James in the belief that it was a memorial against piracy in Borneo waters. The inquiry, which began on September 11, 1854, was still continuing in late October, when James himself took the stand.

'Sarawak,' said James, 'is a private property belonging to myself, and it is clearly impossible that the sovereignty of Great Britain can be acknowledged over Sarawak when it has been consistently re-fused.' He denied the legality of the proceedings, denied the judges' terms of reference, denied that he had killed peaceful citizens. When the judges came to write their final report, they noted that the charges of killing innocent citizens received no support, and could be dismissed. James had asked for a protectorate and talked of handing the country over to Great Britain, but they concluded that he was a vassal of the Sultan of Brunei, and was therefore in no position to make any offer to the British Government. The exhaustive trial decided nothing. Every word spoken at the trial was recorded and printed in an official White Paper, numbering 533 immense folio pages, entitled *Reports of the Commissioners appointed to enquire into certain matters connected with the position of Sir James Brooke, presented to both Houses of Parliament by Command of Her Majesty*. In appearance it is about the size of a first folio Shakespeare.

To the end of his life James regarded the trial as a monumental stupidity. 'Never was there such a farce of an enquiry,' he wrote. 'Humiliation to me, disgrace to the government, injury to the natives, ruin to our policy, from a Commission conducted without dignity or propriety, and all about nothing!' As soon as it was over, he went off to Sarawak, to drown his sorrows. Spenser St. John said it was the happiest time of his life, but it was the happiness of resignation. The trial broke his spirit. Henceforth he was a man of moods, never certain of himself, serene only when he left Kuching behind him and stayed high up in his Peninjau cottage, remote from the world and all its blandishments.

He took long walks, played chess, and sent letter after letter to London, asserting that the trial was a fraud and a farce, or both. 'I am old', he wrote to his friend Templer. 'The fire of my nature burns low, I like easy chairs, I like pleasant books, I do not look for justice in this world——'

With an effort he addressed himself to the affairs of Sarawak. He wrote a memorandum on the subject of recruits for the Sarawak Government, to be hand-picked in England by people who shared his enthusiasms. He did not want college graduates:

Other things being equal, I should decide in favour of the candidate who has least prospects and fewest friends. If a good heart has felt something of the world's wrongs and hardships in youth, it will compassionate the helpless. It is however a mere toss-up; the qualities required cannot be tested; sound judgment and resolute will are not acquired by education, and only improved by practice. A learned fool is as bad or worse a fool than an unlearned one, for he is often a specious fool. Till a man is tried in action, it is a mere lottery.

What he wanted above all were 'poor common mortals, with spirit, gentleness, and love of justice, modified and guided by a strong will'. It was perhaps a self-portrait, not as he was when he first came to Sarawak, but when he was old and white-haired and

F

baffled by the British Government, which seemed to regard him simultaneously as an honourable and cherished ally and as an inter-loper, who had the audacity to found a colony without asking per-mission from London.

All through the history of Sarawak under the Rajahs there was that curious and unhappy ambivalence.

VI

THE REBELS

He seemed, in those days, to have everything he ever wanted. There was the large and imposing palace, with a splendid lawn sweeping down to the river, the air sweet with the scent of jasmine trees. There was his pinnace moored at the foot of the garden, to take him wherever he pleased. There was his large library and his small and precious collection of gold ornaments found in the sands at the mouth of the Sarawak River. He had many friends, for more and more young Englishmen were coming to settle in Sarawak, bringing their wives with them.

Finances were at last on a sound footing, for the Borneo Company had been established in London with a capital of £60,000 to work the mines and pay royalties to the Treasury. Above all, there were all the pleasant rituals of kingship, the consciousness of power, visits from tribal dignitaries, the companionship of Malay nobles. He was the undisputed ruler of 200,000 people, and sometimes as he looked out of his window at the thriving community on the other side of the river, he could hardly believe his good fortune.

Day followed day, with very little change. It was eternal summer, the river muddy and the leaves green all the year round. When the scarlet petals dropped from the flame-of-the-forest trees, new ones came to take their place. Crocodiles basked on the river banks and blue kingfishers flew above the palms. When he grew weary of Kuching, he could always take refuge in his country cottage at Peninjau, high above the plains.

Occasionally distinguished visitors came to stay with him. Alfred Wallace, the famous naturalist, was in Borneo for more than a year, spending many months as his guest. Wallace was then elaborating the theory of evolution which was simultaneously being elaborated by Charles Darwin. He was a man of calm, brilliant temper, who patiently collected every kind of monkey and winged insect, and measured the skulls of orang-utangs, happy in the company of the Dyak guides, who seemed to him as handsome a people as he ever came across.

He had a belief, very puzzling to James, that men were descended from apes. James carried him off to Peninjau, and for a few

83

days they lived alone together in that high eyrie in the clouds. Wallace was struck by the romantic aspect of the place. 'The road to the lodge', he wrote, 'was a succession of ladders on the faces of precipices, bamboo bridges over gullies and chasms, and slippery paths over rocks and tree-trunks and huge boulders as big as houses. A cool spring under an overhanging rock just below the cottage furnished us with refreshing baths and the most delicious drinking water, and the Dyaks brought us daily heaped up baskets of mangosteens.'

Wallace was charmed by Brooke. There was something awe-inspiring in the way Brooke retained the loyalty of 'those head-hunting savages'. They quarrelled, of course, on the subject of human evolution; Brooke refused to believe he was descended from an orang-utang. They talked continually. They laughed and drank wine and sharpened each other's wits, and when he returned to London, Wallace reported that Brooke was the finest gentleman in the Far East and a wonder-worker among the natives.

Spenser St. John, who, as the Rajah's private secretary, had excellent opportunities for studying his employer, said that these were the happiest years of his life. Shrivelled by long years in the East, disfigured by smallpox, his energy sapped by continual bouts of malaria, he nevertheless seemed younger than ever. He enjoyed horseplay, and he liked to take part with his secretary and nephew in debates of the kind which are enjoyed by young undergraduates. He wrote in one of his letters about the arguments which took place at 'The Grove':

> There was tremendous argumentation on the being and attributes of the Deity. Charlie was there in high feather, the room resounded with their voices, and the energetic bangs on the table made the glasses ring. Everybody was an atheist and a pantheist by turns. Charlie and St. John collared Chambers with hard names, and then everybody sat upon poor Charlie, who said that God was everywhere and nowhere at the same time, or words to that effect. Then the company roared at St. John for his heterodoxy, fiercely contesting my definition; but at last it was discovered that everybody meant the same thing, that everybody said it in a different way, and half a dozen times over, and that we were proper and very orthodox at the same time.

So they chattered like starlings, and passed the evenings pleasantly enough, and at the stroke of ten the Rajah made his way to his lonely bed. He never took Malay or Dyak women to his bed; and his asceticism, in a country rich with sensuality, was regarded as miraculous.

Visitors came from Singapore and Labuan, and were always welcomed in his house. He set a good table, liked fine wines, and made every meal memorable. He could draw out a young officer and make him feel the most important person at the table. He had a pleasant gift for flattery, and he especially liked. to play harmless tricks on older people. One day Bishop MacDougall and his wife were invited to dinner. James suggested they might like to eat durians. The MacDougalls objected strongly. Every Malay likes those evil-smelling fruit, which have the odour of corruption about them. 'Well, I'll make 'em eat durian,' James said, and ordered the cook to prepare a durian sauce for the pudding, sweetening it and hiding some of the taste. The MacDougalls complimented the cook.

'Tell me, what do you think of durians?' James asked when the meal was over.

'Horrible stuff!' replied the Bishop. 'I'll never eat it as long as I live.'

'You've already eaten it,' James said, and he howled like a schoolboy.

Years later, when he had abandoned Sarawak, James looked back on those evenings in Kuching with unappeasable nostalgia.

There were, of course, minor pin-pricks. He was still bitterly annoyed because the British Government had not given him the satisfaction he wanted, and he never concealed his bitterness from his visitors. He talked, in fact, much too impetuously about the behaviour of the Government, and some of his diatribes were reported back to England. There was trouble, too, with the newly formed Borneo Company. James wanted his secretary, Spenser St. John, to become the managing director of the Company, and he was alarmed when the company officials overruled him, appointing instead a young Dane, Ludwig Verner Helms. James despised the Dane and liked to describe him as 'a sago-merchant', but Helms, who had been in Sarawak since 1851, proved to be an admirable recruit. Helms had a taste for adventure, and his only fault was that he was interested in balancing accounts. The Rajah detested people who had anything to do with money.

James's quarrel with England ended when Lord Clarendon, the Secretary of State for Foreign Affairs, approved a plan, first outlined by the Rajah's secretary, by which criminal cases in Sarawak were tried by a mixed court; and Lord Clarendon, then at the height of his fame and power, added some comforting words, about the great work accomplished in Sarawak. It was the first note of official encouragement received for some years, and Brooke wrote off at once to his friend Templer in London: 'Clouds have passed away, sunshine has burst upon the darkness of the past years, and I welcome it with thankfulness. The Government has done more than I expected, and our misunderstanding is at an end. I am at charity with all men . . .'

He did not know that Prince Makota and the Chinese gold miners in Bau were preparing to drench the whole country in blood.

The Chinese in Sarawak occupied a special place. They formed a state within a state. They were rich and powerful from working the gold and antimony mines, and they were ferociously nationalistic. Nearly all the four thousand Chinese in Sarawak were members of the dreaded secret society known as the *Tien Ti Hueh*, which had ramifications all over the Far East. They lived in seven or eight communities scattered below Kuching, with their own governors, their own temples, and their own code of laws. Gun-runners were continually bringing them weapons, which they concealed in the forests.

James viewed the growing power and numbers of the Chinese with unconcern. He disliked them, but regarded them as a necessary evil. 'The Chinaman', wrote Helms, 'must have his tea, tobacco, opium and *samsu*, and when he has ready money he must gamble. He is, therefore, an excellent subject to tax, and from the opium, arrack and gambling farms the Sarawak Treasury was largely replenished. The Dyaks and Malays are but poor subjects to tax; they work little and require little.' In this matter at least James was in full agreement with the general manager of the Borneo Company. Since the Chinese helped to fill the Treasury, they should be encouraged. He proposed to deal with them with the same paternal gentleness as he dealt with the Dyaks.

For a long time there had been rumours of growing discontent among the Chinese. As far back as November, 1852, Charles Johnson had reported that the Chinese were secretly collecting weapons for an attempt to take over the country. By 1856 Chinese contempt for the white men had reached such a height that the Imperial Commissioner in Canton was offering thirty dollars for every English head offered him. The Chinese in Borneo were seething with unrest, only wanting a spark to ignite them. The spark came with a casual order given by the Rajah without any thought that it would have fatal consequences.

The Sarawak Government claimed the monopoly of the trade in opium, selling it at considerable profit to the Chinese. The community at Bau was in the habit of taking sixty balls a year. Suddenly the demand for opium fell unaccountably to thirty balls, although the population of Bau was rapidly increasing. James assumed rightly that the difference was accounted for by opium smuggled through Singapore and the nearby Natuna Islands. He insisted that the Chinese pay for the sixty balls, whether they took them or not.

The Chinese paid under protest and did not seem to be unduly disturbed by this new imposition. In November, 1856, vague rumours reached Kuching that the Chinese at Bau intended to surprise the small stockades at Kuching and capture the town. James was on holiday in Singapore, and the government was being administered by Arthur Crookshank, who took the precaution to put fifty men on guard at each of the forts. When James returned, he asked about the defences of the fort, learned about the additional guards, and decided that the danger had been vastly exaggerated. He summoned the Chinese leaders, scolded them, gave them a lecture on the necessity for loyalty, and sent them away with presents. He believed in their fundamental loyalty. It was the greatest mistake he ever made.

On February 18, in the early evening, the chiefs of the gold company at Bau assembled about 600 of their strongest workmen, put all available weapons in their hands, and marched them to Tundong on the Sarawak River, where a squadron of large boats was waiting for them. The workmen were told they were going to attack a Dyak village in Sambas, where some Chinese had recently been killed. Instead the boats sailed downstream towards Kuching.

It was a dark night, with no moon, and everything worked in favour of the Chinese.

A solitary Malay, paddling his canoe at night, overtook them. He was allowed to pass when he explained that he lived eight miles north of Kuching, and his wife and children would be frightened to death if they saw so many boats filled with Chinese coming downstream. The Chinese had no quarrel with the Malays, and allowed him to pass. Paddling furiously, he reached Kuching at about nine o'clock and informed the Datu Bandar about the large Chinese fleet filled with men armed to the teeth. The Datu Bandar was the chief Malay official in Kuching, very close to the Rajah. He listened patiently, and said, 'The Rajah is not very well. We have had similar reports for the last twenty years, so don't go and bother him about it.' It was inconceivable to him that 4,000 Chinese would think of attempting to take over a country inhabited by 200,000 Malays and Dyaks.

At midnight the Chinese pulled silently into Kuching. They had worked out a careful plan of campaign. One party made its way along the creek running behind 'The Grove', while the other continued downstream to the stockades. Their aim was to kill James and capture the stockades. That night only one of the stockades was being manned. James was suffering from the after-effects of a bout of malaria. He was alone in his house except for his English steward, Charles Penty. In one of the bungalows in the grounds slept Harry Nicholetts, who had been appointed resident of Lundu.

He was just eighteen, and had only recently joined the Rajah's service.

The Chinese rebels, armed with muskets and spears, with blazing torches to light their progress, swept across the grounds. What happened then has been well described by the steward:

> The attack took place about midnight with fearful yelling and firing. I hurried out of bed, and met the Rajah in the passage in the dark, who for a moment took me for one of the rebels, grappled me by the throat, and was about to shoot me, when he fortunately discovered it was me. We then opened the Venetian window of my room and saw poor Mr. Nicholetts murdered before our eyes. The Rajah said, 'Ah, Penty, it will be our turn next.'
>
> Then we went to another part of the house, where the crowd of rebels was even thicker. The Rajah seemed determined to fight. While he was loading a double-barrelled gun for my use, our light went out, and he had to do without. The Rajah then led the way to his bathroom, under his bedroom, and rushed out of the door. The rebels, having gathered around poor Mr. Nicholetts' body, left the way pretty clear, and the Rajah, with his sword and revolver in hand, made his way to a small creek and swam under the bow of a boat which had brought the rebels.
>
> Being unable to swim, I ran up the plantation and rushed into the jungle. The Rajah's beautiful house was blazing from end to end and the light reflected for a great distance. Mr. Crookshank's and Mr. Middleton's houses were also burning. At daybreak I heard Malay voices; they, like myself, were running away from the town, which was in the hands of the rebels. They kindly clothed me and took me to the Rajah.

Nicholetts had been cut down while running from his bungalow to the Rajah's house. For some reason the Chinese thought he was the Rajah, cut off his head and stuck it on a spear. All that night they carried the head about in triumph.

Delighted with their success, they went on to attack the nearby Crookshank and Middleton houses. Crookshank and his wife ran out together. Mrs. Crookshank, who was young and pretty—they had been married only a few months before—received a spear wound in her side and was left for dead in the grass near the house, where she lay all night. The Chinese robbed her of her rings, but did not molest her further. Her husband, badly wounded, escaped to the jungle and was later able to make his way across the river and join the Rajah in the house of the Datu Bandar.

The worse fate was reserved for the Middletons. They were particularly hated by the Chinese because Mr. Middleton was the chief of police and a terror to smugglers. He thought his wife and children were following him and were safe in the jungle, but the Chinese had succeeded in cutting off all escape from the house. When the Chinese broke in, she hid in a water jar. A young Englishman named Richard Wellington, a clerk attached to the Borneo Company, was staying with them; he fought frantically to save the children, killing one Chinese with the butt-end of his rifle, but he was overwhelmed.

From her hiding place Mrs. Middleton heard her elder son pleading for his life, while the Chinese laughed. There came the sound of the blow as they cut off the boy's head, and then they kicked the head across the room like a football. The Chinese set fire to the house with torches, and laughed again when they threw the younger boy into the flames. Through all this horror Mrs. Middleton remained completely conscious, noting everything that happened. When the Chinese left, she slipped out of the house and hid in a nearby pond.

There is some mystery about the Chinese attack on the Middleton house, but there is none about the attack on the stockade, which was defended by Charles Adare Crymble with four Malays. Crymble was a hot-headed Irishman, who feared nothing. He saw the Chinese massing for the attack, led by a man holding torches in both hands. They were all yelling and gesticulating. He waited until they were no more than forty yards away, and then he shot the leader with a rifle and fired the six-pounder field-piece loaded with grape into their midst. The Chinese scattered, hiding behind the nearby houses. Their spies told them that the fort was defended by only a handful, and they were in no hurry to take it. At their leisure they lobbed small iron spikes, to which flaming torches were attached over the walls. Crymble and the Malays succeeded in putting out the flames, and waited.

The fort was an arsenal and a prison, and two terror-stricken Malays, one a debtor and the other a madman who had murdered his wife, were in the cells. Crymble decided to let them loose and arm them. The debtor vanished. The madman waited for the first rush of the Chinese, and then in panic and fear turned his rifle on himself and blew out his own brains.

Crymble fought desperately. One of his Malay soldiers was killed, another seriously wounded, and then there was nothing to do except try to escape. He swung down into the ditch, and fought his way through a Chinese mob. He was stabbed at once, but he was wearing a thick coat and was unharmed. He succeeded in making his way to the house of the Datu Bandar, where he joined Crookshank and the Rajah.

At first no one on the other side of the river seems to have known about the attack. According to Paul Tidman, a twenty-year-old employee of the Borneo Company, the general alarm was not sounded until about half-past one. He rushed out of his house and made his way to the mission compound, which was on a hill, giving a good view of the burning houses on the other side of the river. Bishop MacDougall thought the Rajah was dead—at that time the

Rajah was in fact lying in the mud flats, having swum across the river and then fallen exhausted near the bank—and he assumed command.

There were six men and eight women in the mission compound, and the Bishop's plan was to hold the Chinese back until the women could be safely hidden in the jungle. 'The only thing to be done was to make the best defence possible,' wrote Tidman. 'Besides, the prospect of dying fighting was less unsatisfactory than that of being murdered in cold blood.' The Bishop distributed weapons and gave his blessing to the small company of defenders. The sound of shooting could be heard from the direction of the bazaar.

So they waited through the long night, expecting an attack, until the dawn came.

At about seven o'clock, just after dawn, a strange deputation arrived at the mission compound. They were Chinese armed to the teeth, on a mission of mercy. They knew the Bishop had some medicines and they begged him to go with them to the hospital, where some thirteen or fourteen Chinese lay wounded. The Bishop decided to trust them, went to the hospital and tended the wounded. He noted, without too much displeasure, that five of the Chinese had died in the interval.

About this time it was learned that Mrs. Crookshank was lying wounded outside her house, and some Chinese, finding her there, had thrown a covering over her to shield her from the sun. The Bishop heard about her and ordered her to be brought to the compound. The Chinese refused, but relented when the Bishop threatened to have no more to do with them until she was given shelter.

By this time the Rajah had left Kuching. He seems to have reached the Datu Bandar's house at about three in the morning, and soon after dawn he made his way to the little river Siol, which flows into the Santubong, a branch of the Sarawak River. Here he found a large Malay war prahu filled with about sixty armed Malays, and there were a number of other boats escorting the war prahu. His plan was to go to Batang Lupar and organize an expedition to recapture Kuching from the Chinese, who were now all over the town, frantic with victory.

The Bishop had thought there would be a general massacre. To his surprise the Chinese protested that they had no quarrel with the English, only with the Rajah and his government. It was a significant admission, and when some days later the Rajah heard of it he was convinced that Prince Makota had a hand in the affair.

Instead of killing off all the white inhabitants of Kuching, the Chinese were surprisingly helpful. It was a Chinese who informed Helms that Mrs. Middleton was hiding in the jungle. He at once went in search of her and brought her to his house, on the way passing the still smouldering ruins of her own house. Four dogs were tearing at the burned body of her son.

The Chinese had captured Kuching, but had no intention of staying there. They called an extraordinary meeting in the courthouse. A merchant named Ruppell, the Datu Bandar, Helms, and the Bishop were ordered to attend. They found the Chinese captain squatting on his haunches in the Rajah's chair. The courthouse was filled with Chinese, all scowling and gesticulating, half stupefied with opium. They had spent the early part of the morning parading behind the head of Nicholetts which was stuck on a long spear; and they were still convinced that it was the head of the Rajah.

The Chinese captain opened the discussion by stating his grievances. He said the Chinese had been badly treated, paid too many taxes, and were not regarded with the dignity they deserved. The chief offenders had been punished, and he was now prepared to let bygones be bygones. He suggested that Helms and Ruppell should become co-Rajahs—an offer which they respectfully declined—and that the Datu Bandar, who was close to apoplexy and controlled himself only with difficulty, was to be put in charge of the Malays. The Chinese, of course, would rule the country, but since they were accustomed to living in their own settlements, he proposed to lead them back peacefully to Bau. They were to be permitted to carry off all their plunder, and no steamers or boats were to be sent up-river in pursuit.

From the Chinese point of view this was a perfectly reasonable arrangement. They had won a great victory, and deserved to profit by it. Accordingly, they drew up a long contract in English, Chinese, and Malay, and they sealed it in the Chinese fashion by cutting off the heads of two fowls and drenching the documents in blood.

'After which,' wrote Tidman, 'came tea and cigars, and we had to sit another half hour drinking and smoking, and when we left, were obliged to shake hands with the brutes whom with the greatest pleasure we could have shot dead on the spot.'

The Chinese were in a quandary, and they seem to have known that their victory would be short-lived. The Bishop, in his casual fashion, reminded them of the consequences of victory, mentioning that there was still Mr. Johnson to be reckoned with. The Chinese knew that the Rajah's nephew was immensely popular among the Dyaks, and could let loose ten thousand well-trained Sakarangs against them. The Chinese solved this problem agreeably by suggesting that a letter should be sent to the Rajah's nephew, promising not to attack him if he left the Chinese in peace. Johnson, who had already heard about the attack, had no intention of leaving the Chinese in peace.

For the rest of the day the Chinese enjoyed their victory, plundering as they pleased. There were minor skirmishes with the Malays. The white flag of China flew over the stockades, and the head of Nicholetts was carried in procession through the town as a token of triumph almost too enjoyable to be endured.

By evening it became clear that the Chinese would soon be returning upstream. They were filling their boats with loot, carrying off whatever they could lay their hands on—cannon, coins, rifles, silver plate. There were more skirmishes during the night. Suddenly, during the morning, the Chinese decided to evacuate the town. At the last moment they summoned Helms and told him they proposed to take him with them as a hostage: his presence would help to keep off any threatened attacks by the Malays. Helms promptly went into hiding. Fearfully they began to pull upstream.

They had reason to be afraid, because the Malays were spoiling for a fight. The Datu Bandar called a meeting of the Malays and very sensibly urged them to be cautious. There would be time enough for revenge later. The Chinese had taken all the heavy guns, and could quite easily return and retake the town. In river fighting and jungle fighting the Malays would have all the advantages; but with the Chinese established in the town, it would be an altogether different story. So the Malays remained quiet, except for a few young hotheads who pursued the Chinese, defying the orders of the Datu Bandar. Among them was the son of a local chieftain, Patah, 'a sturdy man with a pleasant cheerful countenance'.

Patah swore vengeance. 'Are we going to submit to be governed by Chinese chiefs,' he exclaimed, 'or are we to remain faithful to our Rajah? I am a man of few words, and I say I will never be governed by any but him, and tonight I commence war to the knife against our enemies.' Patah was as good as his word. He manned a light canoe with a dozen Malays, went up-river and captured a Chinese boat, killing the five people in it. The Chinese paid little attention to this small skirmish, and continued on their way.

There were, however, many Chinese merchants in Kuching, and though they protested their innocence, the Malays gave them an uncomfortable twenty-four hours. The infuriated Malays, 'not being in the humour to distinguish one Chinese tail from another', taunted them all day and late into the night. They cut off the head of a dead Chinese and paraded it through the town.

The next day the Rajah, who had reached the Samarahan River, sent up a note to Helms: 'The schooner *Good Luck* is down the river. Hasten on board and write to Harvey [the Borneo Company manager in Singapore] to send us arms and ammunition. I will be with you tomorrow with plenty of men. Meanwhile hold the fort.' Paul Tidman, writing up his diary that day, thought the Rajah was

being a little presumptuous. 'It was', he said, 'like telling the Israel-
ites to make bricks without straw.'

The situation was out of control, and when at eight o'clock in the
evening the alarm was spread that the Chinese were on their way
down again, there was panic in Kuching. The Rajah knew nothing
about the return of the Chinese, and when the Chinese boats appeared, the Rajah himself was coming up the river in a solitary boat
with no men at all. He was fired at by the Chinese and retreated
quickly to the mouth of the river. He felt depressed and hopeless.
He knew he had failed to exercise the proper care. He was still
suffering from fever, and he had not yet recovered from his long
immersion in the river and the hours he had spent on the mud flats,
and he could not forget the horrors of the night when his house was
destroyed and he lost everything he possessed; and for the first and
last time in his life he panicked.

There is no doubt about his panic. It was a horrible and unpleasant exhibition of unalloyed fear. Terrified, he sent an extraordinary message to Helms: 'Offer the country, on any terms, to the
Dutch!'

When Bishop MacDougall heard that the Rajah was capitulating,
he said: 'If the Rajah deserts his country, I must look after my
diocese!'

The Bishop kept his head. He was in all places at once. He succeeded in shepherding the women on to the schooner and sending
them up to the mouth of the river, where they were safe. He inter-
viewed the Rajah, urging him to return and take command. At
Linga, Charles Johnson, sick with malaria like his uncle, had received a distorted account of the rebellion from one of the Malay
scouts, who said: 'Tuan, the news is sorrowful—the Rajah is killed.
Mr. Crookshank is in the jungles and is supposed to be dead, and the
remainder of the European community are either killed or fled in
all directions.' At once at the head of a troop of Dyaks he marched
to the mouth of the river and made contact with the Bishop, but
there was little he could do; and he left it to the Bishop to keep up
the morale of the refugees. 'But for the Bishop', wrote Paul Tidman,
'there would have been chaos. Like us all, he was armed to the
teeth, with sword, double-barrel, and revolver. He recalled the good
old times, when lord-bishops could strike a blow, if need be, in a
good cause.'

Four days passed, and then the miracle happened. On the morning of the fifth day the survivors were still at the mouth of the river,
gazing at the distant smoke rising from Kuching as the Chinese
plundered and set fire to the town for the second time. They were
about to make for the island of Sirhassen, two days from the coast
and ruled by a friendly Sultan, when there was a sudden shout.

Along the coast came the steamer of the Borneo Company called the *Sir James Brooke*. It had come just in time, in the manner of the last-minute rescue of all romantic stories.

The survivors were delirious with joy. The Malays were shouting: '*Kapalapi! Kapalapi!*' (the fire ship) and dancing about like madmen. Paul Tidman tossed his hat in the air and lost it. Helms had thought at first that it was the Dutch ship summoned by the Rajah, and since he was regarded as 'acting Rajah' he was wondering whether he would be forced to capitulate to a foreigner when he saw the name of the ship. The Rajah had seen the smoke rising from the steamer while resting in a war prahu on one of the tributaries of the river, and he soon joined them.

A few hours later the *Sir James Brooke*, with the Rajah on board, steamed into Kuching. The Chinese opened fire from the fort with a blast of grape consisting of balls, nails, and rusty iron. It did no damage. The *Sir James Brooke* replied with its two eighteen-pounders, the first shot, directed by the ship's mate, falling directly on the fort. The Chinese panicked and fled. Paul Tidman wrote it up that day in his diary: 'Out scoured the Chinese like wild hares in March, some dashing up the road, others running through the bazaars, affording practice for the riflemen on board. We steamed slowly up the river, on the side of which the Malay kampong was still burning, and then coming back again anchored off the bazaar. And thus the Company's steamer retook the town of Kuching.'

A victory had been won, but at first there was little to show for it. Kuching was in ruins, for the Chinese had methodically set much of the Malay town on fire, and the smoke still hung over the river. There was only the half-habitable debris of houses, and for many hundreds of yards around the trees were black and leafless. Kuching would have to be rebuilt from the foundations.

For the moment there was no time for rebuilding. The Malays and Dyaks—Charles Johnson had brought up his armed Dyaks at last—thirsted for revenge. They found twelve Chinese from Bau hiding in the ruined town. They were taken to the courthouse, and one, known to have taken part in murders, was summarily condemned to death. By the time he was taken to the green outside, six spears were sticking in him, and he may have been dead when his head was cut off.

The Sea Dyaks wanted to chase the Chinese up the river, but the Rajah was in no mood to allow a general massacre or to encourage their habit of cutting off heads. He invited them on board the *Sir James Brooke*, and instead of fighting from their war prahus, they crowded on to the beautifully built three-masted schooner, examining and toying with everything in sight, shouting and gesticulating at all the mechanical marvels they saw, while an elderly spinster, struck by their physical beauty, 'afforded unceasing amusement by her unequivocal admiration of those lightly-clad warriors'.

The Sea Dyaks and the Malays could be held back for a time, but not for ever. In the end nothing could constrain them from following the Chinese up-river and into the forests. Thousands upon thousands of Dyaks took part in the hunt. They felt the Chinese were legitimate prey, and they killed unmercifully. Some of the Chinese, who had wandered into the jungle, hanged themselves in despair; and at their bodies were found silver spoons and forks stolen from the houses they raided.

The war prahus of the Dyaks, each with thirty men at the oars, soon caught up with the Chinese boats. The Chinese then took to land, making their way to the neighbouring Dutch territory of Sambas. It was a desperate retreat; the Chinese fought courageously, but all the advantages were on the side of the pursuers. The road travelled by the retreating Chinese was littered with clothes, valuables, silver plate, and dead bodies. To keep their pursuers at bay, the Chinese tossed valuable articles in the path of the Dyaks. When there was pitched fighting, the Chinese women and children were placed in a hollow square. It was rugged fighting over impossible territory, but they organized their retreat well. About a thousand were killed on the journey, and some 2,500 survived to reach the border, more than half of them being women and children. They succeeded in taking with them the mysterious sacred stone, called the *Taipekong*, which they had worshipped during their stay in Sarawak.

When they reached Sambas there was more fighting, as they quarrelled over the poor remnants of the loot they had succeeded in bringing over the border. The Dutch attacked them, and plundered them of everything they possessed. Later, with typical Dutch correctness, they sent the loot to Kuching, where it was observed that a good deal of it did not belong to Kuching at all.

The fighting lasted for more than a month. From time to time Dyaks would return with strings of heads, which they cleaned and smoked over slow fires, especially happy when they could do this in full view of the Chinese in the bazaars who sometimes recognized people they had known. Paul Tidman was shocked by the display of heads, and he was shocked by the cunning expressions of the Dyaks, who seemed to be saying to the Chinese in the bazaars: 'If it were not for the very great respect we entertain for the fire-ship's guns, we should feel the greatest pleasure in adding your head to the little collection.'

When all danger from the Chinese had completely come to an end, the Malays and the Dyaks celebrated. On April 15 a prahu gaily decorated with flags and the yellow umbrella of the Rajah went up and down the river. A gong was beaten, and a man standing among the flags solemnly proclaimed a state of peace in Sarawak.

The Rajah was in no mood for festivities. He had been hurt and astonished by his own failure to take precautions in time. Some months later he wrote a brief and not very accurate account of the rebellion, and he explained the Chinese success by pointing to its nihilistic character. 'It was the madness,' he wrote, 'the stark staring folly of the attempt which caused it to succeed. With mankind in general we may trust to their not doing anything entirely opposed to reason; but this rule does not hold good with the Chinese.'

It was a lame excuse, and he knew it. The deaths of too many people could not be so easily explained away. From now on he had to work hard to re-establish his authority and influence. For the rest of his life he was to be haunted by the nightmare of the Chinese rebellion, which plagued him like guilt.

Angela Burdett-Coutts

Rajah Sir Charles Brooke

VII

THE TURBULENT YEARS

THE VISITOR coming to Kuching six months after the rebellion would have wondered if there had been any rebellion at all, for there were no signs of it. The Malay houses, made of wooden board with walls and roofs of attap leaves, had been rebuilt. The Chinese were in the bazaars and were working the gold mines. Finances were in good order, with more and more ships coming to Kuching to remove the goods from the godowns.

A few days after the end of the rebellion the Borneo Company's ship *Water Lily* brought arms, ammunition, stores, and specie for the Sarawak Government, with orders to place at the Rajah's disposal 'the whole resources of the Company in Borneo, so far as they may be made available for the upholding of the Government and the safety of the European and other residents in the Rajah's territory'. More than three thousand men had been killed or driven from the country, but Sarawak gave the appearance of being permanently at peace.

Partly, of course, the climate accounted for it; in that hot land the relics of the war soon vanished. The headless bodies of the Chinese in the jungles soon crumbled into powder, and the Dyaks searched for heads elsewhere. Grief does not last long in the tropics; the luxuriance of the earth hides all sins.

At any other time Brooke might have enjoyed the prospect of rebuilding his country, but he was ageing rapidly and seems to have had little heart for it. He knew only too well that the implicit reliance on his government had been destroyed by a single blow. Spenser St. John, who came to visit him in July, noted that he brooded often and sometimes gave way to fits of melancholy, although he often shone in company. 'I weary of business,' he said once. In June the news of the Indian Mutiny reached Sarawak, and the Rajah, who had deep roots in India, was overcome with shock, 'turning clammy with agitation when he first heard of it'. He felt almost as disgraced and humiliated by the Mutiny as by the Chinese rebellion, but there was of course nothing he could do about it except to hunger continually for the latest reports.

When he first landed in Sarawak, he acted with single-minded determination. At every moment he knew exactly what to do and what was expected of him. Now doubts crept in. He would make up his mind on a course of action, and then change it. He became the prey of rumours. He heard a story going the rounds of the Brunei natives. According to the story the Queen of England was about to have him killed when he humbled himself before the Sultan who intervened in his favour. It was just such a story as any malicious Malay might have invented, but he attached considerable importance to it. To his friend John Templer he wrote in September: 'I have a sensation of mixed pleasure and pain. I wish to do right, but I am not over-confident in my own virtue.' In other ways, too, he showed that he was losing control. He was following the path followed by nearly all heroes: having accomplished what he set out to do with great daring, he lost interest in the venture and entered a strange, many-mirrored world close to madness.

He spoke of living on a steamer with Keppel, presumably ruling the country from the captain's cabin. Presumably, too, the steamer would be moored off the banks of Kuching and it would be heavily armed, so permitting him to bombard any Malays or Chinese who dared to usurp his authority. He spoke very seriously about the ship, described it longingly and explained that he was saving money to buy it. 'I am as stingy as great desires and small means should make me,' he wrote to Templer. 'A penny saved is a screw in the new steamer.'

But more often he spoke of abandoning Sarawak to his nephew, John Johnson, in whom he saw great virtues. John was in Singapore when the Chinese rebellion broke out, and the Rajah sent him a hurried note, telling him to stay there until it was over. Now the young and elegant captain had arrived, accompanied by his wife. James was delighted with her, and installed the couple in the best available house. It was made of palm leaves, but it held a grand piano, and every evening he left his own hut and dined with them.

Perhaps it was a pity, for as time went on he spent less time with the Malay and Dyak chieftains, and more and more with his two nephews and the delightful Annie Johnson, who played the piano well and chattered pleasantly about England. Soon people were whispering that Annie could wrap him round her little finger. In the old days he would spend his evenings with the chiefs, holding court, talking to them in their own language, a strange barbaric figure among his fellow barbarians. Now all that was over. He was tamed at last, and his greatest pleasure was to sit in a corner and nod his head when Annie was playing the piano. His energy was gone. He was very tired.

Though the Malays and Dyaks grumbled, he was still Rajah and his word was law. He could not prevent occasional pirate excursions along the coast, though he complained about them bitterly in his letters and thought of the days when he could hunt them with the help of Her Majesty's navy, but he could, and did, send out expeditions against the occasional Dyak rebellions in the interior. He did not lead the expeditions, perhaps because Annie was expecting a baby and he was watching over her comforts as assiduously as her husband. When the baby was born—it was very fat and its first recorded action was to kick the Bishop in the face—the Rajah felt free to return to England for a long-needed rest.

Even when he was ill, he was not a man who could easily be induced to rest. For him England was a battleground, and he threw himself into the battle unrelentingly. He was continually having interviews with members of the Government to discuss the future of the country. He was on the defensive: his failure to put down the Chinese rebellion immediately was remembered against him. Very weighty questions were being raised about whether Sarawak should become a protectorate, or whether it should be ceded outright to the Crown, or whether it should remain the private possession of the Rajah. He wanted it to remain his private possession under the Crown, to be protected in perpetuity by Her Majesty's ships; and the Government could see very little advantage in adding a new protectorate to the many it already possessed, especially since the financial situation of Sarawak remained obscure.

In London the Rajah spent his days writing an interminable series of reports and memoranda to advance his views, he wrote hundreds of letters; he was continually seeking the attention of the most powerful people in the land. He attended a levee at the palace, where Queen Victoria was graciously pleased to notice him. More important to his purpose, he attracted the attention of the formidable Miss Angela Burdett-Coutts, an English heiress whose philanthropy extended throughout the English-speaking world, and who was especially concerned with advancing the cause of the dark-skinned races. She was the close friend of Disraeli, Dickens, and Faraday. A whisper from her sometimes had the effect of an Order-in-Council. Tall, slender, elegant, she held court in her palatial house at 1 Stratton Street, Piccadilly; and when the Rajah came to her with his troubles, she was swept off her feet.

Angela Burdett-Coutts was not easily swept off her feet. She belonged to the long roster of Victorian philanthropists who combined an intricate moral sense with hard-headed devotion to economics. Born to great wealth, she was determined to use her money as a weapon to advance her humanitarian ideas, and when the Rajah spoke to her about the Dyaks and Malays plagued by their feudal Sultans and by Ilanun pirates, still living in the Middle Ages, her heart went out to them. They must be, they should be protected by the British Government. He seems to have told her little about head-hunters.

The Rajah and the millionairess plotted and planned together. They were happy in each other's company. They were continually dining together. When away from London, the Rajah wrote to her with exactly the right note of humility and encouragement, offering suggestions for the promotion of Sarawak and continually reminding her that she was the most loyal servant of the Empire. She lent him money. She buttonholed ministers. She whipped up interest in Sarawak, and succeeded in persuading the Indian companies to petition the Colonial Office to extend protection to that small and fragile state.

While the Rajah wrote his interminable memoranda, the Colonial Office was also preparing interminable memoranda to be laid before the minister. These memoranda have survived. They are written in the orotund style of the time. There are a great number of words, but very little is said. The Colonial Office had an infinite number of problems to attend to, and it is clear that the fate of Sarawak was not the most pressing.

The Rajah had other worries besides the survival of Sarawak. Shortly after his arrival in England a twenty-three-year-old man with the typical Brooke features presented himself at the hotel, claiming to be his son. There was no doubt about the likeness. The boy was well-mannered, handsome, sensitive, not in the least put out by the knowledge of his illegitimacy. There was something indescribably appealing in him, and the Rajah took his long-lost son to his bosom. Henceforth one of his main concerns was to see that Reuben George Brooke was posted to a suitable office in Sarawak and would be cared for after his death.

No one knows the name of George's mother, but she seems to have been one of the maid-servants in his father's house in Bath. The Rajah never doubted George's claim; on the contrary, he accepted his son with enthusiasm and did everything possible to proclaim to his relatives the existence of this new claimant to his affections. The relatives were properly outraged. They pleaded with him to remain silent, and in return the Rajah sent them long lectures on the duties of parenthood.

He wrote to his brother-in-law on January 9, 1858, a sermon in response to the sermon he had received from him:

My Dear Charles,
    Thank you for your kind letter, and allow me to preach you a little sermon in return. George be assured will do very well, and is receiving the highest education which falls to mortal man. You say I have been precipitate. Can any man be precipitate in doing right? Could I unbeget

George or would you have me sacrifice him because our opinions on education happen to differ?

I have a son—happily or unhappily—but this mere fact should not be a trial of your affection for me, because in telling you of it I do not require you to fall in love with him—only I cannot help loving him myself and doing my duty by him. The misfortune of this is that I am obliged to conceal from George much of what you say, for he is proud and sensitive and did he know your misgivings or hesitation to receive him as a relative, he would not unnaturally draw away from you and repulse you when you wished to be friends.

So dear Charles do not preach any more about it but come to Harrow with Emma and in a week you will find out that George is a dear little fellow—a high-spirited and independent man to be won, but not managed —led not driven—far beyond respectable country clergymen whom he would thrash in a week if they refused to learn from him. Come along then my dear brother and do not let us have any more writing about it. You know how I love you all, but I must do my duty my own way, and do not let my duty interfere with your inclination and if you do not like to love George or love him at the rate of one inch per hundred years I shall not love you the less.

God bless you.
Ever your affectionate brother,
J. BROOKE

This, however, was only the beginning of the trouble with the relatives. They all objected to the existence of George. The 'dear little fellow' did not talk with a refined accent. He had no education, no money, no prospects. Worse still, he had chosen to enter the scene at a time when the most delicate negotiations were being carried out. John Johnson bore the title of acting Rajah and had good reason to believe that he was the duly chosen successor to the throne. He was outraged when the Rajah suggested that George should go to Sarawak and work in some department of the administration. The Rajah had openly declared that George was his son. What was more likely than that George would attempt to usurp all authority? John Johnson had given up a promising career in the Army on the promise that he would inherit the throne; and he saw his whole position menaced by the sudden appearance of a young man whom no one had ever heard of until shortly after the Rajah's arrival in England.

The Rajah did his best to placate his nephew. He did not, he could not envisage a time when his son would have anything except a subordinate position. The young man simply did not possess the qualities needed for leadership. He would amount to nothing unless he was helped, and sending him to Sarawak to assume some very lowly post in the Sarawak service was the best way to help him. 'George is my *illegitimate* son,' wrote the Rajah. 'I wronged him, and as an act of justice gave him my name, but in acknowledging the fact with regret, I gave him no rights, no claims, he has none from his birth, none from my wishes.' So in all manner of ways the Rajah attempted to minimize the importance of his son and to exalt the importance of his nephew. John Johnson was not convinced. There were moments when he seemed to regard the existence of George as a deliberate insult. Secretly, he despised his uncle for bringing a bastard into the world.

The tragedy, of course, lay in the fact that the Rajah and his nephew belonged to different worlds, spoke different languages, and had entirely opposite conceptions of what it meant to be a Rajah. John Johnson had all the virtues and vices of an aristocrat: he was elegant, suave, intelligent, and curiously cold. People spoke of how he wrapped himself in a mist. He liked the Malays, spoke their language, and delighted in the company of Malay princes, unlike his brother Charles, who preferred the company of the Dyaks. He was an excellent administrator, but there was no warmth or passion in him. He possessed the casual inhumanity of an army officer and, unlike the Rajah, he could never tolerate mistakes.

It was in fact a hopeless situation, and John Johnson seems to have known that his tenure of office would be brief. He was fighting a losing battle in Sarawak. For six months following the rebellion the country was prosperous, largely because the Borneo Company was pouring money into it. Now there was almost no money in the Treasury, trade was declining, there were continual small rebellions in the jungle, and the acting Rajah's preference for Malays had annoyed the Dyaks, who were seething with unrest.

Worse still, there was an epidemic of cholera in Kuching. Many of the Malays were affected, and the Chinese in the gold mines were openly laughing at them, saying that God was punishing them for having killed so many Chinese the year before. The people of Kuching were wondering whether they could survive. Even Bishop MacDougall, who usually showed a cheerful face to the world, said that Sarawak seemed to be abandoned by God and by England. 'For a whole year no English man-of-war has visited us,' he wrote, 'and the people begin to doubt whether England has not cast us off.' Sadly he realized that the warships borrowed for expeditions against piracy had been the mainstay of the Rajah's power over Sarawak; and the Malays and Dyaks, who had trained themselves carefully to observe the sources of power, knew perfectly well that they could throw the English out of the country if the Rajah did not receive the protection of the British Government.

According to the Bishop it was a bad year all round, but there was at least one unsuspected piece of good fortune. In November Prince Makota was travelling through the Bisayan country, stopping wherever he pleased to levy fines on the villagers, who were power-less to fight his well-armed guards. He stayed one day at a village called Awang, levied the customary fine and demanded that all the village headmen present him with their daughters for his pleasure. Seven girls were taken on board his boat. The villagers planned revenge.

That night, while the Prince's boat was still moored to the shore and he was enjoying himself with one of the girls behind the curtains, the villagers made their way down to the river bank. They made no sound. They were waiting for the signal, and when the signal came, they climbed on to the boat, slew everyone in sight, broke into the private apartments of the Prince and rescued the girls, only to find that the Prince had fled with two followers in a canoe. It was a very dark night. Suddenly one of the girls seized a torch and shouted to the people on shore that the Prince was quite close to them. Some-one picked up a large stone and threw it with all his might, striking the Prince in the head. He fell overboard and was drowned. It was a strange ending to a Prince who had spent his life in pursuit of all the pleasures of the earth.

Some months later, when the Rajah heard of the Prince's death, he wrote a little sententiously: 'A greater villain· it would be im-possible to conceive, with heart blacker, head more cunning, and passions more unrestrained than those of anyone I have ever know. I say this deliberately of a dead man.'

Only a few days earlier, on October 21, 1858, the Rajah himself had been as close to death as he had ever been. He had spoken many times of dying among the Dyaks and Malays of Sarawak, leading them in some engagement in the jungle, but his first close brush with death occurred in the Free Trade Hall at Manchester, while he was delivering a speech. It was not a very important speech. There was no real reason why he should be at Manchester at all. He felt 'a creeping movement' coming over him, and thought he was dying, but he still had strength enough to walk to the doctor's. He was told he had had a stroke: he would have to abandon his public life for ever. 'I felt,' he said later, 'a shake to the verge of eternity.' Though he lived for ten more years, he never completely recovered.

He was fifty-five, but looked seventy; old, tired, embittered, at odds with himself and the world. More and more during his long convalescence he looked forward to the day when he could retire to a small country cottage in southern England. There he would read his books, write up his journals, and dream of Sarawak, the small kingdom he had carved out of virgin jungle. All he wanted—so he wrote in a letter to Miss Burdett-Coutts—was a small cottage with a sanded floor and a woodbine porch 'to afford me room for speculation'. But the battle was still going on, and there was no time for speculation.

The battle was opened on November 30, when a deputation of more than three hundred of the Rajah's supporters met with Lord Derby, the Prime Minister who had succeeded Lord Clarendon. Lord Derby had already made up his mind: he regarded the Rajah as a mountebank, his title as an absurdity, and his demand for British protection as an impertinence. He particularly disliked 'petticoat politicking' and was not impressed by the fact that many of the members of the deputation were there to please Miss Burdett-Coutts. It was pointed out to him that Sarawak had a reasonable claim to protection because it was in a strategic position and potentially of great wealth, that many Englishmen living there were threatened as long as the country remained unrecognized, and that unless England accepted responsibility for the country, the Rajah would be forced to think of ceding it to a foreign power.

Lord Derby was not impressed by these arguments, and answered that no doubt Sir James Brooke had done some good to the country and had acted with commendable foresight on many occasions, but quite clearly the British Government could not be expected to give military and civil protection to every new state which adventurous Englishmen called into being. He did not call the Rajah a 'common adventurer', but his tone implied that he regarded him as midway between a pirate and a usurper. The disgruntled deputation recognized that it had been out-manoeuvred, and went away. Miss Burdett-Coutts was incensed; but the Rajah, who was still on his sick-bed, derived courage from defeat. He liked a fight, and with Miss Burdett-Coutts at his side, he knew he would win in the end.

He was one of those men who make large plans and despise the accidental, but accidents were always happening, A few days after the meeting with Lord Derby there occurred a small and tragic accident which was to change profoundly the situation in Sarawak. Annie Johnson, the wife of the acting Rajah, died after giving birth to her second son, at the age of twenty-four. She died slowly and terribly, fighting every inch of the way. She knew she was dying. She had been very strong and in high spirits before the *accouchement*, and for four days after the birth she was laughing and talking about the myriad things she would do as soon as she was allowed out of bed. Suddenly there was a relapse. The Bishop, who knew a great deal about medicine, was summoned. He spent the days and nights by her bedside, pressing into service anyone who could be useful, and gave her the last Sacrament as she died in great agony. A microbe had killed her; and with her death John Johnson lost for a while all interest in living. He had loved Annie to distraction, and now he hated everyone. The Bishop, always practical, suggested that a long sea voyage would help him to forget his sorrow, and a visit to England would help him to ensure his succession to the throne. It was perhaps the worst advice he had ever given.

John Johnson sailed for England, and Charles took over the Government. Charles lacked the aristocratic temper. He was quick-witted, generous, a born administrator. He had lived so long with the Sea Dyaks that he looked like one of them, and habitually wore native costume. He mended the roads, pulled down rotting huts and ordered new ones built, and he went on to build a new courthouse and a reasonably well-equipped hospital, something that neither his brother nor the Rajah had done. The Treasury was almost empty, there was no regular communication with Singapore, and the Borneo Company was threatening to pull out; but Charles thrived on difficulties. The government was Charles. Single-handed he was shoring up the ruins. The Bishop wondered how he could do it. 'Poor fellow, he can't pay the government debt, or coin money out of nothing,' he commented, and went on to ask why the government of Charles was such an improvement on the government of his brother.

John Johnson was a broken man long before he reached London. He felt abandoned by everyone, for he had lost his wife and at his first meeting with the Rajah he realized that he had lost the confidence of the man who had once proclaimed him as his successor.

The Rajah was disturbed because he had abandoned his post, because he was always talking about his rights, because he was always whining and creating trouble. He was always implying that his uncle's mental faculties had been impaired as a result of the stroke; and the Rajah, who had once adored him this side of idolatry, came to detest him. He wanted to be proclaimed sole ruler of Sarawak, and the Rajah had no intention of giving up just yet. Negotiations with the Government were still continuing. Miss Burdett-Coutts might still save the situation.

And then there was the matter of the testimonial which the Rajah's friends hoped to raise for him, so that he would no longer be dependent upon money which had to be provided from the revenues of Sarawak. John Johnson regarded the testimonial as a gift to be given to the Rajah 'on the express condition that he retires and gives the Govt. of Sarawak to me'. No one was ever able to explain how he arrived at this unlikely conclusion. He called upon Miss Burdett-Coutts to advance his cause, and was shown the door. He wrote a memorandum about the succession and sent it to her, and it seems to have been returned to him unread. Wherever he turned he found a wall of indifference confronting him. 'I feel like a Dwarf in the hands of some giant Fate,' he wrote; and his aristocratic temper exploded on those rare occasions when the Rajah

spoke to him, begging him to be patient, begging him not to interfere. In Sarawak John Johnson had regarded himself as Rajah and
been addressed by that title. The will of a doddering old man stood
between him and the throne.

The Rajah, however, was not doddering. He knew exactly what
he was doing. He wrote as well as ever. Sarawak was his obsession.
His sole remaining aim in life was to ensure that his possession should
be protected and developed according to his views: he would, if
possible, have on it his own imprint until the end of time.

To frighten the British, he made occasional overtures to foreign
powers. There were half-hearted discussions with representatives
from Holland, Belgium, and France, but they never came to anything. As sovereign ruler of a sovereign state, he was perfectly entitled to hold these discussions. As the close and trusted friend of
Miss Burdett-Coutts, he could not honourably take Sarawak out of
the British Empire. He was playing a pretty game of cat-and-mouse,
playing Napoleon III off against the Dutch, Miss Burdett-Coutts
off against Lord Derby, John Johnson off against Charles Johnson.
It was a legitimate game; he enjoyed it, and played it well, holding
the cards close to his chest; and if he seems sometimes to be saying in
one letter the exact contrary of what he said in another letter, that
was only because he was playing for high stakes and a certain
amount of Jesuitical cunning was necessary. He was a good diplomat, and occasionally a good liar.

That his nephew was not a diplomat was one of the most obvious
things about him. He was always saying the first thing that came
into his head, and the Rajah deplored his lack of finesse. In the
East silence is often the most powerful of all the weapons in the
hands of a ruler; and John Johnson found himself entangled in a
web of silence so strong that many months passed before he was able
to break out of it.

The Rajah chose different weapons for different objectives. For
his nephew there was an all-enveloping silence; for Miss Burdett-
Coutts there was garrulity. He wrote to her an immense number of
chatty letters full of talk about the weather and how she should care
for her health, and because she liked riddles, he made up riddles for
her. They are often like the letters one addresses to a young child.
She evidently enjoyed receiving them; and in her eyes the Rajah
could do no wrong.

At last in the summer of 1859 he was able to tell her he had found
the cottage of his dreams in his beloved Devonshire. The cottage
was only about eight miles from Plymouth, set on a low hill, with
green lawns sloping down to a shallow stream, near the famous old
village of Sheepstor. What particularly attracted him to the cottage
was evidently the site, for it was uncommonly like the site of his

house in Kuching, but instead of the jungle behind him, there was only the vast and empty moors.

Towards the end of July he was writing exultantly to Miss Burdett-Coutts:

> My little 'Box'—that is to be—is snugly situated under Dartmoor—a stream babbles close at hand—wood in plenty and in all it boasts 72 acres of land. I might have searched for ten years without meeting a place within my limits so retired, so near the world and so suited in all respects to my tastes. I have in a week's stay derived great benefit from the bracing and elastic air and I take my daily ride, and walk, to distances I little thought ever to have accomplished again. Yesterday I was five hours on pony-back on the Moor!

Those who visited the cottage were appalled by its barrenness. Almost without furniture, it was so bleak and austere that it frightened his occasional visitors. There were no other houses in sight, and in winter when the fog settled over the moors it was completely lost to view. Yet there is no doubt that the cottage suited his temper. Deliberately he had chosen a place as wildly romantic as any that could be found.

While the Rajah was settling down to a life of contemplation and long-range rule over Sarawak, Miss Burdett-Coutts was actively seeing to his defences. Like Bishop MacDougall she believed that a well-armed ship was worth at least ten regiments of brigadiers and in a burst of affection she offered to outfit and arm any ship he thought he would like. Those were the days when private citizens were still permitted to buy warships and sail them out into Eastern waters. James found the ship he wanted in Glasgow, and transformed it into an ocean-going gunboat. There was some difficulty in finding a suitable name. At one time he proposed to call her the *Iris*, and then remembered the lines of the poem:

> *An Iris sits—*
> *And all amid the horror of the scene*
> *Love watching madness with unaltered men.*

In the end it was decided to call her the *Rainbow*, thus honouring the beauty of Miss Burdett-Coutts, the goddess of the Dyaks, and the calm following a storm. A rainbow appears in nearly all Malay love poems.

James watched the ship sail away, and then returned to his cottage to pursue his half-hearted negotiations with foreign powers. He was still hoping the British Government would find a formula by which Sarawak could be regarded simultaneously as a sovereign state and a British protectorate. Surprisingly, he had made his peace with the enigmatic John Johnson and sent him to Sarawak as acting Rajah, making it clear that he retained ultimate authority. He had no illusions about his nephew. He was permitted to rule only as long as he proved worthy. He was being given a second chance.

Inevitably such an arrangement strained their friendship, for John Johnson felt himself on leading strings, while the Rajah, remembering his continual difficulties with his nephew, kept wondering whether he had chosen well; and he listened eagerly to reports about the activities of Charles. When John outlined his own policy in a long letter to the Rajah, the Rajah answered bluntly in a letter full of undisguised warnings:

8th August, 1860

My Dear Brooke,[1]

I am in receipt of your letter of 1st June and will with a few remarks dismiss the subject of past negotiations. I was not surprised at your differing from me in opinion, but at your deliberately assenting to important measures, and afterwards ruining them by your retraction. It is past— Thus every arrangement, political and personal, which I attempted is at an end. You must continue to administer the government, and send me as formerly regular monthly reports of passing events and yearly a financial statement of revenue and expenditure. Act upon the principles I have laid down, and let Sarawak resemble India in no single respect, more particularly in becoming a military government. Do not introduce a European element of strength to control but to protect the people, and draw the natives more and more around you. . . .

And now, my dear Brooke, I may assure you of my love and reliance upon your integrity, but if we differ, I must govern, and if I cannot guide your measures, I must return to carry out my own policy. My intentions of future retirement must be left to my decision and your ability to carry out the terms: In the meantime you must administer the government as my Deputy, or I must take the reins into my own hands. I have always told you, you could not whilst I lived be free of my control, whether exercised as Rajah or Rajah Tuah [Old, or Retired, Rajah], nor can you ever 'choose your own line of policy', as you now write. You must trust to my love and my judgment, and in due time, I propose formally to transfer the government, but not to confer upon you any power to act independently of me. Your letter calls for these remarks etc. etc. etc. and I rejoice to hear you consider Sarawak secure. It will please me still more, if you report that confidence has been restored and apprehension passed from the native mind.

J. BROOKE

This letter, with its careful threats and implied contempt, did nothing to calm the nephew. The Rajah was simply restating a position, from which it was inconceivable that he would ever withdraw; and while the nephew made little fluttering motions with his clipped wings, he sometimes remembered there was a string tying

---

[1] John Johnson had taken the name of John Brooke Brooke. He often dropped the Christian name, and came to be called Brooke Brooke. Hereafter he will be called by the odd-sounding name he chose for himself.

him to the whipping post. Seven months after Brooke Brooke sailed for Sarawak, his uncle followed him.

In all his letters Brooke Brooke liked to show that Sarawak was at peace. It was not at peace. Serip Mushahor was continually causing trouble. His ambition was to throw all the white men out of Sarawak, and for this purpose he entered into a secret alliance with the Sultan of Brunei. Sago was one of the chief exports, and it was cultivated along the banks of the Mukah River. Suddenly the Governor of Mukah, with the help of many of the Malay nobles of the border river, closed the Mukah River to traders. It was an act of defiance only a little less than a declaration of war.

At the head of a small force, Brooke Brooke sailed for the Mukah River to interview the Governor. When the guns of the fort opened fire on him, he built a stockade. He had brought heavy guns with him, and Charles was on the way with an army of Dyaks. Brooke Brooke was perfectly prepared to counter force with force; and when Charles at last arrived, he immediately set about planning the attack on the fort. The attack was launched and the attackers were scaling the walls of the fort when a steamer suddenly arrived on the scene, training its guns on the English and calling on them to cease fire.

The presence of the steamer shook the English. The timing seemed to have been calculated to the second; and perhaps it had. The steamer was H.M.S. *Victoria*. The order to cease fire was given by Governor Edwardes of Labuan, who had temporarily assumed the post occupied by Spenser St. John, then on leave in England. Edwardes was on good terms with the Sultan of Brunei, and he intensely disliked Rajah Brooke. He was on especially good terms with Serip Mushahor, and he had come to the conclusion that the wily old chieftain had been very badly treated. At this point Serip Mushahor himself arrived at the mouth of the Mukah River. Brooke and Charles came to the not unnatural conclusion that Edwardes, the Sultan, and Serip Mushahor were in league with one another. It was not clear what they hoped to accomplish, but it was certain that they represented a powerful force against the Government of Sarawak.

In the jungle Serip Mushahor had armed the Dyaks; the Sultan of Brunei was threatening war; Edwardes was looking forward to fighting Brooke and Charles. It was a very odd situation indeed, and the two brothers retired with as much dignity as they could muster. Letters were sent to London. Lord Russell found Edwardes' conduct inexcusable, but the harm had been done. Suddenly the Rajah fully recovered from his stroke, decided to visit Sarawak and investigate.

On November 20, 1860, he sailed from Southampton with Spenser St. John. He was in high spirits. He developed a passion for chess, and throughout the journey played with anyone who cared to play with him. He was full of confidence in the future. For a while he stayed in Singapore, watching the scene from afar, allowing it to be known that he had arrived. Then he struck. H.M.S. *Charybdis*, a twenty-one gun corvette, took him to the mouth of the Mukah River, and the fort fell without a proclamation of war or a shot being fired.

The terror of the Rajah's name had accomplished what his two nephews with their armies had failed to accomplish.

He was a little proud of this triumph, and wrote to his friend Fairburn: 'You may congratulate me on this bloodless victory.' He stayed in the fort for some weeks—it was, he said, nothing more than a rude blockhouse about a hundred feet long—and then went off to Brunei for conferences with the Sultan, who welcomed him with royal honours and offered to surrender Serip Mushahor to him, an offer which was gladly accepted.

Naked except for his sarong, the redoubtable old warrior was presented to the Rajah as a captive. There was no trial. The Rajah had asked for him, and that was the end of the matter. There were feasts and exchanges of presents, and a large strip of land famous for its production of sago was leased by Brunei to Sarawak for $4,500[1] a year. The Rajah had accomplished his purpose, and sent off another exultant letter to Miss Burdett-Coutts, telling her quite truthfully that his visit had brought peace and stability to North Borneo.

The Rajah had good reason to be pleased with himself. He had made peace with Brunei. He had settled the troublesome Mukah affair. He had the physical possession of Serip Mushahor, who was not executed, but sent into exile in Singapore. There remained only the question of nominating a successor. The Rajah was seeing Brooke Brooke every day. The young man had recently remarried, and showed every evidence of being in full command of his faculties. He was alert, intelligent, obedient; he looked like a ruler, while Charles looked like a district officer. On September 16, 1861, Brooke Brooke reminded the Rajah that nothing had been settled concerning the succession. He wrote a formal and carefully worded letter:

My dear Rajah,
   I shall be very much gratified if you will publicly install me as Rajah Muda before you quit the country. If you do so, it will not only be a pleasing sign of your confidence in me, but it will strengthen my hands in carrying on the government.
                                        Yours etc.
                                   J. BROOKE BROOKE

Justice demanded that there should be a proclamation and a formal presentation of the Rajah Muda to the Malay nobles; and the

[1] All dollar sums are in Straits dollars.

Rajah, satisfied with the condition of the country and delighted by Brooke Brooke's new attitude, inaugurated his nephew at a gala affair in the courthouse. There were speeches. The Rajah explained that Brooke Brooke would carry on the Government in his absence, but whenever it was necessary he would return. And though he made it very clear that the leading strings were still in his own hands, he never quite defined the rôle he expected his nephew to play. The title 'Rajah Muda' in the eyes of the Malays had the force of 'Crown Prince'. In effect, Brooke Brooke was permitted to act as regent in his uncle's absence. But the question of the succession was not yet settled. For a little while longer the strange game was to be played out, until neither the uncle nor the nephew could remember all the twists and turns of it.

With his nephew installed and the country at peace, the Rajah decided to return to England—the quiet of a country cottage, visits from Miss Burdett-Coutts, long aimless wanderings on pony-back on the moors, the endless writing of memoranda, and daily letters from Harriet Brown, who was Miss Burdett-Coutts's companion and confidential secretary. He had never been able to rest. Too old for war, he organized ducks and geese in battalions, and saw to it that his cows were productive. Deadly serious, but with his tongue in his cheek, he wrote off to Miss Burdett-Coutts an account of how he was organizing his small farm:

> We have two Guernsey Cows which supply the family and feed the pigs with milk—we provide for our neighbour the Curate and send 13½ pounds of butter pr week to market!!! A foal was born yesterday which gives me four colts—the wild ducks are both sitting.

Occasionally there were more questionable activities. On a visit to Totnes he saw some boys bathing in the water-meadows. There were four or five of them, and they were in trouble, for some fishermen saw them and promised them a whipping. The Rajah made it his task to talk the fishermen out of whipping them. He was especially pleased with one of the boys, who had outdistanced the others. He had a long talk with him while he stood naked and dripping in the meadow, and learned that the boy's father was a stonemason and his ambition was to be a shipwright at Devonport. The Rajah took to him at once; adopted him; sent him to school; and spoke of sending him to Sarawak. He had adopted at least four other boys for the same purpose, and they would occasionally come to stay with him at Burrator. Miss Burdett-Coutts was amused by what she called 'your child-gathering', but in time Sarawak was to learn that there were serious disadvantages in recruiting a civil service at the whim of a Rajah.

The Rajah no longer kept a journal, but during his long rides over the moors he seems to have composed those aphorisms which continually appear in his letters—those strange and pregnant phrases which give the impression of having been copied out of a notebook, for they interrupt the flow of the letters. So we find him writing in words which sometimes resound like hammer blows:

> Our responsibility here is for our life-time, and it is by fighting whilst we live, that we guide and control events, according to God's will . . .

> My people are true to me, true to themselves . . .

> The present age will not see that Eastern peoples may be governed and raised by appealing to the pride, and right feeling, which pulsates in their hearts, exactly as it does in those of the western world. . . .

> Directly a man persuades himself he has a divine mission from Heaven, he becomes turbulent on earth. When a mortal speaks in the name of God, it is usually not to bless . . .

They are good phrases, and they testify to his obsessions as much as they testify to his courage and good humour. He was enjoying his premature old age. A constant stream of visitors descended upon Burrator; books arrived in packing-cases; and he was continually exchanging presents with Miss Burdett-Coutts, who invited him to visit Paris to see the great International Exhibition of 1862 at her expense. The exhibition made little impression on him, and he was happy to return to the quietness of his cottage.

Happy and unhappy; for there was always the bright image of Sarawak before his eyes, tempting him like an impossibly beautiful dream. He was still in command, still debating its future in those interminable memoranda, composed in a more leisurely age than ours and full of the most bewildering hair-splitting. Should he leave Sarawak to the King of Belgium? Should Miss Burdett-Coutts be appointed his successor? When, if ever, would the British Government throw its protecting arms around the state and declare it a protectorate?

Surprisingly he drew up a will and bequeathed Sarawak after his death to the now middle-aged heiress whom he sometimes addressed as 'Missus'. To her astonishment and delight Miss Burdett-Coutts became the heir-apparent of the Rajah of Sarawak—'I do hereby nominate and appoint her to be my true and lawful successor in the dignity and office of the Rajah of Sarawak now vested in me, to be held by her, the said Angela Burdett-Coutts, as a public trust for the good of the people.' Unhappily the spectacle of Miss Burdett-Coutts ruling over the naked Dyaks of Sarawak must for ever be removed from our gaze. The Rajah lived long enough to write another will.

Suddenly, while the Rajah was calmly debating the future of his

The Ranee Margaret

Kuching, about 1900

country, something happened in Sarawak to put an end to all his doubts and hesitations. For the second time Brooke Brooke lost his nerve. He had been suffering from malaria; he had lost his second wife and his eldest son; he was in no state to rule; and he was weary beyond endurance of the Rajah's vacillations. Without warning, he wrote a violent and insulting letter to the Rajah, promising a fight to the death on matters of principle. It was such a letter as a man could only write when suffering from a profound depression and in ill-health. He wrote:

> I hesitated not one moment, but resolved to take my own course, and assert my rights and those of the people of Sarawak. Rajah, you must blame yourself. You have overstrained the bow of my patience, and it has broken at last; we must try our relative strength, and all I can say is, that if I prove the stronger I shall always bear in mind that you were the founder of Sarawak, that you *are* my relative, and that you *were* my friend. I don't write this in anger, but in calm determination.

There was only one course open to the Rajah, and he took it. He sailed for Sarawak, determined to punish the upstart. He had no pity. All Brooke Brooke's moral weakness was demonstrated by this incautious letter. Outraged, the Rajah took counsel with Charles, who was home on leave, and who seems to have been perfectly content to contemplate the downfall of his brother. The Rajah planned to go straight to Government House in Kuching; demand an explanation from Brooke Brooke, and the next day he would assemble the people and tell them why the Rajah Muda had been dismissed. It did not happen quite like that. By the time the Rajah had reached Singapore, he saw the advantages of dismissing the Rajah Muda while on neutral territory: there was nothing to be gained by a scene in Kuching. He suspected a conspiracy, and he was sure that others were implicated. There was also the possibility that Brooke Brooke might resort to force. Was it possible that he could rely on help from the Dyaks? Who were his allies? Was the Sultan of Brunei behind it?

All these questions were answered when Brooke Brooke, now thoroughly contrite, arrived in Singapore on February 25, 1863, on the *Rainbow*. The Rajah was rowed out to the ship, accompanied by Charles. Standing on the deck, he mustered the officers and demanded whether they were loyal to the Rajah, and when they all proclaimed their loyalty, he warned them that he had taken command of the ship and henceforth orders would come from him alone. Charles went to see his brother. Brooke Brooke was told that if he promised to submit to his uncle's authority, then the Rajah would meet him at twelve o'clock; if he refused to submit, they would never meet again on this earth.

H

Brooke Brooke was beaten, and knew it. He had no weapons, no possible way of defending himself. He temporized. He asked for a bill of particulars, explanations, reasons; none were given to him.

'Submit,' said Charles. 'Offer to meet the Rajah at midday. I have talked on your behalf. Everything will happen for the best.'

Charles could afford to be relentless. If his brother refused to submit, he had been instructed to give him the letter the Rajah had written earlier in the morning. It was perhaps the harshest letter the Rajah had ever written. It read:

> My Nephew,
>   I disinherit you and banish you from the territory of Sarawak for the crimes you have committed against the State and against myself; but in three years, at your brother's urgent request, I have consented to reconsider your case with a view to the interests of Sarawak.
>
> Your Uncle and Rajah,
J. B.
>
> *Mr. Brooke Brooke.*

At exactly twelve o'clock Brooke Brooke met the Rajah. It was a brief, unhappy interview. Brooke Brooke was cowed. Even if he had wanted to, he was powerless to fight the Rajah, who said calmly: 'I have come, my nephew, to demand an account of the trust I placed in your hands.'

In a mood of abject surrender, Brooke Brooke replied: 'Rajah, I submit to your authority, I cannot resist, and I will do nothing to injure Sarawak, but I have done what I thought I had a right to do. I am ready to leave the country.'

'I think your decision is wise,' the Rajah commented coldly.

That was all, or nearly all. The Rajah, in a letter to Miss Burdett-Coutts, intimates that this was the sum total of the conversation between them, but in fact much more was said. At one point in the discussion Brooke Brooke suggested that it was a matter for the law— he talked of returning to Sarawak to stand his trial as a British subject, to be judged by his peers. The Rajah dismissed the idea out of hand, for it was inconceivable that the former acting Rajah should be put on trial. There was some discussion, too, about Brooke Brooke's source of income in England—the Rajah promised him a pension of £500 a year on condition that he behaved with the dignity of a former ruler. The important thing was that he should return to England as soon as possible.

Then at last the long quarrel was over, and Brooke Brooke disappeared into a fitful obscurity. From time to time news filtered into Sarawak indicating that he was incapable of fulfilling his promises. Once again he was sending memoranda to the Prime Minister or attempting to catch the ear of Miss Burdett-Coutts, who had long ago come to the conclusion that he merited no attention at all.

As his brain faltered, as he saw the crumbling of all his hopes, he was reduced to even more desperate measures. When he threatened to sue the Rajah in the English courts, the Rajah sent him a revised version of the terrible letter which Charles had kept in his pocket during their first interview. It read:

My Nephew,
    I disinherit you for the crimes you have committed against the State and against myself.

Your uncle,
J. BROOKE

The Rajah remained in Sarawak. There were no more triumphant visits to the Sultan of Brunei, no more expeditions against pirates. The years of danger and adventure had passed, and he lived very quietly in Kuching surrounded by his old friends and retainers, an old man who had long since put ambition aside, although he enjoyed ruling his barbaric country. For many years in the upper reaches of the Renjang River the Kayans had been in revolt. They were a treacherous tribe, and liked nothing better than putting out the eyes and cutting the throats of prisoners, or burning them alive. Charles advanced against them at the head of an overwhelming force of 15,000 men, and nothing more was heard of them. But the Rajah took no part in the campaign. He was content to watch from a distance. Towards the end of the year he sailed for England. He never saw Sarawak again.

For five more years he lived in his obscure cottage on the edge of Dartmoor. There were occasional journeys to Bath and the Isle of Wight to visit friends, and the correspondence with Miss Burdett-Coutts continued uninterrupted, but the tone of the letters had changed. Miss Burdett-Coutts gradually lost interest in Sarawak. In her platonic way she had loved the Rajah more than she loved any man; she had been buoyed up by the thought of becoming herself Rajah of Sarawak; but the days of her active interest in a country she had never seen were coming to a close.

She told herself she had done everything that could be reasonably demanded of her. She had secured from the British Government the recognition of Sarawak as an independent state. She had outfitted and manned a gunboat and given large loans to the Rajah. She had fought all his enemies to a standstill, with more passion than the Rajah himself had displayed. It disturbed her that he was making friends with his former enemies. She was made of steel; she thought compassion was weakness; and like lovers who have parted they corresponded in letters which seem to have been carved out of ice. In the small cottage at Burrator life went on pleasantly. The Rajah rode across the moors on pony-back, superintended the milking of his cows, and wrote voluminous letters to Charles. He was still Rajah of Sarawak, and from a distance of twelve thousand miles he gave orders which were received forty days later. Until he died, he would continue to hold the leading strings in his hands.

In Burrator he had time enough and to spare to think out the problems facing the English ruler of an Oriental state. When Charles wrote a book dealing largely with his battles, the publisher asked him to write an introduction. The Rajah wrote the introduction gladly. He had long wanted to compose a testament, a final statement of his aims and desires. So he wrote in a mood of tranquil resignation an account of what he had hoped to do and what he had achieved. He wrote:

> I once had a day-dream of advancing the Malayan race by enforcing order and establishing self-government among them; and I dreamed, too, that my native country would derive the benefit of position, influence and commerce, without the responsibilities from which she shrinks. But the dream ended with the first waking reality, and I found how true it is that nations are like men; that the young hope more than they fear, and that the old fear more than they hope—that England had ceased to be enterprising, and could not look forward to obtaining great ends by small means, perseveringly applied, and that the dependencies are not now regarded as a field of outlay, to yield abundant national returns, but as a source of wasteful expenditure, to be wholly cut off. The cost ultimately may verify an old adage, and some day England may wake up from her dream of a disastrous economy, as I have wakened from my dream of extended usefulness. I trust the consequences may not be more hurtful to her than they have been to me.
>
> Since this I have found happiness in advancing the happiness of my people, who, whatever may be their faults, have been true to me and mine through good report and evil report, through prosperity and through misfortune.

He was an old man and he had long since retired from the combat; and this was his valediction. All his hopes and fears were contained in this moving account of a life lived in the service of an idea, but from this distance we can see that it was not entirely true. Very early in his life he wrote to a friend: 'I go to awake the spirit of slumbering philanthropy with regard to these islands, to carry Sir Stamford Raffles' view in Java over the whole Archipelago.' So he had, but he had gone for other reasons as well. Some demoniac power drove him. He would never have permitted himself an inferior place, and it is inconceivable that he would ever have become a merchant trading between the ports of the Indies. He had no head for figures; was incapable of drawing up a balance sheet; could never concentrate upon details. He had the large view always, and large views incline dangerously towards absolute power, and he had seized power with all the strength and cunning that was in him. He possessed the Elizabethan love for power, believing that some Englishmen are granted a special dispensation by God to wield power to the uttermost.

So he failed, and was sometimes bitterly aware of his failure, for power corrupts and he was aware of being corrupted by it. Again and again in his letters we recognize the authentic note of a man who thirsts for absolute power and will be content with nothing less: he would be Rajah or nothing, But what gives him his particular place in history was precisely his contempt for power once he had obtained it, as he fell more and more under the influence of the people he loved· most in the world. He thought of himself as a man whose aim was to uplift the natives of the Indies to the level of Europe, but in fact he was himself being lifted up to their own level. He made war like the Malays, conducted diplomatic negotiations like them, and came in time almost to resemble a Malay. The beauty of Sarawak and its people seduced him into surrendering all that was English in him; and whenever he returned to England he was like a stranger in a foreign land.

What is strange is that there was so very little change in him. As the years passed, he was still the young adventurer haunted by the thought of an impossible romantic perfection, seeing himself elevated in a position of power and glory. This was the dream, which never completely faded, even when he was an old man doddering on the edge of the wild moorland. In those last years there was something in him which suggested King Lear on the blasted heath, raging against the evil powers of the universe.

Spenser St. John, who visited him about the time he was writing his valediction, says he seemed much stronger. He took his daily rides and walks, talked continually about Sarawak, raged against governments, kept altering his will, and fell into fits of despair. 'Life is going,' he said once, 'and I rejoice in the hope that my death will do for Sarawak what my life has been unable to effect.' He was plagued with the thought that Charles would prove unworthy of his high office. 'Not a single man rising in the service,' he complained. 'Not a man who is really fitted to rule.' Before him there was only darkness and terror, the dream vanishing away, his youthful exploits forgotten, and his example no longer imitated by the younger generation. A strenuous romantic despair had him by the throat, and he raged unceasingly.

Still, there were compensations. The villagers of Sheepstor were friendly to the ageing pockmarked man who carried about with him the aura of kingship, and he was continually sending them presents of food and wine. He was made a church warden. From Devonport, Plymouth, and Totnes young lads came to sit at his feet and listen to tales of Borneo. There were the long rides across the moors, and the inevitable high teas with strawberries and Devonshire cream. He was sinking slowly, but he fought every inch of the way.

To the end he was the romantic in the service of his dream, and he could still hammer out a memorable romantic phrase. When Bishop Colenso was attacked for heresy in South Africa, the Rajah was up in arms in his defence. 'I fight against persecution,' he said, 'knowing that man may be put to death in ways more cruel than burning.'

On Christmas Eve, 1867, he had a stroke which left him paralysed. He rallied, and seemed on the road to recovery when on June 9, 1868, he suffered another stroke, which felled him. He lingered for two more days, and died in the arms of his friend Arthur Crookshank just before seven o'clock on the morning of June 11. He was buried in the spot he had chosen under a great beech tree, only a few yards from the ancient stone cross which stands in Sheepstor churchyard. Some years later a commemorative stained-glass window was placed in the church. The subject of the window would have pleased him. It represented 'the Exaltation of Joseph in Egypt'.

When the news of his death reached Sarawak, the guns thundered a salute across the river and a small melancholy procession with Charles at the head walking under the yellow umbrella made its way to the courthouse. In a weak voice, for he was suffering from fever, Charles announced the death of the Rajah to the assembled Malay nobles and Dyak chieftains, and a few days later he was proclaimed the second Rajah of Sarawak.

No one knew or guessed that he would reign over Sarawak for nearly fifty years.

VIII

RAJAH CHARLES

In James Brooke there was something of the knight errant at the mercy of his dream. Charles was the pure professional, a stern soldier who thought dreaming was the occupation of fools. There was no nonsense about him. He knew what had to be done, and did it, and wrote up his accounts of battles in strict military phraseology, and seems never to have suffered any doubts about the necessity of making war or standing in judgment on his fellow men. Many admired him, but few loved him. His daughter-in-law, who knew him late in life, called him 'a perfectly disciplined, malevolent old man'. He was not malevolent, but no one doubted that he was perfectly disciplined.

In almost every way Charles was the opposite of James. He was hard, precise, quick-tempered, arrogant, and unrelenting in the demands he made on his subordinates. He rarely unbent; James was always unbending. He could be terrifying when he fixed an inferior in the gaze of his cold grey eyes. He was an efficient ruler, who kept a keen eye on the profit and loss accounts in the Treasury. Because his most formative years were spent among the Sea Dyaks, he came to acquire their manners, their ways of thought, their occasional cruelty. James felt close to the Malays; Charles was happier in the company of the Dyaks and the Chinese. His mind worked in Oriental ways, and while James remained English to the core and was always a man of his own time, Charles seemed to belong to a world outside time, coeval with the dark and soaring forests. There were occasions when he seemed to rule as a Dyak chieftain might rule— solemnly, abruptly, feverishly, conscious of his tribal dignity and the presence of the obscure gods.

Charles Anthoni Johnson-Brooke was born on June 3, 1829, at Berrow Vicarage, near Burnham, Somersetshire, the second son of the Rev. Francis Charles Johnson and Emma Frances Brooke, who was James's favourite sister. He was thirteen when he entered the Navy, and sixteen when he fought as a midshipman in the battle of Malludu Bay, being mentioned in dispatches. A drawing made about this time shows him in midshipman's uniform, a sensitive gangling youth gazing languidly into the distance with a suggestion of unruffled composure. The portrait gives no hint of the formidable Rajah he was to become.

He was doing well in the Navy and was promoted lieutenant early in 1852. Quite suddenly he decided to abandon the Navy and serve under his uncle in Sarawak. That summer he took up his duties in the small fort at Lundu in the western tip of the state. For the next sixty-five years he was to be associated with Sarawak. The year before he arrived in Sarawak his uncle had written: 'I am a man of one idea—Borneo; everything else in life is a little snuff that tickles my nostrils; or a sound, or a little sight, for amusement.' From the beginning Charles shared the same enthusiasm.

From Lundu he was sent to the out-station at Linga, where he received a curiously sententious letter from James:

> Do not pull the cords of government too taut of a sudden, and do not be rigid or starched in your views concerning the natives. You must proceed by degrees, and gain their entire confidence, before you can amend all that ought to be amended. Time is the destroyer, but time likewise is the improver; and if our bodies rot in the grave, our deeds will live after us.

James seems to have guessed that Charles would be adept at pulling cords tautly; but he made a good officer. He was still in the shadow of his elder brother, who seemed destined to become the successor. He occupied a succession of minor posts, until in 1854 he was given control of the whole region north and south of the Batang Lupar River. From his headquarters in Sakarran he did his best to put down head-hunting. 'Our Dyaks', he wrote, 'were eternally requesting to be allowed to go for heads, and their urgent entreaties often bore resemblance to children crying after sugar-plums.' He was not prepared to let them have the sugar-plums. As soon as he heard that a raiding party was going out, or as soon as a spy told him that the omens appropriate to head-hunting had been observed, he sent out a party to cut them off or to fine them heavily when they returned. If they returned with heads, he took the heads, which were stored in the fort. All the forts in Sarawak had chambers where the heads were stored, each with an inscription giving the date of capture, the name of the tribe, and the name when known of the original possessor of the head. Charles described how he punished the head-hunters:

> This was steady and unflinching work of years; and before many months were over my stock of heads became numerous and the fines considerable. Some refused to pay or follow the directions of Government; these were declared enemies, and had their houses burned down forthwith, and the people who followed me to do the work would be Dyaks of some other branch tribe on the same river.

My feeling was from the first an intense interest in the people, and I could not very severely blame them for head-hunting. It was an old-established custom of their forefathers, and they considered it their duty to maintain it. Nevertheless my business was to prevent it to the utmost, and the only way of doing this effectively was by a strong hand and steady perseverance. Besides, if these head-hunting parties had not been prohibited, they would have much increased, and our Dyaks, having protection from the Government fort and arms, would have been able to obtain heads with impunity.

By this time the methods of government, which were to survive as long as Sarawak remained under the Rajahs, had been worked out. A series of small forts was spread across the country. Malays and Dyaks who helped to put down head-hunting were always liberally rewarded, and a merciless war was declared on head-hunting because it disturbed the public peace and could always lead to fighting between the tribes. But beyond this, the Government interfered very little with the traditional lives of the Malays and Dyaks. For the Chinese, and later the Tamils from South India, there were complex rules and regulations. For Malays and Dyaks there was only the *adat*, the ancient customary law which had survived through the generations.

Charles showed himself at his most formidable when he led attacks against powerful tribes.

There was a tribe of Dyaks, known as Kanowits, living in the forests. They tattooed their bodies all over, and they were adept in the use of the blowtube and the poisoned dart. At Kanowit, on a bend of the Rejang River, a small fort had been built. In June, 1859, there were two officers in residence. They were Charles James Fox, the Resident of the Rejang, and Henry Steele, the commander of the fort. It transpired later that neither of the men had been particularly well-chosen. Fox was brusque, efficient, easily excited. Steele, a former apprentice on a merchant ship, was more knowledgeable about native ways, but hard on the Dyaks who worked under him. The Kanowits decided to murder them.

On the morning of the attack Fox was calmly digging a trench in the garden attached to the fort. He was unarmed. A Kanowit emerged from the forest, and flung a spear into his back. He pitched forward into the trench, dead. Steele lived a few moments longer. A Kanowit struggled with him, and he was about to get the upper hand when another Kanowit came up behind him and split his head wide open with a sword. He fell dead. The heads of the Englishmen were cut off, and the Kanowits vanished. Everything happened so suddenly that the Dyaks manning the fort were taken unawares.

No one had anything good to say about Fox or Steele, and it is possible that they deserved to die.

Charles however was outraged. He felt, he said later, 'an intense thirst and concentrated desire to seek out and bathe my hands in the blood of those who had murdered our much lamented friends'. He was convinced that the murders were part of a conspiracy organized by Serip Mushahor, but he could not prove it. He could not arrest Mushahor, but he could punish the murderers by sending a well-armed expedition of a thousand Dyaks against them, and when this expedition failed, he formed a second expedition, leading it himself.

There was a pitched battle, with the Kanowits well-protected by a stockade and the Dyaks on open ground. Charles brought up his guns and bombarded the stockade after begging the Kanowits to let their women and children go into safety. The Kanowits refused, and kept on firing at the Dyaks with their blowtubes, killing thirty and wounding many more. There was little poetry in Charles, but he speaks of being stunned with admiration at the beauty of the young warriors who lay dead at his feet, bearing on their bodies only the faintly discernible marks of the poisoned arrows.

This was his first major engagement, and he enjoyed every moment of it. He felt that the Kanowits were worthy of him. He was completely fearless, showing himself in the open. Whenever he found one of his Dyaks wounded, he would rush up to him, pour some brandy between his lips and make him get up and walk; apparently brandy and walking were a sufficient antidote against poisoned arrows. The battle ended in complete victory for Charles. The murderers of Fox and Steele were found, and they were solemnly sentenced to death by having their throats cut, and the same punishment was meted out to the men manning the fort who had failed to prevent the murders. Charles had promised to bathe his hands in the blood of the murderers, and he had succeeded.

The expedition returned to Kuching by way of the Rejang River and the open sea. Serip Mushahor seems to have possessed an ironic turn of mind, and at one point in the journey he boarded Charles's schooner, the *Sarawak Cross*, in the guise of a friendly visitor, even offering to provide a special guard. Charles was furious, but diplomatically concealed his fury, while they faced one another on deck, the slim, darkly sunburned acting Rajah and the stout Malay chieftain with the heavy face and the small pig-like eyes.

> So my course was to meet the Seriff in a friendly manner, without a shadow of suspicion on my brow. And as he sat on one chair, I sat on another within a foot of him; he had his sword, I had mine: both had equally sharpened edges. There was also a guard of armed blunderbuss men on board. We sat and talked cordially on various topics, and he particularly recommended every precaution, as he said he feared many

badly disposed men were about. So after an hour of this hollow friendship we separated, he going on shore again. What would he not have given for my head!

It was a classic encounter, and Charles seems to have enjoyed it almost as much as the chieftain. He regarded Serip Mushahor as his most powerful enemy, one of those men who are capable of creating disturbance while retaining the mask of innocence. He especially enjoyed the encounter on shipboard because the chieftain was accompanied by twenty-five guards, who might easily have killed him. Charles wrote a two-volume book, *Ten Years in Sarawak*, which reads like an extensive military report. Describing his shipboard adventure with Serip Mushahor, he wrote: 'I felt no more fear of danger or death than of washing my hands in the morning.'

Ten Years in Sarawak is rewarding reading only because it shows his mind at work. It was, on the whole, a very simple mind, acute, moralistic, untormented by doubts, capable of making quick judgments: the mind of a man of action, helpless in inactivity. He wanted power. Describing the day he arrived at Lundu, he wrote:

> The morning was beautiful after a pouring night, and as I viewed the surrounding objects, fresh and sweet-scented, with the dew still hanging, I felt as proud as if I had lately been elevated to a very lucrative and commanding position.

In only a few years he achieved that 'lucrative and commanding position', and went on to greater triumphs by absorbing bit by bit nearly the whole of the independent State of Brunei.

Living for long periods alone, with no other white man near him, he learned to enjoy simple pleasures. When three little Dyak girls came to visit him, after having rowed up-river for no other purpose than to see him, he gave them the free run of his bungalow, allowed them to pick all his flowers and wind up his musical box and sleep on mats in a corner of his room. In those days he seems to have had very little to do with native women. 'A good book and profuse perspiration are the indispensables in this country for health and happiness.'

He was always reading: Draper's *Intellectual History of Europe* made a great impression, and to the end of his life he shared Draper's morbid satisfaction in the increasing decay of European civilization. Sometimes, especially when it rained, when it was impossible for him to superintend public works, build roads, organize expeditions or terrify everyone in sight with his display of furious energy, he would relapse into melancholy. He noted once in his diary: 'I can live in lonely jungles but not in Kuching unless I have plenty of work, work, work.' Work was the solvent. Work kept the nightmares at bay.

All through his life he kept a diary. Today, most of the diaries have disappeared, lost during the Japanese occupation of Sarawak. One survives, written in that quick authoritative handwriting which remained unchanged until the last year of his life. It is a small volume bound in calf-skin, showing traces of nearly a century's attrition by white ants, containing the only recorded utterance which shows him at the mercy of his fears. One day in 1867 he heard that Sir James Brooke had suffered a stroke. Though he had been acting Rajah for some years, Charles was suddenly struck by the thought that he might soon lose the man he worshipped this side of idolatry and become the sole ruler of the land. In a shaking hand he wrote:

> The mail has arrived and brought such sad news as near cost me all. Poor dear Rajah again, down with another attack of paralysis. May the recovery again be as complete as before, but the hope is nearly beyond the danger which one knows such an ailment leads one to expect.
> I think—I sigh—and follow round and round a listless circle of ideas, all work has lost its relish as now my imagination pictures a scene of sad prostration with the Rajah who is and has been a friend to me such as I shall never meet again. No one can feel his life as I can, and few know my position even now. I know not how far a change may be brought about as to change my prospects for life—sickness and weakness of constitution brings many changes and old associations and love revive with a tenfold force. But I am steady in my thoughts regarding each trick if I am called on to bear them—and no bad thoughts shall ever be harboured in my breast towards the Rajah if I were to find myself tomorrow or any day a helpless beggar without a farthing. So help me God.
> I am willing so far as frail nature can be to yield up all at his command, or to devote my energy and life to the good work which he has promised to leave me. I feel prepared for the moment which must sooner or later arrive.

More than once Charles had been assured that he would become Rajah on James's death, but there could be no certainty. 'You are my successor, either directly or indirectly, in Sarawak, and the inheritor of the chief part of my private fortune,' James wrote in 1864; but Charles remembered that almost the same words had once been addressed to his elder brother, now languishing in England. The following year Charles wrote to James, saying that if he became Rajah, he would feel 'bound to bear the responsibility and undertake the task to the best of my abilities'. James answered that this plain language gave him satisfaction. 'This matter, then, is finished, and you *are* my successor,' James wrote. James's last message to Charles came from Burrator on April 7, 1868: 'Remember if I die you take possession of Sarawak, for you are my heir by appointment. Be just to our people.' Two months later James was dead.

Charles had been acting Rajah so long that when the time came for the proclamation he was like a man receiving a deed of title for something he had long possessed. People who knew him said there was no change in him. Indeed, he had acted like a Rajah almost from the moment when he set foot on Sarawak.

He had been Rajah for only a few months when he decided to return to England to find a bride. On October 28, 1869, he married his distant cousin, Margaret Alice Lili de Windt, the daughter of Clayton de Windt, of Blundsden Hall, Wiltshire. Margaret was just twenty, an enchanting young woman, well-read and an accomplished pianist. She possessed an exquisite gentleness and feared no one, not even the strange sunburned inflexible man who married her after a brief courtship, and carried her off to a honeymoon at Burrator, as though he wanted her to commune with the spirit of the first Rajah.

After a few weeks at Burrator, they sailed for Sarawak. Margaret was enchanted with the place, especially with the astonishingly beautiful Malays, Chinese, and Dyaks. She adored dressing up in the costume of a Malay princess. Her eyes alight with a secret amusement, she talked to them by signs, and was content to learn from them. Never had she seen such blue skies, such green forests, such tumultuous seething life around her?

Three days after her arrival in Kuching, she received her first shock. Charles casually announced that he was leaving immediately for the headwaters of the Rejang River to put down a Dyak rebellion. He did not know when he would return.

Charles rarely troubled to write to her when he was away on his expeditions; if she had asked for letters, he would have regarded it as a weakness. She was perfectly in command of the situation. She spent nearly all her time with the Malay women-in-waiting who had been chosen for her, walking with them through the town, visiting the hospital, playing the piano, and charming everyone. The new palace, called the *astana*, had been rushed to completion for her arrival; and though it was not over comfortable (for the Rajah liked hard chairs and hard beds), she was supremely content.

When Charles returned seven weeks later, after an unusually bloody campaign, she was bubbling over with her discoveries. In his absence she had learned a good deal of Malay. She knew her way about Kuching. Already she was accepted and admired by the people.

That night Charles gave a dinner party at the *astana*, attended by the European residents and a famous old Dyak chieftain, Appai Mingat. The chieftain had accompanied Charles in his journey through the forests. He was almost senile, but the Dyaks venerated him because he had fought in so many wars. He wore only a kerchief twisted round his head, a narrow loincloth, and a shawl which was falling to pieces around his shoulders. In the early years of the rule of the first Rajah there had been nothing in the least incongruous about the presence of bare-bottomed Dyaks at the royal table, for the Rajah had insisted upon their presence; but the custom had fallen into disuse after the field officers brought their wives to Kuching.

Margaret was much taken by the old chieftain, and during the dinner party asked him to give the famous Dyak war cry. Everyone had said that it was a terrifying and blood-curdling cry. The chieftain obliged, but the war cry proved to be curiously tame. It was very high and thin and piercing, and not unpleasant. The Rajah explained, from long experience, that an old man giving the cry at a dinner table was one thing, but when a thousand maddened Dyaks gave it, it was quite another thing. Margaret bowed to his logic; and when she withdrew a little later to the drawing-room to permit the male guests to enjoy their claret and cigars without the abysmal presence of women, she beckoned to the old chieftain to follow her. She noticed that he had a headache. She wanted to help him, and she had brought from England a wonderful cure for headaches—*eau de Cologne*. She poured it on her hands and then she began to rub it over the old man's head. She was simply fulfilling her duty to assuage suffering wherever she found it, but when half an hour later the Rajah blundered into the drawing-room, now filled with the fumes of *eau de Cologne*, and saw the disreputable old chieftain kneeling at her feet while she rhythmically massaged his head, he exploded. He had not brought his bride to Kuching to permit such intimate attentions to the tribesmen.

Outwardly, the Rajah professed a stern morality. He never allowed her to dance with another man, and never allowed her to wear low-cut dresses—a pity, because she looked particularly pleasing in dresses which revealed her fine shoulders. He forbade undue excitement at Christmas. This, too, was a pity, because she had set her heart on the Christmas festivities. He liked to say, 'I don't believe in fripperies!' Margaret adored fripperies. She bowed to his will, tried to model herself on her husband, but never succeeded in looking the least forbidding. Gaiety kept creeping in.

She was gay even when the Rajah insisted that she should accompany him into the interior. She spent six weeks at the Sibu fort with him, while the Dyak chieftains came to salute their Rajah. War dances were performed in her honour, but she was never frightened, even when there was a sudden raid on the fort by 3,000 Kanowit Dyaks. The Ranee and her Malay maid took refuge behind a piano, while Sepoys and native foot soldiers loaded cannon and manned the loopholes of the fort. Continually amused, reconciled to her fate, admiring her husband while never loving him, she lived as though nothing gave her greater pleasure than being in Sarawak.

Tragedy came early. Three children were born of the marriage, a girl and twin boys. Returning to England in the P. & O. steamer *Hydaspes* in 1873, she lost all her children within a few hours. One day they were well; the next day they were gasping for breath in the raging heat of the Red Sea. No one knew for certain what killed them—cholera, heat stroke, a tin of poisoned milk, were all mentioned later. The children were buried at sea. For the rest of his life the Rajah avoided travelling in P. & O. steamers.

Margaret had not yet given up hope. With fantastic courage she returned to Sarawak and founded a new family. The artist, Marianne North, who visited her in Kuching in 1876, remembered her as a vivid, regal woman whose only delight was to put everyone at ease. She painted, played the piano, entertained the wives of the Datus, and nothing gave her greater pleasure than to sit on the long veranda of the *astana* and look at the small, gaily illuminated town growing on the other side of the river. She was gentle with her husband, but she never deflected him from his purposes, and he never took her advice.

Even in those days he resembled a machine. He worked by a timetable. At five o'clock in the morning, at the sound of the signal gun from the fort, he was out of bed, dressing and bathing by candlelight. At six he took his morning ride along the river bank. When he returned, he usually found a crowd of petitioners at the *astana* gates waiting for him. He listened to their petitions, gave his orders abruptly, and re-entered the *astana*, to emerge a few minutes later in all the panoply of his office, striding down the path that led to the landing stage under a yellow satin umbrella and proceeded by four Malay chieftains, each carrying the gold-handled staff which was the emblem of his office. So to the courthouse, where between ten and twelve-thirty he dispensed justice. His judgments were humourless, but he knew his subjects. Sometimes, like James Brooke, he was tolerant of murderers, especially those who murdered out of passion—they would be sent home with a heavy fine, or would simply be placed in the charge of their relatives. He would rage if any of his European assistants was the slightest bit unpunctual.

The afternoons in Kuching were filled with inspections. He inspected everything. He was determined to make Kuching a modern town. Endlessly puffing at his Manila cheroots, he would order a road built here, a bridge built there, or a new factory for processing oil from areca nuts over there. In the evenings, in the great dining-room lit by hanging oil lamps, with Dyaks waving palm leaves beside each guest, the table laden with silver and crystal, he entertained. These dinners were as formal as the dinners of kings.

On more important occasions he would appear for dinner in his full regalia, wearing his green and gold uniform, his chest blazing with decorations. He would arrange for the most beautiful woman to sit by his side; and if she was the wife of an officer in his service, so much the worse for the officer. He had a keen eye for women, and liked to say: 'A beautiful woman, a thoroughbred horse, and a well-designed yacht are the greatest joys in life.' He never deprived himself of these joys.

When the dinner party was over, the autocrat became a changed man. Instead of the proud ruler, there was a small, white-haired, and desperate man confronted with the horror of his own loneliness, for over many years Margaret remained in England and many of his evenings were spent alone. At such times he would write page after page in his small leather-bound journals, and afterwards he would grapple with the latest French novel. He had a vast library of French books. He read the books aloud, alone or in the company of his French valet Alphonse, and the Dyaks, hearing his voice, thought he was conversing with the spirits.

The Rajah's attitude towards France and the French language bordered on idolatry. In his considered judgment English was an uncouth, barbarous language, hardly worth speaking; and he preferred French or the strange gutturals of the Dyaks. He was steeped in the glamour of Napoleon, and knew all his hero's battles by heart —this knowledge helped him to win his own small battles against the Dyaks. He had no faith in the English newspapers; his knowledge of world politics was based on the careful reading of the *Figaro*, which he received when it was four or five weeks old. He always had a French valet in his service, and nearly always he stayed in France on his way to England. Yet to the end of his life he spoke French with an atrocious accent, and it always puzzled him when he passed through Paris to discover that so few people understood him.

In his curiously dictatorial way he loved Margaret, but she frightened him a little. His manner of authority had been learned in a hard school; Margaret also possessed an authority of her own. She could be stubborn, and he would permit stubbornness in no one. In the end Margaret learned to bow before his stubbornness, but she never completely accepted the inferior position in which he sought to place her. For more than half their married life, she lived apart from him.

In those early years, however, she remained by his side. Kuching was still a small town enjoying little communication with the outside world: a single steamer made the journey to Singapore every two weeks. The European community consisted of only three married couples and five or six bachelors. Sarawak was still poor and burdened with debt; the time of diversification of produce had not yet come. But afterwards, whenever she thought about those years, Margaret found herself preferring them to the years that came

later. It was a time of simplicity, contentment, and a dancing delight
in life. She delighted in the company of the Malay women, but it
was the nearly naked Dyak warriors and their wives who most enchanted her. Bristling with swords and spears, with tigers' teeth inserted in the upper part of their ears, and huge black and white
hornbill feathers rising from their heads, they resembled 'Pan and
the other sylvan gods I have read about in fairy tales'.

In April, 1875, she accompanied Charles on his first visit to the
Baram River, never previously explored. Margaret was prepared
to be excited by the journey, but she never guessed how excited she
would be. Two days up-river they came to a Kayan long-house.
Charles sent one of his officers on shore to tell them the Rajah
wanted to talk to their chiefs. The officer was told there was a curse
on the place, and since such curses were frequent, Charles decided
to wait on his yacht until the curse had evaporated. He waited for
two days, and then sent a message that he was coming ashore. It
was obvious that the curse was a diplomatic one, which could only
be removed by diplomatic means, and soon it became clear that two
representatives from the Government of Brunei were in the long-
house hoping to create trouble. Unarmed, Charles marched up to
the long-house, climbed the notched ladder, and took his place in
the middle of the long-house on a block of yellow wood, hurriedly
put in place to serve as a throne.

Margaret was not to be outdone. She followed her husband up
the notched ladder and sat beside him on another throne of yellow
wood. Charles spoke to the chiefs, reminding them that he had come
as a friend and as their Rajah. It was a long conference; Margaret
grew impatient and asked to see their wives. Charles was not too
pleased—he saw no very great advantage in the presence of the
women. At last the women came, led by the wife of the senior chieftain. She came slowly and steadily, swathed in white cloth from the
waist downwards, her black hair hanging over her shoulder and
bound in fillets of golden straw, pale and beautiful, her face lowered.
Margaret could hardly contain her excitement, even when she observed that there were tattoo scrolls all along the woman's legs as
they flashed between the slits of her skirt. There was something in
the stately appearance of the beautiful woman which reminded Margaret of a Greek goddess about to perform a sacred rite.

In this she was not being at all over-enthusiastic. Many have commented on the beauty of the Dyaks, especially the young women and
the boys.

Margaret was so entranced by the woman that she pulled off the
thin gold chain she wore round her neck and slipped it over her
head. There were sudden smiles among the womenfolk, and then
the Kayan princess fell at Margaret's feet and fondled her knees,

I

quietly happy, gazing up at her. Charles was staring grimly ahead, listening to speeches, Margaret would have liked some approbation from her husband, but none came. Afterwards came the slow descent down the notched ladder and the journey downstream, with a storm brewing out to sea, so that for two days the yacht sought the shelter of the river, and food ran out, until there was only a single tin of strawberry jam, but Margaret never forgot the incident in the long-house, when she sat on her throne, and received the adoration of the Dyak princesses.

Like James Brooke, Charles had only one thought—Sarawak. Slowly Sarawak was growing, coming out of the doldrums of the seventies. Gradually trade improved. There were now large areas cultivated with pineapples; roads were being built; the standard of living was increasing. Marianne North, the artist, said that Kuching seen from the *astana* resembled Cologne and Mayence, so many were the lamps glittering there. In fact, it was still a small village. Charles was squire of the village and gamekeeper of all the forests around. In time he hoped to acquire even more valuable estates.

Among the important matters which engaged his attention was the possibility of extending the frontiers of the State. When he became Rajah, he inherited a territory which extended from Cape Datu on the Sambas border to Cape Kidurong, a small promontory seven miles north of the mouth of the Bintulu River. This was not the territory originally acquired by Sir James Brooke from Rajah Muda Hassim, but a vastly increased area, for the first Rajah had acquired by treaty the whole of the Rejang Basin in 1853 and a further stretch of coast beyond the Bintulu River in 1861. The second Rajah thought the time had come for another big bite of Brunei territory.

Sultan Omar Ali was dead. In his place there was an even weaker Sultan, Abdul Mumin, whose age was unknown, but he was believed to be over eighty. He was a fat, portly, dignified gentleman, who smiled frequently and ruled weakly, at the mercy of his advisers. The Rajah was sorely tempted by the Baram territory, and in 1868 he asked the Sultan to cede it to him in return for an annual payment. The Sultan refused. Enraged, the Rajah, who had a very low opinion of the Bruneis—he said they were 'debased, sordid, exacting and unreliable'—decided to punish the Sultan.

The opportunity came about a year later when the Sultan of Brunei sent him an official letter, with the seal fixed high up on the paper. Charles believed, or pretended, that the seal had been deliberately fixed in this fashion to insult him; and he concluded that the overweening pride of the Sultan needed to be punished and there was already in existence a convenient method of punishing him. He would fine the Sultan by withholding two-thirds of the annual tribute which Sarawak paid to Brunei according to the ori-

ginal agreement between Sir James Brooke and Sultan Omar Ali.
If necessary the Rajah was prepared to go further. He would with-
hold the whole of the tribute.

Charles had many other weapons, and he used them all. He suggested to the British Government that Brunei no longer deserved to
exist as an independent state; the British should immediately assume a protectorate over it. At the same time he induced the Sultan to open the ports of Brunei to Sarawak traders and to demand
no exorbitant custom duties. Step by step he was attempting to
weaken the authority of the kindly, doddering old man.

Almost by instinct Charles was being driven to territorial expan-
sion, but many other forces were at work. As he saw it, he was
fighting for the life of Sarawak, which had never been in so great
danger. The weak Sultan was the prey of every adventurer who
came to Brunei, and at any moment any one of the great powers
might step in and assume control. Already a large part of northern
Borneo had fallen into the possession of a strange mountebank called
Charles Lee Moses, who arrived in Brunei in 1865, ostensibly to
take up his duties as United States Consul. Almost immediately he
acquired from the Sultan a ten-year lease on the greater part of
northern Borneo. A certain Joseph Torrey thereupon bought the
lease, for which Moses had paid $9.50, and styled himself Rajah of
Ambong and Marudu and Supreme Ruler of the whole of the
northern portion of Borneo.

Charles regarded Moses and Torrey as land speculators, who had
no intention of settling among the natives or ruling over them.
They were small men and could be fought to a standstill, but what
if a more powerful figure entered the scene?

In January, 1875, his worst fears were realized. For a reputed
$15,000 Torrey sold his possessions and titles to Baron Gustavus von
Overbeck, a man with excellent connections and a brilliant brain,
then consul in Hong Kong for the Austro-Hungarian Empire. The
Baron, who disposed of vast sums of money and who was said to be
on intimate terms with the Austrian Emperor, was a man to be
reckoned with. He worked slowly and secretly. He visited Brunei
and acquired from the Sultan all the territories, river, lands and
provinces lying in the area between Kimanis Bay on the north-
west coast of Borneo and the Sebokoe River on the east, an area of
30,000 square miles and a coastline of 850 miles. For this huge
territory he was prepared to pay an annual tribute of $12,000, with
a further annual tribute of $5,000 to the Sultan of Sulu, who claimed
some rights in this area. The Baron proceeded to call himself
Maharajah of Sabah and Rajah of Gaya and Sandakan, cautiously
omitting any claim to be Supreme Ruler of the whole of the northern
portion of Borneo.

Charles watched these events with mounting alarm. He hated the Baron with a bitter and unappeasable hatred, speaking of him always as though he were the devil incarnate. These events only whetted his determination to destroy Brunei root and branch. Unlike the Baron he had no vast sources of income at his disposal. In this extremity he turned to the Borneo Company, which had been managing the trade of Sarawak under licence from the Rajah, and obtained from them the promise of £20,000 on condition that he obtained the permission of the British Government to negotiate with the Sultan of Brunei to take over the control of the Borneo coast as far as Malludu Bay. The Sultan and any other Rajahs with claims to the territory would simply be pensioned off, and the state of Brunei would disappear.

The plan came to nothing. The British Government, alarmed by the Baron's activities, stepped in. The Baron sold his rights to an English partner, a chartered company was formed in 1881, and the administration of the northern tip of Borneo fell into the hands of the British North Borneo Company with headquarters in London. It was not a company in any ordinary sense. The British North Borneo Company was a private government modelled on the East India Company, which had once ruled over most of India.

Charles had failed to bring the whole of North Borneo into his grasp. He did, however, succeed in the following year in acquiring control of Baram. Brunei, which had once ruled over the whole of Borneo from Cape Datu to Malludu Bay and beyond, had become a buffer state between Sarawak and the chartered company. It was to suffer the fate of all buffer states, as the two giants competed for the few remaining territories in the possession of the Sultan.

Gradually over the years Charles swallowed up large portions of Brunei. The largest area, Baram, was ceded to him in 1882. Trusan followed in 1884, Limbang in 1890, and Lawas in 1904. Brunei was left as a small triangular appendage, completely surrounded by Sarawak on three sides, so small a state that it was hardly worth destroying.

By 1890 Charles was ruling over a country as large as England and Scotland, with the help of about twenty European officers. In a single hour he would give orders for new public works, arrange the sailing of Government steamers, hear an appeal in the courts, transfer a Government officer, and order an expedition into the interior. He was minting copper coins, and printing postage stamps with his own portrait on them. As an independent sovereign he devised his own punishments, gave orders when and where there should be planting, chose his own Bishop of Sarawak, and even trained his own army of Rangers.

When he gave the Government chaplain the task of editing the

Sarawak Gazette, he issued full and detailed instructions about how the paper should be edited; and when the Reverend Mr. Kemp introduced some mild criticism of the existing court procedure, the Rajah thundered: 'I must confess that I was rather surprised to see in the last issue some criticism on the alteration in the regulation of our courts. As the paper is printed by the Government Press, *I think it is a little out of place.*' There was no more criticism of the courts, and the *Sarawak Gazette* retains to the present day a morbid and paralysing dullness.

In the eighties and nineties of the last century Sarawak was still a country of mystery. Visitors were not encouraged; there were no hotels; few of the valleys had been adequately explored; and over large regions the Rajah exercised only a nominal sway. Borneo was still the dark mysterious continent of Lingard, Almayer, and Lord Jim, a land of yellow rivers rolling down from the legendary and unknown mountains of the interior. Occasionally in the newspapers there would be reports of 'men with tails' living in the high mountains of Sarawak.

In those days trade was largely restricted to the export of gutta percha and sago; oil and rubber were unknown. Some tobacco was grown, but the experiment was abandoned after it had cost $60,000. Foreign exports included diamonds, birds' nests, bêche-de-mer, and bezoar stones, these last providentially provided by the monkeys and porcupines in the forests. In 1890 the total revenue was $413,000, the total expenditure $363,000. Whatever else Charles was doing, he was not making a fortune.

Surprisingly, few minerals were found: only enough cinnebar, antimony, and alluvial gold to whet the appetite. In 1896 Charles spoke of working the oil deposits at Miri in the Baram district, but it was many years before the wells were dug.

Charles was not vitally interested in increasing the wealth of the country, but he was dedicated to increasing its extent. When the district of Limbang was taken over in 1890 as the result of a direct *coup de main*—he took possession of it and argued with the Sultan of Brunei afterwards—he caused to be printed in the *Sarawak Gazette* a statement which was inaccurate and misleading.

> The annexation was brought about by the constant appeal of an oppressed race to His Highness the Rajah's keen sense of fairness and to the philanthropic nature which had descended to him from his distinguished relation Sir James Brooke.

By dint of repeating these claims he came to believe them. If he had had his way, Sarawak would have included the whole of Borneo. When British North Borneo came into existence, he told the Governor he 'intended to proceed up the coast and stir up the minds of the natives'. He never carried out his threat, and people wondered what had come over him that he should be so.mild.

The truth was that he was beginning to change. Middle-age came upon him abruptly, and he was losing his appetite for adventure. Sarawak was becoming settled, provincial, a little dull. In 1891 he mentioned that he had spent thirty-nine years in Sarawak, thirteen spent in suppressing head-hunting, thirteen on 'expeditions and more peaceful pursuits', and thirteen on 'regular political and social duties'. Though a pirate fleet approached Kuching as late as 1917, the great days of adventure were already past, or were passing, by the end of the century.

Still in the long-houses in the deep interior the head-hunters went about their work. Unknown to the Rajah and his small band of policemen the women in the Dyak settlements danced and held up the smoked heads of long-dead enemies and covered them with kisses and chanted to their children:

> *Listen well, my little rice-basket,*
> *Grandfather's head hangs over the fire.*
> *Go and avenge us:*
> *Do not let us give you milk in vain.*

IX

THE OLD VICTORIAN

IN THE early years of this century when Charles Brooke, Rajah of Sarawak, Knight Grand Cross of the Order of St. Michael and St. George, visited England, everyone knew of it. He was a legend out of the remote past. That short, sunburned man, with the long, white silky hair and the grey searching eyes deep set under bushy eyebrows, carried himself as men expected a white rajah to carry himself: brusque, commanding, strangely remote. It did not trouble him in the least that the Court Circulars sometimes announced him as 'Charles Brooke, Esq. (Rajah of Sarawak).' Workmen in Cirencester, where he spent so many winters, knew him as a king in his own right and cheered him when he rode down the streets.

As he grew older, he grew more mellow. His passion was still Sarawak, but hunting with the hounds had become the avocation he prized most. He was happiest wearing a scarlet riding coat and top hat, and racing over the fields after foxes. He introduced racing to Sarawak, and on one occasion rode his own horse. No one dared to compete with him, and he was an easy winner. Thereafter he never rode to races in Kuching again, but contented himself with a pony ride every morning, and every evening he would solemnly drive his pony cart into the countryside.

Though mellowed, he still had his blunt old-fashioned way of dealing with problems. When his son Vyner introduced the motorcar to Sarawak, keeping it in the *astana* grounds, he simply ordered a servant 'to remove the dirty thing and put it somewhere else'. Age made him irascible, but it also permitted him the luxury of occasional acts of tenderness. Sometimes, as he grew older, he would talk at length of the expeditions he had led long ago against the Dyaks, and no one ever reminded him when he confused one expedition with another.

To the end he remained a Victorian, with a Victorian skill in solving problems. During a cholera epidemic the Chinese in Kuching paraded through the streets, carrying a naked man sitting in a chair entirely fashioned of sharp swords. The man's head rolled from side to side, his tongue protruded, and only the whites of his eyes could be seen. The procession was accompanied by a deafening clashing of cymbals. Charles ordered the Chinese to stop. They did not stop. He summoned the Chinese towkays, and told them that if they did not stop he would order the guns of Fort Margherita to level all the Chinese shops. They stopped.

He was always having trouble with the Chinese. Once, when he heard rumours of another Chinese rebellion, he ordered the towkays to meet him outside the town. He had a small army of Dyaks with him. He reminded the Chinese about the rebellion of 1857, and how many had died in a tragic rear-guard action fought through the forests to the Dutch border, where they were interned and all their possessions were taken from them. The chilling voice gave no quarter. Suddenly he pointed to the Dyak chieftain standing beside him and said: 'If you dare to rebel, you will suffer the same fate, and these Dyaks will be only too happy to cut off your heads!' Then he dismissed the Chinese and returned to Kuching.

In England the Rajah lived almost exactly as he lived in Sarawak. He hunted, looked after his stables, attended his immense aviary filled with birds from the Indies, read innumerable French novels, and lived the life of a country gentleman, never happier than when he was sitting on his favourite horse. 'Everyone ought to hunt,' he declared. 'Clears the blood. Keeps you young.' But he continued to hunt long past the time when most men give it up, and people whispered about his relentless display of masculinity and wondered at the causes. It was observed that he was more tender to his horses and his birds than he was to his friends.

As usual, he was living his life to the full. He was always collecting trophies. The Dyaks cut off human heads, and the Rajah filled his house in Cirencester with the heads of foxes. He built a small museum to house his mementoes from Sarawak: the most impressive object in the museum was a thirty-foot python which still contained the undigested body of a large pig. He had such a love of shooting that one of his daughters-in-law wondered why he did not shoot the birds in the aviary.

For a long time he had been separated from his wife Margaret, who divided her days between a house near Genoa and another at Ascot, near the races. Margaret never showed the slightest interest in races, but she adored Sarawak. He never permitted her to go out there, and it was rumoured that he feared her power over the natives. He wanted to be the sole ruler of his kingdom.

Among the hard-riding gentry of Cirencester he was regarded as something of a character, abrupt and sharp-tongued, with no small talk. Women were fascinated by his strangeness and his title, and by his gallantry. He was more than a man: he was a legend from a remote Elizabethan past, and he possessed an Elizabethan coarseness and an Elizabethan delicacy. They said of him that he was as relentless in the boudoir as on the hunting field.

He was not always hunting. As he grew older, he became more and more preoccupied by the future of Sarawak. Better than any man, he knew the temper of the Orient, and foresaw the rise of great Oriental powers which would threaten the colonial powers. In 1907 he published a small brochure in London under the title: *Queries, Past, Present and Future. By the Rajah of Sarawak.* Forty years had passed since his first book. This brochure assumed the character of a valediction, a warning to the European powers to mend their ways while there was still time.

One passage was amazingly prophetic:

> Happy, thrice happy, the country that has no colonial or distant possessions to trouble it in the present or in the future. Happy the people who can be contented with being thriving and rich upon their own native soil, as the Swiss. . . . My own opinion is that before we reach the middle of this century all nations now holding large Colonial possessions will have met with very severe reverses, and that the tens of millions of Europeans will not be able to hold their own against the hundreds of millions of Easterns who are daily gaining substantial power.
>
> Forty years hence China and Japan, and in all probability Russia, will join, and acting together, will be able to place millions of armed men in the field to walk through India or wherever else they may desire to pay off old scores. These are substantial truths looming in the future, and one fears a remedy is difficult, if not impossible, to find. The whole of Europe will have to combine to stand against such a force as these three countries would show.

Today these substantial truths are a commonplace, but it was a very different matter in 1907, when Russia was still reeling from the blows inflicted by Japan and her own revolutionaries, and the Chinese Empire was falling into a decline. The Rajah put the date of the grand alliance of China, Russia, and Japan at 1947. The alliance of China and Russia did in fact take place in 1949.

This small brochure, which covers only fourteen pages, contains other prophecies. Not all have been fulfilled, but so many have been fulfilled and so accurate was his vision into the future that they are worth quoting. He wrote:

> England will lose her colonies to the strength of China and Japan, who will oust her and will, in the place of the present governments, establish independent ones under their own protection. Or the Colonies, Canada, Australia, and New Zealand, will, of their own accord and energy, declare themselves independent, under their own flags, and with their own laws; and in such case it scarce be needed to add that they together will form a confederacy and commonwealth with the United States, as equals with, and not as subordinate to, the latter. The old rules of the English bureaucracy cannot be fitted to manage our rising Colonies in any way in an efficient manner, nor with the elasticity which is now necessary.
>
> The blunders that are now being so repeatedly made by the State

offices are so palpable that an opportunity of obtaining real sympathy between the English and the Colonials never seems to be given, and *time only widens* the breach. India to a certainty will be lost to us . . .

So he goes on, striking sparks with flint, impervious to the logic of bureaucracy, aware only that there was one overriding factor which entered into all equations in the East, though usually omitted in the mathematics of Whitehall—the native mind. Already in 1907, in his view, the dark races were in rebellion against the bureaucratic West. 'The fault', he wrote, 'lies in ourselves as governors, and mostly arises through want of care and of knowledge of the native mind. It is the many little disregarded trifles which gradually swell into importance, until the neglect becomes an open sore and festers into gangrene.'

Some fifty years before he had listened to 'an old veteran of the Indian service'—he is evidently referring to Sir James Brooke— who bitterly accused the Indians of ingratitude for bringing about the Mutiny. James had raged against the horror of the Mutiny, and for all those ensuing fifty years Charles had studied its causes from the seat of power. He thought the Mutiny could be explained very simply. 'The people were never questioned as to their wishes, and later on, when they demur or show forcible opposition, they are called rebels and are shot down.' He accused colonial officials of employing expediency as their most potent weapon.

He foresaw a time when the dark and coloured races would be masters of their own soil, and there would come into being a mixed race in the East:

There will probably come a time—and the sign of this looms in front of us—when the dark and coloured races will have their day of power. We have advanced too far, and this can be said of nearly all the nations of Europe. The system of aggression must stop, and it may be justly said that we have been the pioneers who have laid the seeds of education and many other systems through the conquered Colonies which will eventually lead to reduction, partly or wholly, of our power throughout the world, and that we shall have to serve as second-rate, instead of being the superiors. The whites cannot be annihilated, but will be fused into a mixed race and element, to become inhabitants of the Eastern hemisphere, better adapted than pure whites to stand the climate and earn a livelihood in the open exposure of the sun.

We stand on the verging pinnacle at the present time, and so many begin to see that our rule is not, nor ever has been during the last century in particular, adapted pacifically to advance the interests of the aborigines of the East; it has arisen to too high a standard, upwards or onwards, according to our own light, without due consideration to the existing circumstances.

He examined the fate of the native populations in all the British colonies—in Australia they were killed off, in New Zealand there were years of warfare to subdue 'as fine a race as ever trod God's earth'. Endless battles in India, skirmishes in Burma, the brave and hard-working Kaffirs fought to a standstill in South Africa, small wars in Somaliland, Afghanistan, and Tibet. Egypt was under British occupation, and he wondered whether 'a small cloud, apparently no bigger than a man's hand, may gather force through the Mohammedan world in Europe and Asia and burst into a hurricane'. What was the purpose behind all these annexations and occupations? Was it so that the wise men of England could say, 'Just look at the invaluable benefits we confer on native races by our superior example, by teaching them the Gospel and converting them to Christianity'?

Far in advance of his time, and far in advance of our own time, he thought of a revolutionary way of dealing with colonies. They should be thrown open to the world, not maintained as private estates by the colonizers.

Why not open up all such countries—conquered as they are called—to all the world, whatever flag the new-comers may fly? We talk of South Africa and Australia for the English, which is a shamefully narrow view to hold in this grand era of civilization.

We seem generally to be walking backwards into an exploded form of barbarism, instead of embracing the whole world in a common brotherhood, and taking humanitarianism as the right doctrine to be followed. We close our hearts in a narrow-minded exclusivism, as did the Dutch and the Spaniards centuries ago.

Hardly anyone else in his time dared to say these things, or even thought them. Yet all of these statements in their various ways were logical inferences to be drawn from his own autocratic rule in Sarawak. It was as though, in that small legendary state, he was hammering out the ideas of the future. There is a sense in which *Queries, Past, Present and Future* must be regarded as one of the most important documents of imperialism.

Charles saw the world through the eyes of the natives. Like them he seemed to possess a knowledge of the art of divination. While the British Government maintained an Olympian calm, secure from all blandishments and from all ghosts, he looked into the glass and was terrified. He foresaw new conjunctions of colonies: India would go; China would become a great power; the rising strength of America would be felt in the East. No wonder he became a legend in Whitehall, and senior officials quaked in their boots at his coming.

It was typical of the man that he should search for the realities, not the appearances, of power. For him real power lay in the overwhelming affection he felt for his subjects, himself a patriarch guiding them along the paths of—was it progress? He was not sure where he was guiding them, but he knew, as few men have ever known, the satisfaction of helping them in their day-by-day affairs.

But the days when he could rule his people effectively and efficiently were nearly over. An old man, half deaf, half blind, no longer in full possession of his faculties, his mind often wandering, he allowed power to fall more and more into the hands of his son. In public he was still the Rajah, but in private he surrendered to his loneliness and misery. He seemed weary of life as he paced the veranda of the *astana* in the evenings, reading aloud passages of Molière, his favourite author, and humming French songs. Then his only companions were the *chikchaks* running up the walls and the Malay servants who, with the cruelty of the young confronted with the old, imitated behind his back his gestures, his gruff voice, and his prolonged silences.

In England he showed the best side of his character. In his odd ferocious way he was kind and understanding. He rarely permitted himself the luxury of resentments. In Sarawak, suffering from fever and brooding over the succession, he often found himself echoing his uncle's complaint: 'There is none worthy to rule after me.'

The old man's last years were haunted by the thought of what would happen after his death. Towards the end of 1913 he decided once more to put his ideas about Sarawak on paper. These thoughts were expressed in a political testament intended for his successors.

It is a disturbing document, for it reveals his strength and his weakness, his public hopes and his private fears. For him Sarawak was the very breath of life, and sometimes, as he wrote, he wondered whether his sons shared his own passionate faith in the country. He had been the autocratic ruler, bearing upon his shoulders the whole burden of government, remembering everything, rarely deputing any task to others.

He wrote:

I urge that the policy and methods of government of Sarawak as hitherto carried out by the first British-born Rajah and myself may not be departed from after my death. I cannot help feeling anxiety lest the attractions of Europe may prove too strong a temptation to my successors, who may not be prepared to give up the luxury of life in the West in order to live in the East and devote their lives and energies for the good of an Eastern people. If that should prove the case, the future of Sarawak after my life is over will remain unstable and uncertain.

Therefore I wish to impress upon each and every one of my successors the necessity of establishing himself in Sarawak immediately after his accession, and of taking up life there and carrying on the Government of the Country on the lines laid down and followed by my predecessor and myself, and of not allowing Western attractions to separate his mind from the inhabitants and the interests of the State. Let him devote himself to the duties of the Government, let him consult and employ his brothers and other members of our family and the tried and faithful servants of the State to aid and assist him in his task, and let him keep the Sarawak State Advisory Council in England together as a substantial support to his unique position and great inheritance, the duties of which he is honour bound to fulfil to the best of his ability. Then he may call himself a true Rajah of the Country.

Otherwise he will never make a Rajah of an Eastern people of the same type as his predecessors. Unless my successors are prepared to live and govern on the lines above laid down, I should wish the Sarawak flag to be hauled down for good and all, and the era of the British-born Rajahs of Sarawak to be brought to an end.

So he wrote in the year before the First World War, goaded by anxiety, demanding from his successors the same remorseless and unremitting devotion to duty which he demanded from himself. He wanted them shaped in his own pattern, and he knew they would not be shaped in his pattern. When he spoke of hauling down the Sarawak flag, he meant exactly what he said. He would have hauled down the flag in his own lifetime if he had felt that his successors would be unworthy of him.

Again and again in the political testament, he reverts to the problem of rulership. What is the good ruler? How shall he devote his time? How much money should he possess? What should be his relations with his subjects? It appalled him that some future ruler might be so blinded by the magnificence of his own office and titles that he would forget his heavy responsibilities. No; the proper role of the Rajah was to be 'the slave of his country and his people' He must surrender himself wholly to the good of Sarawak, never forgetting that he is the servant of the Malays and the naked Dyaks:

In order to do his duty properly and effectually, it is necessary that the Rajah should spend at least eight months of each year in Sarawak at his post unless his health or other unexpected difficulties or old age prevent. As Rajah he should be the slave of his country and people. Otherwise the Raj will merely be the form, a display, a title to be kept up in England and not a reality. The Rajahs of Sarawak should have but one home, and that Sarawak.

He was writing at a time of prosperity—a dangerous prosperity. There was no public debt. Two large hospitals, a dry dock, a museum, a barracks, and public bathhouses had been built out of revenue. There were metalled roads, and a pipeline from the mountains brought fresh water, and all this had been paid for. There were also six steamships belonging to the Government. He foresaw a time when the riches of Sarawak might tempt speculators to enter the country, with the inevitable result that the white men would occupy a privileged position, and the dark men would be thrust to the wall. 'The main consideration', he wrote, 'should be an honest and upright protection afforded to all races alike, and particularly to the weaker ones.'

These were general statements uttered with passion and devoid of legalisms. They meant what they said. The State *must* be administered for the natives, otherwise it had no meaning. As for the succession, he made it very clear that he expected his two sons, Vyner and Bertram, to rule jointly. There must be no changes in the form of the State, and no large public works should be inaugurated unless there was agreement between the brothers. Bertram was to be allowed free access to the *astana* at all times, and he was to be shown the same respect that was paid to his elder brother. 'It is my firm belief', he wrote, 'that it will require both of them working hand and heart together to keep the edifice on a firm base.' He demanded that Bertram be given the title of Tuan Besar at his death, and he concluded the political testament: 'With these my last wishes I bid my two sons Adieu and may they both prosper.'

This moving document shows him wrestling with his angel. Throughout there are doubts and hesitations, half-formed thoughts, sudden brilliant flashes of illumination. It was more carefully composed than the short book he wrote six years before. More than fifty years had passed since his uncle, the first Rajah, had said to him: 'The head cannot long be separate from the heart.' And now at last head and heart were united.

Yet there were still many problems to be solved. A new age was coming to birth. Sarawak was a small principality ruled by a patriarchal sovereign who possessed in native eyes some, if not all, of the aura which surrounded the first Rajah.

When the war came, Charles was in England, as vigorous as ever. He was ruling Sarawak from Cirencester, as his uncle had ruled it from Burrator. His task, as he saw it, was to keep his country alive, while the nations of the earth were busy killing each other. He heard there was a shortage of rice: laws were accordingly passed against profiteering. But panic raced through Kuching when it was learned that over two thousand bags of rice had reached Sarawak from Singapore, and no more were coming. The Chinese hoarded; the Malays hoarded; and people began wondering whether Sarawak might not die of starvation.

Sarawak played almost no part in the war. No German raiders came to her shores. Almost none of her products except oil and rubber were useful to the war effort; neither oil nor rubber were yet being produced in large quantities. The young field officers who had taken service under the Rajah were flocking back to England to join the Army. From Cirencester Charles issued a stern decree forbidding them to leave their posts, and when they still insisted on going to

England, he terminated their service. 'No one who leaves me for this war', he wrote, 'will return to me.'

These were harsh rules, but he was a harsh man fighting for the survival of his country, while the German armies pushed through Belgium and came close to reaching the Channel ports. He was asked whether he cared to contribute to the Prince of Wales' Fund, the great war charity of the time. He answered that he needed every penny to help Sarawak, and contented himself with a token gift of £50 and some hospital clothing for the troops and the Belgians. He thought of the war only as it threatened Sarawak. He was like an old lion watching over its young. And when winter came and the armies seemed about to settle in a long stalemate he made plans for returning to Sarawak.

He was in his eighty-sixth year when he made the journey to Sarawak for the last time, a peppery old man full of fight and fierce impudence. He still regarded himself as the equal of men half his age. He still laid down the law. He permitted the Sarawak Advisory Council to meet in London, but rarely sought its advice and rarely confided in it. He still read vast numbers of yellow-backed French novels and talked French in his atrocious accent at the slightest opportunity. He was back in his old hunting grounds, giving orders, watching over the future. But increasingly as the months passed, and news of the war became more ominous, he wondered what would happen to Sarawak after his death.

Shortly after his arrival in Sarawak he summoned a meeting of the Council Negri, and there he spoke about matters which had rarely been spoken about publicly before. He was haunted by visions of Sarawak given over to a new and hitherto unimagined enemy. He said:

I beg that you will listen to what I have to say, and that you will recollect my words, and endeavour to call them to mind to my Successor. I can only be responsible during this, my lifetime. I have lived in this country now for over sixty years, and for the greater part of that time as Rajah. I know that I feel as you do in every way regarding the present and the future for the existence and welfare of the inhabitants. I think, after so long a period, you will allow me to open my mouth and give my opinion truthfully.

Has it ever occurred to you that after my time out here others may appear with soft and smiling countenances, to deprive you of what is solemnly your right—and that is, the very land on which you live, the source of your income, the food even of your mouths? If this is once lost to you, no amount of money could recover it. That is why the cultivation of your own land by yourselves, or by those who live in the country, is important to you now. Cultivation by strangers, means by those who might carry the value of their products out of the country to enrich their shareholders. Such products should be realized by your own industries, and for your own benefits. Unless you follow this advice you will lose your birthright, which will be taken from you by strangers and speculators who will, in their turn, become masters and owners whilst you yourselves, you people of the soil, will be thrown aside and become nothing but coolies and outcasts of the island.

His voice was failing. Even as he spoke, he seemed to be weakening. At the end of his speech, he said: 'I am old, and cannot live many more years, if any. I have had a long life, but my cord must have very nearly reached its end. I now bid you goodbye.' For a little while longer he sat in his straight-backed chair, unmoving. Then he pulled himself together and marched out, squaring his shoulders like a guardsman.

In that strange speech, filled with overtones of disaster, he seemed to be saying that Sarawak was in danger of being overwhelmed by mysterious men 'with soft and smiling countenances', who would exploit the country to the uttermost. Was he thinking of the Japanese or the Colonial Office? It was the last speech of any consequence he made, and he seems to have spent the last months of his life contemplating the nightmare.

But the work of government had to go on. There were small Dyak uprisings, but these were easily quelled. His son, Vyner, had returned to England, hoping to join up, and Bertram was already in the Army, and the Rajah was continually writing to his London office, urging that his sons be exempt from military duty. Months passed, and it was not until February, 1916, that a certificate of exemption was issued by the Secretary of State for the Colonies permitting officials of the Sarawak government to leave the Army.

The first and most important person to be affected by the certificate of exemption was Vyner, who left London for Sarawak late in March. Vyner was given the government of a vast area in the Ulu Rejang and the Batang Lupar, but almost immediately the Rajah fell ill and Vyner was summoned back to Kuching. The old man's heart was giving out. He had a swollen ankle, and the swelling passed to his leg. He called it 'a touch of gout', but he knew better. There were fits of dizziness, and he was forced to take to his bed. He was a bad patient, always restless, and when everyone thought he was dying, he would suddenly appear on the veranda of the *astana*, huddled in a great blanket, reciting fragments of long-forgotten French poetry.

Surprisingly, he rallied. Telegrams to England from Kuching described his amazing progress. 'Rajah's condition serious' was followed by 'Shade weaker' and this in turn was followed by 'Rajah progressing rapidly'. He refused to die, and made plans for returning to England on the Japanese mail steamer *Katori Maru* in December, forgetting that every time he returned to England in winter

The Dyaks, who compose the greater part of the population of Sarawak, are a handsome race. (*Right*) A typical Dyak beauty

(*Below*) The son of a chieftain of the Kayan tribe preparing fire in the traditional manner

(*Above left*) A Sea Dyak boy; in the past his ancestors included the pirates who caused James Brooke so much concern. (*Left*) A young tattooed Dyak warrior. (*Above*) A Dyak chieftain, wearing his traditional dress

he always suffered from bad colds even when in good health. The damp weather always upset him, and Chesterton House was one of those mansions which retain the damp in their walls.

He reached London at the beginning of February, 1917, and stayed at the Hyde Park Hotel. The fog settled down; Zeppelins flew overhead. It was the worst time of the war. He coughed continually. He knew he was dying and spoke of being buried in his beloved Sarawak. He said once: 'Sarawak is my honour and my pride. In any baser earth I should perish.' From the Sea Dyaks who had been the friends of his youth he retained the belief of survival as an imperishable spirit wandering among the jungles and the sandy shores.

He was thin and withered, and his body was almost transparent. Yet he remained in good spirits, talked often about his grandchildren, and showed much tenderness to the women who flocked around his bed. With the spring he improved a little, and was removed to Chesterton House: he never left his bed. There was now no Rajah in Sarawak, for Vyner had fallen seriously ill and had gone to Colombo to recover.

The old man suffered from terrible spells of coughing, choking interminably. In the intervals of quiet he seemed to be gathering his strength, but this would be exhausted with the next fit of coughing. He was suffering from oedema of the lungs. No one knew how he could survive so much punishment. He was coughing up large pieces of lung. His heart was failing. There had been delays in obtaining the release of Bertram from the Army, but at last in April he was permitted to join his father at Cirencester. Vyner decided to hurry home to be with his father, but when his ship reached Lourenço Marques he realized he had very little hope of seeing the old Rajah alive and returned to Sarawak. The Rajah died at noon on May 17, 1917. It was a very quiet death, and for some days previously he had seemed to be on the road to recovery.

All the funereal trappings which surround the death of a potentate were provided for this man who hated 'fripperies'. There were long obituaries in *The Times* and *The Observer*; there were official condolences; there were the inevitable memorial services, one at Cirencester, the other in the Chapel of the Order of St. Michael and St. George in St. Paul's Cathedral, with the King being represented by the Earl of Kintore. The King sent a telegram to Bertram:

> The Queen and I desire to express to you the deep sympathy with which we have received the sad news of the death of the Rajah of Sarawak whom I valued highly both as a loyal subject of my own and as the distinguished ruler of a friendly state. We assure you and the members of your family of our deep sympathy in your bereavement.
>
> GEORGE R.I.

K

The Rajah had spoken so often in the past about being buried in Sarawak that his body was embalmed and placed in a vault, and there it remained for two years. Finally it was decided to bury him next to his great-uncle. It was thought perhaps that the massive rough-hewn grey stone of the moor was a more fitting tomb than the crumbling stones of Sarawak.

He was buried beneath a beech tree in the little churchyard at Sheepstor, in a rough granite tomb, beside the tomb of the first Rajah, far from the earth of Sarawak where he had hoped to lie.

Of the three Rajahs of Sarawak he was the strangest, the most un-approachable, the most relentless. Indeed, there was little that was characteristically English about him. He resembled those early Crusaders from France who stormed across the Mediterranean to take Jerusalem by force, and for him Jerusalem was a wild and tropical Eden, where the natives lived in happy nakedness. He belonged to the Middle Ages. When his reign came to an end, Sarawak was startled to discover that it had suddenly jumped into the modern world.

X

RAJAH VYNER

WHEN, AS a very old man, Charles Brooke wrote his valedictory *Queries, Past, Present and Future* with its strange prophecies about the future of Asia, he gave much thought to how he would bring the pamphlet to an end. In a few pages he attempted to present his mature philosophy, all he had ever wanted to say about the trials of kingship and the tasks confronting the West in the East and the emerging patterns of civilization as he saw them. He had said it all, and there remained now only to gather all the threads of his argument together. He had been reading the famous *Instructions of the King to the Dauphin*, written by Louis XIV, and it occurred to him to quote the words of the King to his successor:

> My darling, you are going to be a great King, but all your happiness will depend upon your submission to God and the care you take to succour your people. To attain that, avoid making war; that is the ruin of peoples. Do not follow the bad example I have given you in that respect. I have entered into war too lightly, and sustained it through vanity.

Quite clearly Charles was addressing the words to his successor, whoever he should be. It was not so much that he had himself made war to the ruin of his country, though in fact he had made war without remorse and on occasion rejoiced in bloodshed; but he was demanding in his successor a peaceful temperament, a sense of compassionate duty greater than any he had himself possessed. He had been a man of violence. He asked that his successor should be a man of peace.

So it happened, very much as he hoped it would happen. Vyner was a man of peace, who took no delight in bloodshed, and ruled with humanity and compassion.

In our present age the peaceful despot is something of an anachronism. When a man possesses supreme power and uses it only for the good of the people we are inclined to view him with suspicion. We wonder at his motives. Inevitably we suspect that his benevolence derives from weakness, and his compassion from frailty. Why, we ask ourselves, does he not fall into the many pitfalls which lie open to all those who exert absolute power?

Vyner was not faultless. He made mistakes and regretted them, and went on to make more. His childhood was dominated by his stern father, who regarded any sign of weakness as a crime, and by his beautiful and accomplished mother, who regarded him as a nincompoop because he did not share her passion for literature and the arts. He admired his parents without loving them. Neither of them suffered from shyness, but his own shyness only grew with the years. He possessed a physical beauty which was almost impudent. There was a demon in him, but it was not the corrosive demon of inflexibility. He was restless, garrulous, trusting, painfully sensitive, never sure of himself, and so he deliberately hardened himself and conquered his restlessness by making Sarawak the great passion of his life. He had much in common with Sir James Brooke, and almost nothing in common with his father except an inextinguishable affection for the Sea Dyaks, among whom he spent so many years as a district officer that he was able to claim that he knew the interior of Sarawak better than either of his predecessors.

Charles Vyner de Windt Brooke was born in Albemarle Street, London, on September 26, 1874, only a year after the deaths of the three children in the Red Sea. Soon after his birth the Ranee Margaret was summoned to Kuching, and the boy spent his first year in the care of Bishop and Mrs. MacDougall in England. He was two when he was taken to Sarawak for the first time, and it was remembered that he screamed with terror when he heard the royal salute of twenty-one guns. He stayed only a few months, and came out to Sarawak again when he was twelve, this time accompanied by his two younger brothers, Bertram and Harry.

Once again it was only a brief visit. He returned to England, went to a private school, and then to Winchester, where he distinguished himself in athletics. He made few friends, suffered atrociously from earache, and defended his younger and weaker brother, Bertram, against allcomers. The brothers were inseparable, until Bertram was sent off to Heidelberg for a cure. Vyner was beginning to realize that schools do not necessarily bring the best out of their pupils.

He was happier at Magdalene College, Cambridge, which he entered after a third brief visit to Sarawak. He was growing up into a tall, lean, astonishingly handsome youth, with a flair for thinking out problems to the end and an unalterable hatred of bullying, whether it was the bullying of his father or of the senior boys at Winchester, who 'hazed' their juniors by holding them over candle flames with their trousers pulled tightly around them. There was also the more delicate bullying practised by his mother, which consisted in inviting her sons to meet her distinguished visitors, and while the boys sat tight-lipped on the edge of their chairs, she would ask them why they were so foolish whenever they opened their mouths.

There was no malice in her. It was simply that she could not understand why they had no love for the arts. Her husband would have preferred sons who were dauntless, possessed of all the heroic virtues. She would have liked a family of poets. Instead there were three boys distinguished by recurrent ill-health, all of them appallingly shy, and none of them seeming to possess any gifts.

They did possess gifts, but they were not the more obvious gifts their parents were looking for. The brothers were intensely loyal to one another, and each was determined to seek his salvation on his own merits. They had their own codes of behaviour. They knew what they wanted. They had all worn the cut-down clothes of their father, but not one of them showed any disposition to follow the father's example. They had a particular reason for detesting the snobbery which goes with wealth and power: they were not wealthy, and in those early years they were curiously unaware they would ever reach positions of power. The Rajah sometimes spoke darkly of abdication. It was not at all certain that Vyner or Bertram— Harry was so often ill that he was rarely considered—would ever become rulers of Sarawak.

At Magdalene College Vyner found himself for the first time among people he genuinely liked. He spent his allowance prodigally, bought horses and was in debt to his father for many years afterwards. Undergraduates were strictly forbidden to fight the townspeople, but Vyner found himself in many fights. Once he was attacked by some navvies who kicked him unconscious: he remembered hearing the cracking of three ribs, and then everything turned black. It annoyed him when he woke up to find the whole of the front of his best blue suit covered with congealed blood. There was a court scene, the navvies were given a light punishment, and Vyner royally offered them sixpence each for their pains.

In August, 1897, after six years' absence from Sarawak, Vyner was gazetted in the Sarawak Government Service, attached to the Rajah's staff. He was then twenty-three. He stayed only a few months in Kuching, and the following February he went to work as a district officer at Simanggang under the Resident, Demetrius Bailey, renowned for his enormous yellow handlebar moustache. For the first time he came in daily contact with the head-hunters.

From the beginning it had been the Rajah's intention to train his sons in the field. He had not approved of Vyner's fights, his occasional gambling, or his reputation for levity. The boy laughed too much. It was time he was submitted to a harsh discipline, and the Rajah hoped that Simanggang would provide just the kind of discipline he needed.

In fact Simanggang was about the worst place he could be sent to. Bailey was one of those suave officers who make a good impression upon their superiors, clever and charming in a robust Irish way, but quite incapable of managing the daily problems of an out-station. He drank too much. He was lazy. He had no sense of discipline, and did not care very much what happened to the natives under his control. Vyner, who could not yet talk Malay, found himself in an elaborate conspiracy to conceal the real situation at Simanggang. Most of the work at the out-station fell on his untried shoulders. To him fell the task of keeping proper documents, checking records, vaccinating the Dyaks, and seeing that law and order were observed. He was judge, prosecutor, garrison commander, chief medical officer, and office boy all at once. He also acted as the local barber, for Bailey suffered from tremors brought on by drinking and his young assistant was deputed to shave him every morning, because when he shaved himself he was always cutting his face to ribbons.

Bailey was a symbol of what was wrong in Sarawak. He had been hand-picked by the Rajah, had county and aristocratic connections, and when sober possessed impeccable manners. He came from the same class as most of the other officers in the Sarawak Government Service. There was nothing in his birth or upbringing which predisposed him to command tribes of wild head-hunters. The Rajah was perfectly aware of the unsatisfactory nature of some of his appointments, but there was little he could do about it. About this time he was writing: 'I sigh for some of the old hands that could not read or write, but could work, and had more sound wisdom in their little fingers than many popinjay gentlemen of the present day carry in their heads.'

Bailey was one of those 'popinjay gentlemen', belonging to the long line of besotted empire builders described by Somerset Maugham. Vyner himself was closer to those old hands 'that could not read or write, but could work'. He genuinely liked the Dyaks. He had a flair for helping them and solving their problems, and was quickly learning their language. He had a vast sense of humour and extracted amusement from almost everything connected with the daily lives of the Dyaks—he was amused rather than frightened by the grinning heads in the long-house. He enjoyed their dances. He was even beginning to enjoy the complete absence of ordinary comforts which went with life in the forests. In those days one did not take a sleeping bag: one slept stretched out on the floor in the Dyak long-houses, while the heads kept watch.

There was no telegraph, and few letters; orders came by runner from Kuching; very infrequently the Rajah came on a tour of inspection. Life at Simanggang became a series of improvisations. He was living like Robinson Crusoe, surrounded by a host of friendly and murderous Dyaks. Once a Dyak ran amuck, cutting another

Dyak almost in two with a sharp parang. Vyner hurried to the scene to see what he could do. The Dyak's entrails had spilled out of his stomach and lay beside him. Knowing very little about medicine, Vyner carefully stuffed the entrails back in the man's stomach fold by fold and sewed up the huge wound, while the awe-struck villagers gaped. 'Do you know,' said Vyner later, 'everything was perfectly all right except that when the Dyak began to speak, his voice came out of his navel.'

The stern high-blooded man, who ruled his little empire from the veranda of the *astana* in Kuching, would not have been amused. He would have thought the levity misplaced. 'I must keep the collar on throughout my life,' Charles said once. Vyner wondered what collars had to do with naked savages, and like Blake he was prepared to 'damn braces' through most of his life.

He could not always, of course, live in the unrestrained freedom of a desolate outpost, dosing natives with castor oil and attending to the wants of his superior officer. Occasionally there were uprisings in the interior, and these had to be put down. On May 2, 1900, a punitive expedition left Muara for the Trusan River, where the wily old chieftain Okong had raised the flag of revolt. The Murut chieftain had killed a great number of men and had served notice that he intended to kill more. Some fifteen long-houses were in his possession, and he commanded perhaps three thousand armed Dyaks. The expedition consisted of four European officers, six hundred Dyaks, a hundred Rangers, and a hundred Malays. They spent ten days marching over the mountains, climbing through jungles and along precipitous slopes, always in danger of attack from the enemy hidden in the forests. They were plagued by the heat, by mosquitoes, by long treks through swamps. Remembering the expedition many years afterwards, Vyner recalled how he was strangely lighthearted and excited throughout those intolerable days when danger lurked in the crackling of every leaf.

Okong had his spies in the forests, and watched their progress and set traps for them. When at last they came in sight of the long-houses, there was no sign of the enemy, but all the long-houses were surrounded with poisoned bamboo spikes. Twelve Dyaks were severely wounded by the spikes. There were occasional brief skirmishes, but no pitched battles. It was a curiously ineffective affair, for Okong was in hiding, watching them while remaining himself unseen, and they never knew when he would suddenly emerge and fall on them. In the steamy heat they set about punishing him by removing whatever they could find in the long-houses, and by slaughtering his cattle. Then they burned the long-houses, and made the long weary journey back over the mountains to Muara.

There were innumerable raids of this kind, all following the same pattern. Little had changed in the sixty years since Sir James Brooke led his first expedition against Balidah. There were the same poisoned spikes, the same enemy lurking among the trees, and at the end the same black smoke-cloud hanging in the sky, heads and jars removed as punishment, a few bodies lying in the long grass, soon vanishing, for nothing survives in that heat. Astonishingly few lives were lost in those expeditions.

Sometimes there were holocausts, caused by flood, drought, cholera, or the plague. They did not happen very often, but when they did, men remembered them to the end of their lives.

The year 1902 started quietly. In January Vyner returned from a holiday in England, and the next month found him appointed Resident at Muka and Oya, a district embracing two small rivers flowing into the China Sea. He administered justice, inspected the long-houses, and wrote up his brief reports. His report in May spoke of the satisfactory work of road-building performed by prisoners, the export of sago flour, and the arrival of a ship bringing a much needed supply of rice. That month the Rajah returned from England and heard about rebellions in the upper part of the Batang Lupar River on the frontier. He could never tolerate rebellion. His method was to attack at the first sign of disorder. An expedition was fitted out under the command of Vyner and FitzGibbon Deshon, who was then the Resident of Kuching. The Rajah accompanied the expedition as far as Simanggang on the upper reaches of the Batang Lupar River. They slept there only one night. There had been rumours of cholera in the area, but the Rajah was inclined to laugh at them—he was himself in excellent health and no one had *proved* the existence of cholera. When Vyner reported the next morning that two men had died, apparently of cholera, outside his bungalow during the night, the Rajah became livid. 'Absurd!' he exclaimed. 'We have ten thousand men under arms all ready to attack the enemy, and all you can think of is cholera! The expedition goes on!'

No one ever argued with the Rajah, who returned to Kuching with the satisfaction of having sent the expedition on its way.

The expedition consisted of more than 800 native war prahus, from forty to sixty feet long, each vessel carved and painted, with streamers flying and figureheads representing snakes, bulls, and crocodiles. For the first three days the flotilla made its way noiselessly and secretly up-river, making for the headquarters of a Dyak chief called Bantin. They were quiet summer days, and there was no sign of the cholera. On the third day the cholera struck. Deshon was not alarmed: he thought it was contained in only a few boats. But as the boats paddled steadily upsteam, and men died one by one, their skins turning blue, Vyner became convinced that an epidemic of cholera had seized upon the whole fleet.

Deshon, who had a healthy fear of the Rajah, at first insisted on continuing the journey. He was the senior partner in the enterprise, and there were no doctors on the expedition to certify that it was in fact cholera. Suddenly it was decided to turn back. The Dyaks were dying by hundreds, suffering agonizing cramps, collapsing only a few hours after the disease attacked them. Horror descended on the expedition. Boats drifted past, laden with dead Dyaks whose arms hung limply over the water. When orders were given to make camp on the river bank, it was no better. The Dyaks died like flies. They rolled screaming down the grass slopes into the river, preferring to die by drowning than to suffer the agony of the last stages of cholera. Shallow graves were dug, and the Dyaks were buried hurriedly; and then there occurred that phenomenon which is familiar to all those who have witnessed a cholera epidemic—the dead writhed and twisted in their graves. A few recovered, and some of those who had been lightly buried were able to walk down to the boats and make the journey to Simanggang, where the epidemic assumed more frightful proportions. Of the ten thousand who set out, more than two thousand died, and in Simanggang the bodies were stacked like cordwood and set on fire. For days the town reeked of the smell of burning corpses.

The expedition was a catastrophic failure, and Vyner never quite forgave his father for ordering it after he had been warned. Soon the epidemic spread across the whole of Sarawak, which had already suffered a similar outbreak ten years before. Curiously, none of the sixty or so Europeans living in the State were affected.

In the following year Vyner was made Resident of the Third Division, embracing the large area around the Rejang River. His reports, written in the customary dry and official style, speak of imports and exports, the planting of rice, the state of local finances; and interspersed with these figures on the economics of government are precise statements of raids by head-hunters—one day eighty women and children had their heads cut off in a long-house on the Rejang River, while their men were working in the fields. Once more there was a punitive expedition, an attack on a long-house, poisoned spikes, the destruction of the head-hunters' property. Vyner did his work well, and the Rajah, who once thought him the least worthy of his three sons, now changed his mind completely. An order appeared in the *Sarawak Gazette* for June 4, 1904:

I, RAJAH OF SARAWAK, do hereby inform all those whom it may concern that my son and successor VYNER RAJAH MUDA will henceforth take a portion of my duties, and make Kuching, the Capital, his principal residence, that he will take my place in the courts of law unless any question be submitted to me for any decision, that he will be entitled to use my swallow-tailed flag on shore and on board at the main, and also entitled to have the yellow Umbrella, the emblem of Royalty, when he goes to Court or wherever he may see fit to use it. . . .

There were many reasons, of course, for this change of attitude. The Rajah was growing old; Sarawak was going through troubled times; and there was need of a younger man at the helm. Vyner had shown that he had steady nerves. He had shown, too, that he was perfectly capable of taking the reins of government in his hands. Henceforth, whenever the Rajah was absent from Sarawak, his son became acting Rajah of the state, entitled to all the honours and all the burdens which go with absolute monarchy.

Vyner had been proclaimed Rajah Muda as far back as 1891, when his birthday, September 26, was ordered to be celebrated as a national holiday. In a speech to the Council of State the Rajah said that seven days after his own death Vyner should become Rajah of Sarawak. The seventeen-year-old boy had borne the title of Rajah Muda, but this was a very different thing from being Rajah Muda in fact. Now he was receiving power when affairs were going none too well in Sarawak.

The country was still suffering from the effects of the cholera epidemic; the large area of Lawas on the borders of Trusan had been incorporated into the state, and there was the possibility that the British Foreign Office would raise formidable objections to the seizure of land belonging to the friendly state of Brunei; and there was trouble with the Chinese Secret Societies.

The trouble with the secret societies was perhaps the most ominous. It was the fourth time since the rebellion of 1857 that the Chinese had formed these societies. They were astonishingly powerful, brutal, and widespread. Chinese who refused to pay tribute were murdered. Because the Chinese formed the merchant class in Sarawak, the secret societies formed a kind of super-government over them; and the Government of Sarawak could not tolerate their existence.

It was not easy to root them out. The Orchid Society, centuries old, with its headquarters in San Francisco and Singapore, had passed under the control of Sun Yat-sen. Tribute in the form of money and weapons was being sent continually to this obscure doctor who was relentlessly hammering at the decadent Ch'ing Dynasty. The Rajah's police went to work. They rounded up suspects. They discovered tracts and pamphlets, and had them translated. They were able to discover the signs and passwords of the Orchid Society, which had branches all over Sarawak. They found many banners bearing the devices of the revolutionaries:

We are strong, and spread in all directions;
We command the hills and rivers, despise us who dare!
In Fukien a black flag is flying,
And Kansu is the gathering place!

In the end it was the Orchid Society which overthrew the three-hundred-year-old dynasty of the Ch'ing Emperors and made China a republic.

The Sarawak police were lucky. They were able to arrest the leaders of the local branches of the secret society, and send them out of the country. The conspiracy was scotched. The Government, too, was lucky, for the Foreign Office, not without some reluctance, finally approved the transfer of the district of Lawas to Sarawak. The country was lucky, for at long last it was beginning to enjoy prosperity.

The old order was passing. Vyner was in charge, and the Rajah spent less and less time in the country, his brief appearances which rarely lasted more than three or four months being described as 'annual visits'. There was now hardly anyone left who had known Sir James Brooke. In 1906 there died at the age of about ninety-four the old Datu Bandar, who had fought by the first Rajah's side against the Chinese rebels. Early the next year Angela Burdett-Coutts died at the age of ninety-two and was buried in Westminster Abbey. Only three years before, Sir Henry Keppel, once captain of the *Dido*, later First Sea Lord, had died quietly in bed. He was ninety-five. Most of those who had been connected with Sarawak lived long lives.

There was change in the air. Twenty-five thousand people lived in Kuching, and it was said the population of Sarawak was close on 700,000. Every year trade with the outside world was increasing. And there were notable signs of change in Kuching itself—in 1906 there were street lights for the first time. The lights were always going out because the Swedish producers of the incandescent petroleum gas had not counted on the vagaries of Kuching weather. Still, the people of Kuching could lift their heads high, no longer suffering the taunts of the people of Singapore who had had street-lighting for thirty years.

More wealth came to the country when oil was discovered in Miri in 1909. Charles Hose had suspected its presence in large quantities twenty-five years before, when he was a young district officer in the Baram district, but the first well was not put down until 1910. Soon Miri was being recognized as a potential oilfield of great importance. The Rajah signed a concession with the Anglo-Saxon Oil Company. He had feared the inroads of European businessmen, grumbling about the way they would inevitably exploit the natives, but he began to relent. In that year he permitted two hundred acres of land at the mouth of the Sarawak to be sold to an American company. Here artificial rubber was manufactured. The estate was known as Goebilt. This strange name concealed the identities of two American millionaire families—the Goelets and the Vanderbilts.

Vyner had his roots in this new developing age. Unlike his father, who refused ever to ride in a motor-car (though he had no objection to travelling in trains and steamships), he was among the first to drive a motor-car in England, and he was the very first to drive one in Sarawak. He enjoyed speed, liked tinkering with machines, delighted in plans for modernizing Sarawak with the utmost speed. But all his plans came to nothing when in the early months of 1910 he caught a chill while fishing in the rain, and for some weeks hovered between life and death. He was removed to Singapore and operated on for an abscess of the liver. Another abscess formed, and then another. Finally in May, very weak, he was carried on to a ship and sent back to England for a long convalescence which lasted throughout the rest of the year. He was pale and thin, and had the air of a dying man. In Kuching people whispered that they would never see the Rajah Muda again.

In February, 1911, surprised Government officials, opening the pages of the painfully official *Sarawak Gazette*, with its calendar of saints days, lists of ships' arrivals and departures, and reports from out-stations—all the reports resembled one another, and the only news referred to an occasional rape or murder—were struck by the brief announcement of the engagement of the Rajah Muda to Sylvia Brett, the youngest daughter of Viscount Esher. The engagement was followed almost immediately by the wedding.

The wedding, which took place at St. Peter's Church, Cranborne, Windsor Forest, was inevitably a social event. Both the Rajah and the Ranee Margaret were in England. For once the Rajah permitted himself the luxury of riding to the church in a motor-car, sitting bolt upright, half terrified out of his life. The bride moved in court circles, and her wedding presents came in imperial profusion. King George and Queen Mary sent a blue enamel diamond and pearl brooch bearing the royal cipher. Lord Rothschild sent a diamond watch. The Duchess of Albany sent books, and J. M. Barrie sent a necklace. Some two hundred glittering presents testified to the popularity of Sylvia Brett. Vyner was a little shaken to discover that the only visible marriage gift which he could put beside those of his wife was a clock given him by his father, presumably to remind him of the virtues of punctuality.

Sylvia was small and vicacious, graceful and debonair. She had a pretty wit, which she shared with her sister Dorothy, later to become the intimate friend of D. H. Lawrence. Like Vyner she suffered from a paralysing shyness. Characteristically, Vyner, who had known and admired Sylvia for eight years, had to fight a major battle with himself before he dared ask for her hand in marriage.

Vyner was happy, but the Rajah regarded the marriage with considerable reserve. Bored during the wedding reception, he turned to the first man in sight and barked: 'How do I get out of this damned house?' and was answered kindly enough by the father of the bride, who escorted him to the door. The Rajah was inclined to regard the Eshers as upstarts and rich *parvenus*, without substance. He was afraid Sylvia would lead Vyner into the fast-living café society of the time. He wondered whether Vyner, with his flashy cars and his air of a young man-about-town, would prefer the fleshpots of London to the long ardours of life in Sarawak.

At the time the young couple knew nothing about the hesitations which filled the mind of the Rajah. They went off to Italy for their honeymoon, where Vyner galloped through the museums, leading a protesting Sylvia in his wake. He wandered wherever his feet led him, flippant and carefree. He would go to a railway station and wait until he saw a train that pleased him, and then take it. He carried an ancient and worn guide-book, and it amused him that most of the information was wrong, and that nothing happened as they expected it to happen. Vyner rejoiced in caprice; Sylvia would have preferred a well-planned honeymoon in some quiet resort with no mountain climbing and no helter-skelter adventures in search of adventure, and sometimes she wearied of Vyner's wild good humour. Rome bored her, and only Sorrento hanging perilously over the cliffs against a flaming blue sky entirely delighted her. She was glad to return to England, and to receive a new nursery rhyme composed by George Bernard Shaw in her honour:

> Ride a cock horse
> To Sarawak Cross
> To see a young Ranee consumed with remorse,
> She'll have bells on her fingers
> And rings through her nose
> And won't be permittted to wear any clo'es.

The marriage had begun well, and the lovers were left to their own resources, while the Rajah paid his annual summer visit to Sarawak, returning to England as usual for the hunting season in the autumn. King George had approved the granting of the title 'His Highness' to the Rajah Muda with precedence over the heirs of Indian Princes. It was arranged that the Rajah Muda would bring his bride to Sarawak in the spring of the following year.

Before this could happen, the old Rajah suffered an accident which profoundly altered his character. His horse stumbled into a blind ditch, and he was thrown. His eye was pierced by a branch.

There was an operation, which he bore courageously, and thereafter he wore a glass eye. Hard and relentless before, he grew harder and more relentless; and for the first time a note of bitterness can be detected in his letters.

In the hospital he had time to think about the succession at great length. Brooding, he came to the conclusion that Vyner could not be expected to rule Sarawak alone, but needed to be buttressed by the authority of his brother Bertram and by an advisory committee, perhaps operating from London. It was an unworkable solution to a pressing problem, but he held to it with grim determination. He was becoming increasingly unhappy with the Eshers, suspecting them of exerting undue influence over his son. 'Vyner has more or less married into unsafe surroundings,' he wrote: To safeguard Vyner, he outlined to Charles Willes Johnson, his nephew and also his legal adviser, a plan of succession by which Vyner and Bertram would rule together. He wrote in April, 1912:

> I am contemplating a move which I feel will much strengthen my successor's position in case of his being surrounded by those who would wish to grab Sarawak when I am no more—would turn it into a money bargain—and the British Government would be the first to encourage this movement, as they naturally would like the country added to theirs to assist to pay for their shortcomings in Singapore and its surroundings. As a safeguard against this I wish to bring Adeh [Bertram] to the fore and install him with honours in the position of heir presumptive in case of Vyner's death or his bearing no male issue . . .

The implications were clear—Bertram was to possess royal power, receiving the customary twenty-one-gun salute and possessing powers almost as great as those possessed by the Rajah Muda. Once again there was to be repeated the long-drawn-out 'quarrel of the succession' which plagued the last years of Sir James Brooke.

When the Rajah wrote this letter to his nephew, Vyner had already sailed for Sarawak with his bride, to take up his duties. He knew nothing of the circumstances of the letter. He arrived at Kuching in a blaze of excitement. Flags waved. Small boys swam beside the ship bringing him to the *astana*. There were speeches and parades, with guards of honour under the hot sun, and the Chinese towkays gave a reception such as they had never given before. All Kuching was caught up in the excitement of welcoming the heir to the throne and the young bride who smiled at his side.

Eighteen days later the Rajah himself arrived, and almost immediately he made known his intention to grant royal honours to Bertram. When Vyner insisted that the arrangement was unworkable, and that there could not be two rulers of the country in the Rajah's absence, the Rajah simply pointed out that he had authority to do as he pleased. He drew up a proclamation which read:

I, Charles Brooke, Rajah of Sarawak, do hereby decree that my second son Bertram Brooke, heir presumptive to the Raj of Sarawak in the event of my eldest son, Charles Vyner Brooke, Rajah Muda of Sarawak, failing to have male issue, shall be received on his arrival in the State of Sarawak with a Royal Salute and honours equivalent to his rank.

I further decree that he shall be recognized in future by all the inhabitants of Sarawak as being a part of the Government of the State and that such recognition shall be duly registered in the records of the Supreme Council of Sarawak.

C. BROOKE,
Rajah.

The proclamation duly appeared in the *Sarawak Gazette*, sandwiched between a note on the observance of the Rajah's birthday and the announcement of the prize-giving in the Malay schools.

Vyner, knowing that Bertram was expected to arrive towards the end of June, decided to act quickly. He adored his brother, who was solid, handsome, and efficient, but he remembered that Bertram's last visit to Sarawak had occurred in 1895, seventeen years before. At that time Bertram was only nineteen. He had never been sent to an out-station, and knew almost nothing about conditions in Sarawak. Vyner could only conclude that there was a dark plot to reduce his authority, and wrote a hurried letter to his father announcing that he was not prepared to tolerate a situation in which his powers would be curtailed by someone who hardly knew the land. He was particularly perturbed by the words of the proclamation declaring that Bertram would be recognized as being 'a part of the Government of the State'. The Rajah replied, pointing out that the words meant only that Bertram was an officer in the Government recognized and appointed by the Rajah. He accused Vyner of being jealous of his brother. Vyner denied the charge. Hot words were spoken. The Rajah went on to accuse Vyner of disloyalty and disobedience, and suggested that he leave the country. Outraged, Vyner took the first available boat to Singapore.

The storm was over; and in the long silence following the storm the Rajah had time to secure his defences. He told himself that Vyner had behaved abominably, but the Eshers had behaved more abominably still—they were evidently trying to take over the country. He had never given Vyner independent power. As Rajah, he was entitled to do exactly as he pleased, and why should Vyner refuse to receive his brother with a royal salute? In this absurd situation all that remained was to provide 'a course of safety' independent of Vyner's tantrums. In his most magisterial manner he wrote: 'My wish is now that Vyner has separated from me.' Charles, though casual to grammar, meant what he said.

Bertram had no desire to usurp the position of his brother and he was a little puzzled by the turn of events. On his arrival he was greeted with the royal salute and walked under the yellow umbrella, the emblem of royalty. Every evening he was invited to the *astana*, where the Rajah plied him with questions and discussed every subject under the sun. Still more significantly, when the Rajah decided to pay a diplomatic visit to his neighbour, the Sultan of Brunei, Bertram and his wife accompanied him. Bertram, with the title of Tuan Muda, received the honours due to the heir presumptive to the throne.

One day, shortly after the arrival of Bertram, the Rajah went for a long walk in the woods at the foot of Mount Matang. When he returned, he wrote off an angry note to his nephew, Charles Willes Johnson, defending a situation which seemed already to have passed beyond his control. He had decided to return home. He would leave the country in charge of a Resident, while ruling it from a distance. It is the letter of a man who is tired and a little frightened, but still, at the age of eighty-two, in amazing fettle, full of pride in his achievements and determined not to slacken the reins of power.

> Vallombrosa—Matang
> August 25, 1912
>
> My dear Charley,
>   Vyner now tries to make himself equal to me. He can show nothing to prove that I ever made him an equal, but there it is, he is as the Ranee says a fly in a spider's web. Everything in the country from one end to another is in a very flourishing state. Revenue, trade, planting, etc. etc. all equally prosperous. Where is the C.O. [Colonial Office] going to find a *casus belli* to touch me or the present rule in Sarawak? The Eshers and Bretts may have other views and wish to put Vyner above me, but I am not afraid of their evil influence. They will cut against a file . . .
>   I am pretty strong and have just come in from a six mile walk over the lovely mountain where I have a bungalow built 44 years ago. I am bringing home a lot of birds. I have 152 of different kinds, if half reach England I shall be happy . . .
>   Vyner and party left for England before Adeh and Gladys arrived—there have been a good many unpleasant half hours.
>
>> While stands the Coliseum, Rome will stand,
>> When falls the Coliseum——
>
> Your afft. Uncle,
> C. BROOKE

So the summer passed, and soon the Rajah was making preparations for returning to England, to hunt with the hounds. He was still distressed by Vyner's behaviour. 'I look on Vyner as in the hands of his wife's party and not to be relied upon,' he wrote to his nephew in October from the Hyde Park Hotel. To his lawyer he spoke warningly of 'the evil of an absentee, weak and extravagant des-

Rajah Sir Vyner Brooke

The Rajah and Ranee of Sarawak : Sir Vyner and Lady Brooke in England

potism', but he told the same lawyer that he resolved to make no change in the succession. He was beginning to relent. Vyner, too, was beginning to relent. Somehow—no one quite knew how—it might be possible to strike a balance between the claims of common sense and the demands of an old man haunted by the thought that no one could rule as wisely as he had done.

One day he relented sufficiently to accompany Vyner in a shopping expedition in London. They paused outside a taxidermist's shop, where the eyes of tigers, leopards, and bears were on exhibition. Vyner suggested amiably that his father might like to wear a tiger's eye. 'I will, too,' the old Rajah said, and they walked into the shop and bought several dozen eyes of several dozen beasts, and the old Rajah wore whatever struck his fancy. When he returned to Sarawak, it would sometimes happen that a glass eye fell in the mud when the war prahus were being beached. Then the Malays and Dyaks, in sudden frenzy, would search for the lost eye until they found it, all the while quivering with fear at the loss of so sacred an object. To the end of his life Charles used his glass eye to the best advantage.

Meanwhile he was still fighting 'the war of the succession'.

What was happening was in fact very simple and very understandable. The Rajah had been an autocrat of autocrats; he had ruled Sarawak almost single-handed for fifty years; he was beyond the reach of English laws; through him Sarawak had vastly increased its territory; he was a law to himself. He was more than a man. He was a legend, and legends are irreplaceable. Since he could not hope to see Sarawak ruled by another man of legendary accomplishments, he saw only one solution—those who had known and served Sarawak best should form a kind of Cabinet advising Vyner and Bertram, who would rule jointly, in a delicate balance of power.

Through the remaining months of the year the Rajah endlessly debated the situation with his advisers. The Sarawak State Trust Committee, with power to receive and check and supervise the revenue reports from the Treasury, was brought into existence by proclamation. The Rajah was not altogether happy with the final product of these interminable discussions, and called it 'rather a long-winded rigmarole'. Still, he had designed an instrument of government which gave him some assurance for the future. In December he spoke of abdicating. In the following February he was saying: 'I doubt if I am justified in giving up the reins, knowing as I do that so many desirable things, if I do, will fail. I think I must bide my time, and go on as I am now.' And in March, when he heard of troubles in the interior, he wrote characteristically with his old fire: 'This I shall have to put in order by fair means or foul.'

In his impetuous way the Rajah returned to Sarawak, determined

L

while there was still breath in him to see that his law was obeyed. He saw that the rebellion was quashed, instituted a Chinese Court to deal with the affairs of the Chinese, and returned to England, where he made his peace with Vyner—an uneasy peace, for neither had in any way retreated from his original position. The next spring Vyner went out to Sarawak and ruled alone, as he had so often ruled before. He was still in Sarawak when the First World War broke out.

The Rajah knew his place. With the war spreading all over the world, with German colonies in the neighbourhood of Sarawak, and with the economy of Sarawak inevitably dependent on the fortunes of the war, he took the first available boat to the East. It was inevitable that he should take charge in time of war. It was perhaps just as inevitable that Vyner should return to England, hoping to join up as a private.

There was no longer the Rajah Muda; there was only the tall forty-year-old private, who had spent a third of his life as a reigning prince. He passed his medical tests, and was looking forward to army life when orders came from the Colonial Office forbidding his enlistment. He joined an Anti-Aircraft regiment. He worked as a labourer in Shoreditch, shaping aeroplane parts. No one was aware that the obscure workman in overalls, standing all day at the lathe, known simply as C. V. Brooke, might at any moment find himself under orders to sail from England and rule over an Eastern principality. In 1916 the Rajah summoned him, and with his wife he took the long slow journey to Sarawak.

The war had so far produced very little effect on the country. New oilwells had been sunk; there was increased production of rubber; there were rebellions among the Balleh Dyaks; a mutiny had been quelled in Singapore, and its reverberations were felt all over the neighbouring islands. The Japanese were allied to the British, and only the occasional German raiders were to be feared.

The Rajah no longer believed that Vyner was the pawn of the Eshers and Bretts. All quarrels were forgotten. To signify his approval of the Rajah Muda he issued an extraordinary proclamation placing the control of the Rejang area entirely under him:

> This thirtieth day of September, 1916, I wish marked as an important epoch in the history of Sarawak, for I have today handed over the control of the Dyaks of the Ulu Ai or interior of Rejang and Simanggang districts together with all correspondence concerning these districts to my son and successor the Rajah Muda.

It was almost his last official act. In a few days he took to his bed, and by December he was a dying man. In the late spring of the following year he was dead.

On May 24, 1917, seven days after his father's death, Vyner was rowed across the Sarawak River in the State barge to be proclaimed Rajah.

It was one of those cloudless days when the sun beats unrelentingly from a brazen sky, the hottest day he had ever known. He wore a green and gold uniform, and he felt, as he always did on State occasions, abysmally nervous. On the steps of the Government Office the Malays, Dyaks, and Chinese were waiting to greet him. He had been reading Government reports, and it occurred to him that not all the auguries were favourable—the pepper crop had been a failure, and the export of sago had stopped altogether. And since Sarawak depended on its exports for its very existence, he could only hope that the war would end soon and put an end to the poverty which was slowly descending on the people.

The nervousness vanished as soon as he began speaking. Speaking in Malay in a surprisingly loud and clear voice, he said:

> I make known to you Datus, Pengirans, Abangs, Inchis, Chiefs and all classes of people in Sarawak that I will on no account interfere with the Mohammedan faith or with any other religions or faiths of the people.
>
> As the white *labu* and the *kundor* fruit show white when they are split, so too is my heart unblemished towards you.
>
> My people, rich and poor, never be afraid if you are in trouble and have anything to complain of. I wish you all to tell me so that I can help you: therefore never be afraid to come to me.

So he went on, while the sun was reflected from the stone steps and the crowds hung on his words, using sometimes the great, heavily weighted words like 'straightforwardness, truth, and justice' and 'to maintain and strengthen the government of the country', but in fact all the important things had been said in the opening sentences. The armoured hand of Charles had gone; a lighter hand now ruled the country. One could not imagine Charles saying, 'As the white *labu* and the *kundor* fruit show white when they are split. . . .'

For twenty-four years men were to hear the characteristic voice of the third Rajah of Sarawak. After him there were to be no others.

XI

THE END OF AN ERA

On another hot day a year later Vyner took the oath of accession. Once again he was ferried across the river in the State barge, once again there were garlands and waving flags, bands blaring and people cheering, and once again he found himself wondering what all the fuss was about and why the ancient rites of initiation into kingship were attended with so many ceremonies. He did not enjoy ceremony. He did not enjoy putting on his green uniform with its heavy gold brocade—the uniform had been put aside and forgotten, and part of the morning was spent in repairing the damage caused by moths. He could talk with a crowd of five hundred naked Dyaks and be happy, but a solemn investiture was something else altogether. He was shy and miserable as he walked under the yellow umbrella and took his place in the courthouse, his wife by his side and his brother Bertram following a little behind, bearing the sword of state on a yellow, tasselled cushion.

The Dyaks had come from hundreds of miles away to witness the ceremony. Immense spreading hornbill feathers rose out of their tangled hair; their ears were pierced with tiger-cats' teeth; bead necklaces hung at their throats; their sword hilts were tufted with goats' hair dyed crimson. With blue tattoo marks all over their bodies, they provided the proper barbaric background to the scene.

So during that long morning, while he listed to the official speeches and prayers, and saw the Sword of State displayed to the people, and heard the sudden tumult as the Dyaks raised their spears and uttered their terrible war-cry, he found himself at the disadvantage of being in a curious way remote from the scene. As he promised to obey his father's will and to uphold the constitution, and looked at the venerable old Malays who tottered about the platform, men who had served his father and were almost as old as his father would have been, he seemed to be living on some remote island where the ancient customs were still practised. It was July 22, 1918, and in Europe the war was still being fought.

Then it was all over and he was marching out into the sunlight. There was a twenty-one-gun salute from the fort, the smoke from the guns lying on the river. In front of him there lay years of heavy responsibility, continual visits to out-stations, and problems that would be insoluble or would depend for their solution on the vagaries of international trade.

A year before, on the day when he was proclaimed Rajah, he had wondered about the extent and legality of Sarawak's claims in the north. Charles had vastly increased the territory of Sarawak, but he had never troubled to show the title deeds to his eldest son. Vyner wrote to Charles Willes Johnson: 'I have the very haziest idea about our possessions in the north of Sarawak. Never have been informed what they are. I should like to know if the original documents are in safe-keeping.' The original documents were in fact in safe-keeping; but there were other problems, most of them caused by Charles's inveterate habit of doing things in his own way without consulting anyone.

The value of land was rising. Charles had made it a practice to grant land to the Chinese near Kuching for a few dollars an acre. It began to look as though Kuching was being surrounded by a solid ring of Chinese property owners. Was this the best thing for the State? Then trade: pepper was falling, and the rice crop unsatisfactory—it was to become a failure in the following year—and there was no rise in sago, and few ships were coming to port. The best news was the slow growth of the inexhaustible Miri oil-fields.

In those early years Vyner went about his work cautiously. It was one thing to know the country as acting Rajah; it was an entirely different thing to be the sole fountain of power. So he went about the State, visiting all the important centres, listening carefully. The second Rajah had slept with a pistol under his pillow and a sword by his side; Vyner went about unarmed.

Occasionally there were moments of barbaric splendour, as when tribes which had been at war with one another were compelled to make peace. At these ceremonies the tribal chieftains changed into supplicants before his throne. Pigs and hens were ceremonially killed, their blood sprinkled on meal, and the meal was solemnly eaten by the chieftains. They pledged each other in bowls of *tuak*, exchanged holy jars, and received gifts from the Rajah in token of peace. At such times the Rajah would make a speech to them, not unlike the speeches which fall from the lips of Red Indian chieftains in the pages of Fenimore Cooper:

> The oaths that you will utter I confirm with my word, and should any-one reopen the feud, he shall become my sworn enemy, and I shall demand the life of anyone who takes the life of another. Henceforth there is no more feud: as witness the blood of these pigs and the exchange of these jars.

Therefore I present you with a spear, *kuna* and *pua*, to hand on from

generation to generation as a seal from myself that the spirit of strife
between these tribes has now been laid to rest.

Remember my words, all you chiefs.

I have spoken.

But though the peace-making ceremonies were to occur at intervals throughout Vyner's reign, the Dyaks themselves were being
drawn slowly into the era of modern industrialism, and the old barbaric ceremonies were gradually losing their importance. Head-
hunting, except for occasional forays, was coming to an end. The
very few officers who administered the State, rarely more than
twenty, possessed strange new weapons for putting down crime.
Radio communication had been established between Sibu, Miri, and
Kuching in 1918. Soon flying-boats would come. People spoke of a
time when there would be electricity in the remote Dyak villages.

Life in Sarawak during the twenties went on at 'an increasing
tempo, but except in the oilfields it was not vastly different from the
tempo in the time of Charles. It had been a leisurely country, and
so it remained, while the Dyaks cultivated their rice fields and tapped
their rubber trees, moving fast only when they shot over the rapids of
their innumerable rivers.

The early years after the war were boom years, with oil and rubber
standing high in the world's markets. In 1921 there was produced at
Miri 170,000 tons of oil; in the next year the figure shot up to
400,000 tons. So it went on, Sarawak quietly prosperous and the
natives reasonably content. Vyner's task, as he saw it, was not to
interfere too much in the traditional customs. He spoke of building
new roads, and a few short lengths of road were built: the Malays
and Dyaks continued to use the rivers and paid very little attention
to the official road-building campaign.

Occasionally there were brief flurries of excitement. Somerset
Maugham, looking even then like an elderly crocodile, arrived for a
brief visit and wrote some satirical stories about the white men in the
out-stations; and since there were only a few white men in the country, who believed they were faithful to their wives, they were a little
alarmed by his stories. There were regattas and horse races. Books
arrived, and their titles were solemnly listed in the *Sarawak Gazette*,
which had not notably changed its format or its contents since it was
founded in 1870.

Life could have been boring, but was not. White men in the
tropics do not drink themselves to death with *stengahs*; they very
rarely keep native mistresses; they are usually too busy to indulge in
complicated pleasures. With Malays, Dyaks, Chinese, and Indians
all around them, and with a growing country to serve, they were
kept occupied. Only one went mad, but he had a streak of madness
in him long before he came to Sarawak.

Something should be said about this extraordinary man, because he played a strange rôle in the history of Sarawak. His name was Gerard MacBryan, and he was the son of a doctor who kept a mental hospital in Box, near Bath. Tall, graceful, with unusually bright eyes and an ivory-white skin, he was one of those men who have only to enter a crowded room to make everyone instantly aware of his presence. He was eighteen when he entered the Sarawak Government Service in 1920 after a brief career in the Navy. He did well as a cadet, and was gazetted for duty in Sibu. Later he became Vyner's private secretary and married a Malay girl.

Gerard MacBryan was a man of vast enthusiasms. He talked of a great Moslem Empire stretching from Morocco to the Philippines, and spoke of how it could be brought into being in his own lifetime. He seems to have believed that he could be the agent which would bring about this new empire, and when Vyner grew weary of him and dismissed him, he became a Moslem and made the *hajj* to Mecca with his Malay bride. The story of that hazardous journey has been told by Owen Rutter in a book called *Triumphant Pilgrimage*. Rutter seems to have disliked him, and describes him as 'lean and rather shabby with a nose I always associate with King's Counsel'. Rutter met him at a bad time, when he was on the eve of one of his periodic attacks of paranoia.

They said of Gerard MacBryan that he had more concentrated charm than all the other district officers combined, that he was a master of intrigue, and that if he wanted anything badly enough, he usually got it. Failing to bring about a Moslem Empire, he returned to Sarawak. He was sane, brilliant, completely in command of himself. He arrived in the spring of 1927 and was put in charge of the *Sarawak Gazette*, which remained as portentously dull as before under his editorship. He became Vyner's secretary again. He lived in a little lodge just behind the *astana*. At intervals Vyner recognized the symptoms of a breakdown, and then he would be quietly dismissed. When he recovered, he was made secretary again.

When MacBryan went mad, he went completely off his head. Once in South Africa he appeared naked at a party, and afterwards explained that he thought he was invisible. Sometimes he thought he was a dog, and came crawling across a room, barking at the top of his voice. Thinking that he was God, and that therefore everything belonged to him, he stole from shops and alms-boxes, and his friends were reduced to quivering trepidation, wondering how to prevent him from being arrested. He knew the lunacy laws backwards and forwards. He would disappear for long periods in asylums, to emerge calmly with an appearance of great sanity.

He was a brilliant linguist, an expert jeweller, a scholar in the customary laws of the Malays. He was popular with the Malays and

Dyaks, and usually hated by the Government officers. At one time he seems to have thought of marrying into the Rajah's family and becoming the next Rajah of Sarawak. At another time he appeared at the coronation of the Sultan of Brunei and disputed with the Sultan's attendants about the validity of the coronation ceremony. He claimed to be the possessor of 'the golden hand', a kind of golden sleeve worn by the Sultan only during his coronation, and since it was not used during the ceremony, the coronation had not in fact taken place. Vyner was always dismissing him and taking him back again; and his services were used during the complicated discussions on cession which came at the end of Vyner's reign. He died in Hong Kong in 1952. He was living like a Chinese in a cheap Chinese hotel, and it is possible that he was murdered.

Adventurers like MacBryan were the exception. The officers who made up the Sarawak Civil Service were usually men who were pre-pared to live hard lonely lives in out-stations. They were hand-picked by Government officers in London, and as many as possible were chosen from distinguished families. In Charles's time officers sometimes elected to serve without pay, but those days were over. They were given extensive holidays in England and they could look forward to substantial pensions after only twenty years' service. At least one former officer of the Sarawak service enjoyed a pension for forty years.

The depression at the end of the twenties hit Sarawak hard. Happily, the exports of the country were sufficiently diversified to enable the country to survive. In 1929 exports amounted in Straits Settlements dollars to $63,000,000, and by 1932 they had dropped to $13,500,000. Just in time Sarawak pepper became established under its own name in the world markets, and while 19,000 piculs of pepper were sold in 1929, 71,000 piculs were sold in 1932. Gold exports also increased from $35,000 in 1929 to $400,000 in 1932. In Sarawak these dull figures were coloured with romance.

Sarawak weathered the depression and enjoyed the benefits of the minor boom in rubber in 1934. It lay outside the tin belt, which stretches across Malaya, but its very considerable wealth did not depend, as the wealth of Malaya depends, on two primary sources, rubber and tin. Sarawak has oil, pepper, rubber, gold, coffee, tea, tapioca, and timber. Once it was thought to be potentially one of the world's great producers of quicksilver, but the supply of scarlet rocks which exude quicksilver under heat soon petered out. Oil produced the greatest wealth of Sarawak, and still does.

As Vyner saw it, his task was to govern the country without ap-pearing to do so. There were the occasional moments of great pano-ply when he was attired in the green and gold uniform, wearing a cocked hat, receiving the ceremonial swords from the Malay nobles.

But those moments were rare. He liked to saunter through the bazaars, wearing a white drill suit, his shirt open at the neck, his sun helmet resting on the back of his head, talking to Chinese coolies and Malay fishermen and anyone else who had anything to say. He made it abundantly clear that anyone who wanted to talk to him need stand on no ceremony. He followed his father by taking court cases in Kuching until a Chief Justice came from England, and like his father and like Sir James Brooke he had a casual approach towards head-hunters and murderers. At one time nine convicted murderers were working as gardeners in the grounds of the *astana*. In Sarawak death sentences were followed by summary execution by firing squad. Vyner had a habit of quashing death sentences and imposing hard labour instead.

After ruling Sarawak for eight or nine months, he usually took a holiday in England. His brother Bertram would be summoned to act as Rajah in the interval. Bertram was the work-horse who would shoulder any task given to him by the Rajah. He was quiet, scholarly, diffident, deliberately unspectacular. He had been a famous oarsman at Cambridge. During the First World War he was an artillery officer, and his greatest love was for the Army. His title was that of Tuan Muda, a Malay term corresponding to Royal Prince, while the title of Rajah Muda was given to the heir to the throne.

The Tuan Muda's task was to hold the fort in the absence of the Rajah, and since all his life had been spent under the shadow of his father and his father's successor, he developed the habits of service until they became almost indistinguishable from a kind of slavery. Without Vyner's spurts of brilliance, and without his talent for talking casually with everyone he met and in this way feeling the pulse of the people, Bertram possessed a love for Sarawak greater than that of any man of his time.

In many ways Bertram resembled his mother; Vyner resembled no one who had ever existed in his immediate family. As he grew older and more assured of his power, he lost his diffidence. He liked telling stories. He liked dice games, and he liked drinking with a few chosen companions. If he remained to the end a little frightened by the three daughters born to him by his marriage to Sylvia Brett, this was understandable. They were all strikingly and dangerously beautiful, and possessed more than a normal share of Brooke charm. They were charged with electricity, and knew it, and they could usually twist their father around their painted fingernails. Leonora, the eldest and quietest, married the Earl of Inchcape. The romantic escapades of the younger daughters, Elizabeth and Valerie, filled the headlines, sometimes to the undisguised horror of their father and their grandmother, the Dowager Ranee of Sarawak.

There was nothing prudish about the Dowager Ranee Margaret. It was simply that she belonged to an earlier age and was baffled by the age which brought in the Charleston, the radio, and the aeroplane. In her own way she could be relentlessly daring. It was in her house near Genoa that the wife and two sons of Oscar Wilde were sheltered after the trial which sent Wilde to prison. She had an instinct for knowing genuine artists, and cultivating them. A list of her friends is a roll-call of the talents. She knew Elgar, Henry James, W. H. Hudson, Bernard Shaw, H. G. Wells, C. W. Nevinson, Ernst Toller, and a host of others. She could remember Elgar lighting a bonfire and sitting on a camp stool to watch the flames rising until at last they were burned out, and then he strode deliberately into the music room and 'wiggle-waggled his pen over music paper'. She spent long hours at her house in Ascot while Henry James unburdened himself of his troubles. When they met they were inseparable, and when they parted, they were always sighing for the next meeting. Of the hundred letters from Henry James now in the possession of her granddaughter, Lady Jean Halsey, only one will be quoted here:

> Lamb House, Rye, Sussex.
> August 16, 1902
>
> Dearest and best Ranee,
>
> I saw this a.m. in the *Times* an account of how Vyner had escaped with his life from a cholera-stricken expedition of the most gallant kind in Borneo, and it made me think of you afresh and more remorsefully as the mother of princes and soldiers.
>
> Of course you don't sleep on both ears, but of course also you are gallant enough for anything. And then there was your brother starving somewhere in a coat or shipwrecked on a desert isle! [1] but you are used, I take it, to *him*, and that is his metier and his glory. I hope with all my heart that for the rest you are not in a period of alarm.
>
> I am unimpeachably here and I am very little anywhere else. The conditions of my existence here are inducing premature old age, but that is their only fault. It would take 10 years off my shoulders to see you. In which assurance, believe me, dearest old friend, yours always and ever,
>
> HENRY JAMES

Margaret wore her years well. She was one of those small women who give an impression of great height and she could sail into a room like a ship with all her sails flying, and when Melba and the Dowager Ranee of Sarawak entered a room together it was a little overpowering: a whole fleet of sailing ships seemed to have entered. She was still playing the piano when she was over eighty. She embroidered, and exchanged embroideries with Queen Mary. She

---

[1] Henry James is referring to Harry de Windt, the explorer, who usually appeared in photographs wearing an enormously heavy fur coat, in which he appeared to be drowning.

spent hours making enamelled ornaments and jewellery. She read everything written by her friends, and continually encouraged them when they were dispirited.

She believed that *Lord Jim* was the best book ever written about the islands of the East Indies, and when she sent Conrad her own book of memoirs with a letter praising his work to the skies, he answered with a letter of such touching humility and veneration that it seems to scorch the page:

Oswalds, Bishopsbourne, Kent.
June 15, 1920

MADAM,

I am immensely gratified and touched by the letter you have been good enough to write to me. The first Rajah Brooke has been one of my boyish admirations, a feeling I have kept to this day strengthened by the better understanding of the greatness of his character and the unstained rectitude of his purpose. The book which has found favour in your eyes has been inspired in great measure by the history of the first Rajah's enterprise and even by the lecture of his journals as partly reproduced by Captain Mundy and others. Even the very name of the messenger whom you so sympathetically appreciate was taken from that source. Jaffar, if you remember, was the name of the follower and favourite servant of Pengeran Budrudin, who brought to the Rajah his master's ring and his last words after that prince with Muda Hassim and others had been treacherously attacked and murdered in Bruni.

Your Highness is not mistaken as to my feelings towards the people of the islands she knows so well and has presented so intimately in the volume of her life in Sarawak. It was never my good fortune to see Kuching; and indeed my time in the Archipelago was short, though it left most vivid impressions and some highly valued memories.

For all my admiration and mental familiarity with the Great Rajah the only concrete object I ever saw connected with him was the old steamer 'Royalist', which was still in 1887 running between Kuching and Singapore. She was a venerable old relic of the past and the legend, I don't know how true, amongst all the officers in the Port of Singapore was that she had been presented to Rajah Brooke by some great lady in London.

I beg to subscribe myself Your Highness's
most faithful and obedient servant,
JOSEPH CONRAD

Conrad was ill when he wrote the letter, and part of the letter was dictated to a secretary and typewritten. When he went over the letter, he changed the small 'g' of 'great Rajah' into a capital in his own hand. Throughout, he gives the impression of a man blinded by the light beating down from the throne, while quietly and firmly repaying in her name the debt he owed to Sir James Brooke.

To the end Margaret collected authors and artists with impeccable taste. She died quietly, at the age of eighty-seven, on December 1,

1936, as enviable in her dying as she was in her life. This 'mother of princes and soldiers' always believed that her descendants would continue to rule over Sarawak. Ten years after her death the rule of the white Rajahs of Sarawak came to an end.

When the Second World War came, no one in Sarawak had any illusions that the country would remain unaffected. The Japanese were no longer allies of the British, but of the Germans. As soon as the Japanese decided upon the conquest of the Archipelago, Sarawak would be in the direct line of fire.

All through 1941 the Japanese were strengthening their position on the mainland of south-east Asia. American reinforcements poured into the Philippines; Australians were preparing positions in North Malaya; the Dutch were preparing to defend Java. All through the summer and autumn a Japanese attack on the islands was expected. Vyner noted with some bitterness that the British Government had no intention of defending Sarawak. It could hardly have been otherwise. There were no troops to spare, and every logistical and military consideration pointed to the paramount importance of defending Malaya and the huge naval base at Singapore.

There was nothing to be done except to hope that somehow there would be no Japanese attack at all. There were periodic air-raid drills at Kuching, and plans were made to blow up the oilwells at Miri. Beyond that, there was little that could be done.

Meanwhile, in an atmosphere of extraordinary tension, with the shadow of Japan falling over the country, it was decided to proceed with the celebration of the centenary of the proclamation of Sir James Brooke as Rajah of Sarawak on September 24, 1841. For Vyner the date had a very particular significance. He had decided long ago that the time of autocratic rule was coming to an end. He had ruled for twenty-four years. He was nearly seventy, and could not expect to hold his office much longer. The centenary celebration provided him with a long-sought-for opportunity. On September 24, 1941, exactly a hundred years after Sir James Brooke came to power as an autocrat answerable to no one, he would proclaim a new constitution, giving power—a much larger share of power than they had ever enjoyed before—to the people. Instead of an autocrat, there would be a constitutional monarch.

The constitution is not a completely successful document. It was written hurriedly, too many hands were involved in it, and it attempted too much. It proclaims that Sarawak is the heritage of the people of Sarawak, held by the Rajah in trust for them, and the sole legislative authority is vested in the State Council, composed of fourteen members of the Sarawak Civil Service and eleven representatives of the races inhabiting Sarawak. There was no question of giving votes to the primitive Dyaks, but for the first time Dyaks, Malays, and Chinese were represented in considerable numbers.

Orders of the State Council were binding on the Rajah, who could no longer disburse money without the Council's approval. In the preamble to the constitution the Rajah announced that he intended to commemorate the centenary 'by terminating for ever the era of autocratic rule which has so far characterized our government'. In effect, much of the Rajah's power was being inherited by the European members of the Council. But though the document possessed some obvious flaws, it did constitute a clean break with the past. The Rajah could no longer initiate laws, though like the American President he could veto them. He could no longer collect taxes or hold trials or make appropriations from the State Treasury. He had become, like all constitutional monarchs, the prisoner of his ministers.

With the new constitution went a new attitude towards the Government of Sarawak. Was there, after all, any great need for continuing the monarchy? Speaking late in March, he hinted at the possibility that in a few years the monarchy would have outlived its usefulness. He said:

> I have always been positive, as was my father, that it was never the intention of Sir James Brooke to establish a line of Absolute Rulers. What he set out to do was to protect the natives of Sarawak, the real but backward owners of this land, from exploitation and oppression, until such time as they could govern themselves.

More and more, as the months passed and the Pacific War drew nearer, he found himself thinking of the time when, in the interests of the natives, it might be necessary to step down. A distinguished Governor of British North Borneo, the last of the chartered companies, had once written him a cheerful letter, describing himself as an anomaly writing to an anachronism. Vyner was half-inclined to agree that autocratic rule was an anachronism.

The new constitution in Sarawak was celebrated with a fanfare. There were speeches, galas, horse races, triumphal archways. The Dyaks, Malays, and Chinese paraded in ceremonial costumes. At night Kuching was a blaze of lights, and by day the river was crowded with every kind of boat, all of them beflagged and garlanded. The Japanese were only three months away.

During the first days of the Pacific War the Japanese were too busy to send any great force against Sarawak. On December 23 a Japanese squadron was sighted off Miri, proceeding down the coast towards Kuching, which was reached the next day. Japanese troops, dressed for jungle warfare, landed from armour-plated barges. The

Europeans were rounded up and thrown into internment camps. Kuching celebrated the worst Christmas it had ever known.

Many stories of heroism were told of those early days of the Pacific War. The General Manager of the Sarawak Oilfields refused to escape in the ship which had come to evacuate Europeans because the Asiatic members of his staff were not allowed on board. At the moment when the war broke out, the Rajah was in Australia. C. D. Le Gros Clark, the Chief Secretary, elected to stay, though he could easily have escaped. In January, 1942, he wrote in the internment camp:

> For long I have been appalled at the calamity gradually approaching this innocent people of Sarawak. By the inexorable march of circumstances, forced on a people who had little or no say in their development, war has come to Sarawak with all its sufferings and hideous results.
>
> With these people of Sarawak, among whom I have spent many years of my life, I have determined to remain and to share with them their sufferings during this period of trial.
>
> I do not regret this decision. I am proud to share with my companions in captivity this honour of hardship during a war which affects the lives of millions throughout the world.
>
> I could not have it otherwise.

Le Gros Clark was murdered by the Japanese during the last months of the war.

The Japanese plundered Sarawak at their leisure. The oilwells had been destroyed; and their anger at losing the oilwells spilled over in causeless brutality in the camps. During the whole course of the occupation almost no news of Sarawak came to the outside world. Silence settled down on the land of rivers and forests.

Early in 1942 a forester stationed on the Rejang River was making plans to escape into Dutch territory when he heard that some women and children from Kapit were also hoping to escape in the same way. He left his forest and came to Kapit, and began the desperate task of shepherding a crowd of fifty women and children in river boats up to the Dutch frontier, over treacherous rapids, and across the high mountains of Central Borneo. By a miracle the refugees reached the Dutch military post of Long Nawang. The forester returned to Kapit, having promised the Dyaks he would stay among them to organize whatever resistance was possible and to help them grow rice. He felt that the whole expedition had been dangerous and futile, and he would have refused to lead them out of Sarawak if he had not received direct orders from a Resident, who had escaped in the same party.

Within days the Japanese learned that the refugees were in Long Nawang. They sent a small raiding party, captured the fort, lined up the women, and told the children to climb into the trees. They machine-gunned the women and amused themselves by picking off the children one by one. Altogether fifty women and children were killed in a few minutes. Of all those who had taken part in the expedition only two Europeans escaped.

The story of the children falling from the trees somehow symbolized the defencelessness of Sarawak. It haunts the imaginations of the white people in Sarawak, who can rarely bring themselves to talk about it.

Just before the capture of Singapore Vyner flew from Australia to Batavia, hoping there was some way he would be able to organize resistance in Sarawak against the Japanese. He asked to be flown into Borneo, but the Dutch were already preparing to abandon the large area of southern Borneo they once controlled. They said Vyner was too old to be a guerrilla leader, they had no planes to spare, and nothing was to be gained by an attempt to raise the Dyaks against the Japanese. Vyner argued, but in vain. He did not return to Australia until Wavell was about to leave Java, and the whole Archipelago was about to fall into enemy hands.

He flew to Melbourne, staying there for the next months, organizing a provisional government which was as powerless and ineffective as most of the provisional governments of that time. He lived obscurely in a flat in South Yarra, cooked his own meals, drank afternoon tea, took long walks in an old raincoat, and hugged the radio. Towards the end of the year he sailed for England.

All through the war years he was haunted by the helplessness of his country. He blamed the British for not putting up a token defence in Sarawak; he blamed himself for not being able to return to Sarawak and to die there. Nearly all his friends were in Sarawak, and he assumed they were all dead.

By 1944, when the tide was turning, he was seventy, and he had almost lost hope of seeing Sarawak again. His brother Bertram, two years younger, was in charge of the provisional government. From the Colonial Office that year came urgent inquiries about the Rajah's intentions once Sarawak had been recaptured by British forces, and it was suggested that the existing treaties should be reviewed. The Rajah replied that Sarawak was a sovereign state under the protection of Great Britain, now under alien rule 'owing to the unavoidable inability of the Protecting Power to preserve it from invasion'. He was in no mood to surrender his country at the whim of a Colonial Secretary. If it was to be given to Great Britain, it would be given at the proper time, under peaceful conditions, after discussion with the survivors among the State Council and the native chiefs. He would not be hurried. He hinted that a drastic change in the treaty arrangements was probably inevitable, and then retired to a country house in Berkshire to await the end of the war.

In Sarawak the war ended on September 11, 1945, when Australian forces landed in Kuching. Just before the end a Chinese, who had spent the occupation in hiding, ran out to Fort Margherita, hauled down the Japanese flag and flew the Union Jack. The Japanese, who had been expecting an invasion, panicked and fled into the forests. A few more Japanese heads were added to the collections in the long-houses. After forty-five months of occupation, Sarawak was free.

Alone, on his own responsibility, Vyner decided the time was soon coming when Sarawak would have to take its place among the possessions of the British Commonwealth. The wealth of the country had been destroyed by the invaders. Vast amounts of capital would be needed to set Sarawak on its feet again. No doubt these vast sums of money could be raised on the international money market, but only at the price of allowing foreign exploitation. It had been the intention of Sir James Brooke that the final legatee of the country should be the King of England; and Vyner was content that Sarawak should become a possession of the King. He made inquiries among the native chiefs, who were puzzled and stunned at the thought of coming under direct British rule—to some it seemed a betrayal of trust, to others who were more far-seeing it seemed the only solution to a problem which was beyond the power of one man, or a group of men, to solve, but even then they would have preferred the continuation over a transitional period of Brooke rule. They knew the Rajah. They did not know what the British had in store for them.

In February, 1946, Vyner decided upon drastic measures. Without warning, he issued a proclamation from London, urging the people of Sarawak to accept the King of England as their rightful ruler. The proclamation, written in the ornate style of an imperial rescript, reads oddly in English, but it was not primarily intended for the English-speaking reader. It was written for those who speak Malay and Dyak and who are accustomed, even when speaking to one another, to employ a flowery, resounding, and feudal vocabulary. The proclamation reads:

> We believe that there lies, in the future, hope for my people in the prospect of an era of widening enlightenment and of stability and social progress, such as they have never had before. We regard the acceptance of the cession as the consummation of the hopes of the first Rajah of Sarawak.
>
> It is constitutional that all authority derives from the Rajah. The people select the Rajah, and what the Rajah advises for the people is the will of the people. I am spokesman of the people's will. No other than myself has the right to speak on your behalf. Not one of you will question whatever I do in his high interests. No power nor personal interest shall

subvert my people's happiness and fortune. There shall be no Rajah in Sarawak after me. My people will become the subjects of the King.

It is now drawing near the time when I will come to you.

Expect me soon.

This is for your good: My royal command.

Now there was no turning back, no possibility of changing the course of history. Those flowery phrases concealed a note of defiance. What had to be done had been done, and Vyner never for a moment regretted it.

But if Vyner thought that by means of a simple proclamation he could bring Sarawak into the orbit of the King of England, he was mistaken. His brother Bertram, who had served him loyally for many years as acting Rajah when Vyner was away from the state, heard of the proclamation in a broadcast from the B.B.C. He was shocked to the core. He remembered that by his father's political will Vyner was 'urgently enjoined' to make no changes in the State without consulting him. He had not been consulted. He had in fact been kept in complete ignorance of the course of events leading up to the proclamation. Vyner answered that as the Sovereign Ruler of the State he was not bound by the wishes of his father: no prince or king can operate by edict from the tomb. He had done what he had to do with full consciousness of his responsibility, knowing that his brother would be pained, but helpless to manage the affair in any other way. If Sarawak should ever be given to Great Britain, it was better that it should be given now, in the aftermath of a war, than at some later date when it might be more difficult to make the gift cleanly.

Others besides Bertram were shocked. Bertram's son, Anthony Brooke, who had been declared Rajah Muda in 1939,[1] found himself deprived of his inheritance. Even before Vyner issued the proclamation, Anthony Brooke said: 'I will fight tooth and nail any proposal that Sarawak shall become a Crown Colony before the people of Sarawak have been consulted under their own constitution.' As he saw it, there was no reason at all for the cession, and Sarawak, even in the modern world, might continue its independent existence with only slight modification, like Brunei and the Malay States which continued to be ruled by their Sultans. He regarded the cession as a betrayal. Vyner regarded the continuing existence of Sarawak as the private domain of the Brooke family as an anachronism. There could be no compromise between them.

Others besides Anthony and Bertram Brooke questioned whether Vyner had any right to surrender the state to Great Britain. Tedious

---

[1] Vyner withdrew the grant of the title nine months later. On April 1, 1941, Anthony's father was appointed 'Heir to the Raj, to be proclaimed as soon as news reaches Sarawak of the Rajah's death'.

and complex constitutional problems were involved. The treaties signed between Sarawak and Great Britain, the political testaments of the first two Rajahs, the documents which went to make the constitution of 1941—all these might be examined without anyone being any the wiser about the exact powers possessed by the ruling monarch. What kind of state was Sarawak? It paid tribute to Brunei, but it had eaten up most of Brunei. Its foreign affairs were by treaty controlled by the British Government. Its protection was guaranteed by Great Britain, and its reigning monarch remained in some strange way a British subject. There were no rules which applied to a cession of this kind. A lawyer examining the case with all the documents before him might conclude that the matter would have to be settled at the Court at The Hague, for there existed no other body capable of adjudicating between sovereigns. But in this case the sovereign ruler of Sarawak had freely granted the state to another sovereign. If Bertram or Anthony Brooke objected, to whom should they appeal?

Not for the first time the Brooke family was bitterly divided. Anthony Brooke fought the cession on many grounds. It was illegal, unconstitutional, undemocratic. It threw Sarawak to the mercy of the bureaucratic officials of the Colonial Office. There had been no referendum; the natives were not consulted; there existed no strong desire in Sarawak for rule by the Colonial Office. If Sarawak was taken over by Great Britain, it would amount to British territorial aggrandizement as a result of the war. When it became known that Sarawak was already being described as 'a colonial territory' in a White Paper published by the Colonial Office, and had already been allocated a sum of £1,500,000, he wrote in a letter to *The Spectator*: 'The pen, with so bold a stroke, may well be mightier than the sword, but apart from the question of this nation's honour, is there not something just a little unrealistic about jugging an uncaught hare?'

Questions were asked in the House of Commons. It was felt that the Rajah and the Colonial Office might be acting a little too abruptly. The hare had in fact been caught, but there was something to be said for examining it before deciding whether to put it in the pot, or to let it free. Anthony Brooke attempted to arouse public opinion against the cession. Members of Parliament were beginning to insist that a commission of inquiry or a parliamentary deputation be sent to Sarawak to ensure that the transfer was in the best interest of the people.

Vyner was tempted to maintain a lofty silence, but when an article appeared in the *Sunday Times* above the signature of the distinguished historian Arthur Bryant, proclaiming that 'Sarawak had flourished on traditional native lines tempered by British idealism' and was about to be forced into an 'imperial strait-jacket', his temper snapped. He could see no purpose in continuing the romantic fiction that Sarawak was another Shangri-La. The Rajahs of Sarawak had ruled as benevolent despots, but they had possessed neither the capital nor the equipment to rule the state to the best advantage of the people. There were never enough hospitals or schools. Few roads had been built. Some of the practices of the Rajahs had been disastrous. It was time for the moment of truth.

He wrote:

What now is the stark truth about Sarawak in the past? My father's policy was to support the virile Sea Dyak tribes against all other tribes. Frequent expeditions, resulting in indiscriminate slaughter, were sent to subdue the recalcitrant natives. *Corvée* was the inveterate practice and the Malays loathed being ordered to take part in expeditions and to give gratuitous labour. There was no free Press, no means whereby the natives could ventilate their grievances without the haunting fear of incurring the displeasure of local British officers, who acted as 'little tin Gods', and no adequate educational or medical facilities for the mass of the people.

The State revenues were mainly derived from opium, gambling, pawn and spirit farms, head and exemption taxes. The mineral wealth of the State was monopolised. And the small rubber holdings, which Mr. Bryant extols were established at the cost of extinguishing thousands of acres of rice lands—rice being the staple food—with the result that poverty was rife whenever the price of rubber fell.

In all the criticisms which have appeared in Parliament and Press I have sought in vain for a single constructive suggestion which might contribute towards the establishment of a happier and brighter future for the natives. All that is urged is a return to 'the good old days'. But those days were good only for the British residents and not for the natives.

The attitude of the people towards cession is summed up in letters that have reached me from the heads of the Malay and Chinese communities. They say, 'We pledge our unreserved support for whatever measures Your Highness determines to pursue, since we know full well that the paramount interest of Your Highness is the welfare of all the people of all the races dwelling in Sarawak.'

So, in a mood of resignation, knowing that Sarawak could not survive in the world of atomic bombs unless it was brought into the Commonwealth, distrusting most of his advisers and especially those former members of the Sarawak Civil Service—those 'little tin Gods'—who were urging him to continue as an autocratic ruler, Vyner set about the last stages of the transfer of power. For very nearly fifty years he had been associated with the Government of Sarawak, and when he left by air for Kuching in April, 1946, he knew the pang that comes to all men who uproot themselves late in life.

He was losing more than Sarawak. Many of his friends were

against the cession. His brother Bertram was determined to fight to the bitter end. His nephew Anthony, who led the campaign against what he called 'the betrayal of Sarawak', was an even more irreconcilable enemy. Others besides the immediate family objected to the transfer of power. Among them were many of the Datus and Dyak chiefs. It began to seem that the battle to be fought out in Kuching would be between forces that were very nearly equal.

It was not a good time for going to the Far East. All Asia was in ferment. There was war between the Dutch and Indonesians. Chinese guerrillas were fighting in the jungles of Malaya. In French Indo China the civil war was beginning which was to lead to the expulsion of the French.

After four and a half years' absence Vyner came to Kuching in a flying-boat from Singapore. A royal salute of twenty-one guns boomed from Fort Margherita. The Dyak chiefs, the Malay nobles, and the Chinese towkays were waiting for him. For the last time there were enacted all the ceremonies which accompanied the home-coming of a Rajah. There were speeches of welcome, and the presentation of a sword by a Malay noble whose ancestors were rulers of Sarawak. Then it was all over, and Vyner entered the *astana*, which he once thought he would never see again.

During the war the Japanese Governor of Sarawak had taken up residence in the *astana*. Nearly all of Vyner's books, nearly all his possessions had perished. Hundreds of letters and documents written by Sir James Brooke had vanished in the flames.

For some reason Vyner had decided to bring with him on the aeroplane journey from Poole to Singapore the centenary stamps printed in 1941 to commemorate the centenary of Brooke rule over the country. For the last time those handsomely produced stamps were sold in the post offices of Sarawak.

For seventy-five days Vyner ruled over Sarawak. He met his old friends, decorated those who had served bravely in war, and briefly examined the collections of Japanese heads amassed by the Dyaks. He sauntered through the streets of Kuching as he had done long ago. He was at home again. Once more there was the familiar man in the sun-helmet walking through the bazaars and talking familiarly with any coolee who wanted to speak to him. He was the last of the Rajahs of Sarawak. He was seventy-two, and ready to go.

Three weeks after the arrival of the Rajah, Bertram flew out to Sarawak in a desperate last-minute attempt to prevent the cession. He satisfied himself that the natives were not yet ready to surrender Brooke rule, but he was helpless before the combined powers of the Rajah and of the Colonial Office. Returning to London, he made a direct appeal to King George VI, concluding his appeal with the words:

> I am emboldened to write as I have done by the urgent appeals addressed to me in most touching terms by the Malay and Dyak Associations of Sarawak to champion the fight of those communities for the retention of the State's independence and by my profound conviction that there is at this time among the natives of Sarawak an overwhelming feeling of bewilderment and betrayal and the loss of confidence in the reality of the Atlantic Charter principle which Great Britain undertook to support.
>
> Your Majesty will graciously believe that at my advanced age I have no selfish desire in this matter and that I am and shall be your Majesty's most loyal and humble servant.

Bertram was fighting with blunted weapons, for a Rajah and great officers of state had already made their decisions, and his own powers were nebulous. In fact, no one could make any reasonable estimate of the will of the people. There could be no ballot boxes among those primitive tribes scattered about the forests and along the banks of the great rivers which form a network throughout Sarawak. There were no recognized organs of public opinion. Two Members of Parliament, constituting an unofficial commission of inquiry, visited Sarawak and reported that the people seemed hopelessly confused by the situation. The cession bill was voted in the Council of State. Of the twenty-six non-European members thirteen members voted against cession and twelve voted for it.

To Vyner, it seemed that the country was in danger of being split into two camps, and this was all the more reason for stepping down. He executed the instrument of cession, and on July 1, 1946, in the sombre white and brown courtroom at Kuching, an under-secretary read the decree which ended the rule of the Brooke family. Only a few Chinese and Malays were present, and no Dyaks attended the ceremony. The Rajah sent a message, saying that he had every confidence that Sarawak would benefit by the cession, and the King welcomed a new country into his immense Commonwealth. Significantly the King spoke of bringing Sarawak to 'a higher stage of social and economic development than has hitherto been possible'.

Vyner had done what he set out to do. He had no hesitations. He thought it had been done cleanly, and it was absurd to accuse the British Government of acting with unnecessary haste, for he had himself insisted on haste and forced their hand. In its time the rule of the white Rajahs had fulfilled a need, but no single man could rule a country as large as Sarawak in the modern age. He flew back to England in a mood of careful composure, feeling as a man feels when he has lost his most precious possession, and still thinks it is for the best.

Then it was all over—the battles, the hunting of pirates, the long expeditions into the interior, the ancient treacheries in the Sultan's court, the withered heads dancing in the wind. For a century Sarawak had been a legend, a remote and almost unknown kingdom in the East, where few white men entered. Now at last Sarawak was opened up. Medical teams flocked to the country; education was improved; roads were built. The Stone Age Dyaks entered the world of the jet plane without a qualm.

For a hundred years a single family had ruled over those rivers and forests as a private preserve, dedicating themselves to the service of the natives. They left their mark on the country. They had shown a way of ruling which was in advance of their time, for they had thrown paternalism to the winds. Again and again the Brookes insisted that the Dyaks and Malays were the equals of the British, and were to be treated with the utmost respect.

In the days when he was still fighting against pirates, James Brooke wrote: 'Sarawak belongs to the Malays, Sea Dyaks, Land Dyaks, Kayans, Kenyahs, Milanos, Muruts, Kadayans, Bisayahs, and other tribes, and not to us. It is for them we labour, not for ourselves.' In fact he had loved the Dyaks and Malays to distraction, and believed himself the luckiest of men alive to be among them. For him, and for the Brookes who came after him, Sarawak always wore the colours of an almost impossibly beautiful dream.

Today the old Rajah, living in London, surrounded by the mementoes of a long reign, the great oil paintings hanging on the wall, Malay krisses and Dyak ornaments on the mantelpiece, watches the world as it passes. Though he wears a sports jacket and flannel trousers, he still looks like a Rajah, and there is the faintest hint of grandeur in his gestures. He smiles easily. He lights a cigarette, pours himself a drink, settles down in the easy chair by the window, and talks about Sarawak.

'You know,' he said recently, 'I've been all over the world, but I never found a better place than Sarawak, or a better people. I was the luckiest man in the world to be the Rajah.'

SELECT BIBLIOGRAPHY

Baring-Gould, Sabine, and Bampfylde, C. A. *A History of Sarawak under its two White Rajahs 1839–1908*. London: H. Sotheran & Co., 1909.

The Borneo Question: or, The evidence produced at Singapore before the Commissioners . . . Singapore: A. Simonides, 1854.

Brooke, Sir Charles. *Queries, Past, Present and Future*. London: Planet Press, 1907.

Brooke, Gladys. *Relations and Complications*. London: J. Lane, 1929.

Brooke, Lady Margaret. *Good Morning and Good Night*. London: Constable & Co., 1934.

Brooke, Lady Margaret. *My Life in Sarawak*. London: Methuen, 1930.

Brooke, Lady Sylvia. *Sylvia of Sarawak*. London: Hutchinson & Co., 1936.

The Facts about Sarawak. London: Balding and Mansell, n.d.

Foggo, George. *Adventures of Sir James Brooke*. London: E Wilson, 1853.

Gomes, Edwin. *Seventeen Years among the Sea Dyaks*. London: Seeley & Co., 1911.

Hahn, Emily. *James Brooke of Sarawak*. London: A. Barker, 1953.

Helms, Ludwig. *Pioneering in the Far East*. London: W. H. Allen & Co., 1882.

Hose, Charles. *Fifty Years of Romance and Research*. London: Hutchinson & Co., 1927.

Hume, Joseph. *A Vindication of the Character of Sir James Brooke*. London: J. Ridgway, 1853.

Jacob, Gertrude. *The Raja of Sarawak*. London: Macmillan & Co., 1876.

Keppel, Henry. *The Expedition to Borneo of H.M.S. Dido*. New York: Harper & Brothers, 1846.

Keppel, Henry. *A Visit to the Indian Archipelago in H.M.S. Maeander*. London: R. Bentley, 1853.

Longhurst, Henry. *The Borneo Story*. London: Newman Neame, 1956.

MacDonald, Malcolm. *Borneo People*. London: Jonathan Cape, 1956.

McDougall, Harriette. *Letters from Sarawak*. London: Wheldon & Wesley, 1854.

Mundy, Sir Rodney. *Narrative of Events in Borneo and Celebes*. London: J. Murray, 1848.

Pfeiffer, Ida. *A Lady's Second Journey Round the World*. London: Longman, Brown, Green, 1855.

Report of the Proceedings at a Public Dinner given for H.E. Sir James Brooke . . . London: Baily Brothers, 1852.

Rutter, Owen. *British North Borneo*. London: Constable & Co., 1922.

Rutter, Owen (ed.). *Rajah Brooke and Baroness Burdett-Coutts*. London: Hutchinson & Co., 1935.

Rutter, Owen. *The Pirate Wind*. London: Hutchinson & Co., 1930.

Rutter, Owen. *Triumphant Pilgrimage*. London: Harrap & Co., 1937.

'Scrutator'. *Borneo Revelations*. Singapore: Shaick Kyam, 1850.

St. John, Sir Spenser. *The Life of Sir James Brooke, Rajah of Sarawak*. Edinburgh: W. Blackwood & Sons, 1879.

St. John, Sir Spenser. *Rajah Brooke*. London: T. F. Unwin, 1899.

Templer, John C. (ed.). *Private Letters of Sir James Brooke*. London: R. Bentley, 1853.

Wallace, Alfred. *The Malay Archipelago*. New York: Harper & Brothers, 1869.

INDEX

Titles marked with an asterisk have restricted rights